Misconceiving Merit

Misconceiving Merit

Paradoxes of Excellence and Devotion in Academic Science and Engineering

MARY BLAIR-LOY AND ERIN A. CECH

The University of Chicago Press   Chicago and London

The University of Chicago Press, Chicago 60637
The University of Chicago Press, Ltd., London
© 2022 by The University of Chicago
Published 2022
Printed in the United States of America

31 30 29 28 27 26 25 24 23 22   1 2 3 4 5

ISBN-13: 978-0-226-82011-8 (cloth)
ISBN-13: 978-0-226-82015-6 (paper)
ISBN-13: 978-0-226-82014-9 (e-book)
DOI: https://doi.org/10.7208/chicago/9780226820149.001.0001

Library of Congress Cataloging-in-Publication Data

Names: Blair-Loy, Mary, author. | Cech, Erin A., 1982– author.
Title: Misconceiving merit : paradoxes of excellence and devotion in
    academic science and engineering / Mary Blair-Loy and Erin A. Cech.
Other titles: Paradoxes of excellence and devotion in academic science
    and engineering
Description: Chicago ; London : The University of Chicago Press, 2022. |
    Includes bibliographical references and index.
Identifiers: LCCN 2021054318 | ISBN 9780226820118 (cloth) |
    ISBN 9780226820156 (paperback) | ISBN 9780226820149 (ebook)
Subjects: LCSH: Scientists—Rating of. | Science—Social aspects. |
    Work-life balance. | Scientists—United States—Attitudes. | Science
    teachers—United States—Attitudes. | College teachers—United States—
    Attitudes. | Discrimination in higher education.
Classification: LCC Q175.5 .B55 2022 | DDC 306.4/5—dc23/eng/20220112
LC record available at https://lccn.loc.gov/2021054318

Contents

List of Tables and Figures vii

1 Misperceiving Merit, Excellence, and Devotion
   in Academic STEM 1

2 The Cultural Construction of Merit in Academic STEM 19

3 The Work Devotion Schema and Its Consequences 39

4 Mismeasuring Merit: The Schema of Scientific Excellence
   as a Yardstick of Merit 68

5 Defending the Schema of Scientific Excellence,
   Defending Inequality 95

6 The Moralization of Merit: Consequences for Scientists
   and Science 125

Acknowledgments 153   Appendix 155   Notes 175
References 213   Index 237

Tables and Figures

Tables

1.1   Delineating the Work Devotion Schema and the Schema of Scientific Excellence in Cultural Definitions of Merit in STEM 7

1.2   How the Schemas of Work Devotion and Scientific Excellence Reproduce Inequality 13

1.3   How the Schemas of Work Devotion and Scientific Excellence Are Bad for STEM Professionals and Scientific Innovation 15

3.1   Means and Standard Errors of Dependent and Independent Measures ($N = 266$) 47

3.2   OLS Regression Predicting Respondents' Reports of Flexibility Stigma in Their Departments with Demographics, Family, and Work Circumstances ($N = 266$) 48

3.3   OLS Regression Predicting Log Average Articles Published per Year Using Demographics, Job, Research Time, and Motherhood Status ($N = 266$) 50

3.4   OLS Regression Model Predicting Log Salary Using Demographics, Job, Productivity, and Motherhood and Fatherhood Status ($N = 266$) 62

3.5   OLS Regression Models Predicting Persistence Intentions and Job Satisfaction with Flexibility Stigma and Controls ($N = 266$) 64

A.1   OLS Regression Models Predicting Self-Conception Measures with Gender, Race/Ethnicity, Department, and Career Stage 171

Figures

3.1   Average Values on Work Dedication Measures and the Work Dedication Scale 42

3.2   Predicted Work Dedication by Gender, Underrepresented Racial/Ethnic Minority (URM) Status, LGBTQ Status, and Parenthood Status 42

3.3   Mean Hours Spent on Childcare on Weekdays and Weekends, on Total Work per Week, and on Research per Week, by Parenthood Status of Children Under Sixteen 49

3.4   Predicted Values on Productivity Measures by Parenthood Status of Children of Any Age 51

3.5   Predicted Salary by Gender and Parenthood Status, Net of Department and Demographic Measures ($N = 266$) 63

3.6   Predicted Values on Three Outcome Measures, by Low (First Quartile) and High (Third Quartile) Reported Levels of Flexibility Stigma (FS) 65

4.1   Scholarly Productivity Measures, by High and Low Values on Assertive, Relational, and Diversity-Promoting Self-Conceptions 82

4.2   Reward and Respect Measures, by High and Low Values on the Self-Conception Measures 84

5.1   Faculty Assessments of the Fairness of the Tenure Process at Case University (Percent Who Somewhat or Strongly Agree) 98

Figures in Appendix

A.1   Mean Values on Perceived Characteristics of Successful STEM Professional 172

A.2   Averages on Each Strand of Scientific Excellence Schema, by Broad Disciplinary Field 172

A.3   Schema of Scientific Excellence Strands versus Self-Conceptions, by Gender 173

A.4   Schema of Scientific Excellence Strands versus Self-Conceptions, by Race/Ethnicity 174

ONE

Misperceiving Merit, Excellence, and Devotion in Academic STEM

Few beliefs are as sacred to scientists, engineers, and mathematicians as the belief that science is a meritocracy. As a system of advancement and recognition, meritocracy is thought to reward those who produce the best work in science, technology, engineering, and math (STEM). This belief in meritocracy is especially strong in academic STEM, where the most innovative work and the brightest scholars are presumed to rise to the top.[1] In our study of STEM professors, most believe that the best scientists ascend through the ranks to full professor status and national and international prominence solely on the basis of their creative brilliance, assertive leadership, and intense devotion to discovery. Kristen, a biology professor, described scientific excellence like this:

Someone who really goes after a question with intensity . . . really incisive, insightful, drilling down to a problem. . . . In terms of clear metrics of excellence, you know, people who really make discoveries that shed new light and really transform and move the field forward. . . . People who are always pushing things forward and in an aggressive way.

The scientists we researched were confident that they could recognize merit in other scientists and reward it fairly when they see it.[2]

Yet inequities in how STEM professionals are respected, treated, and represented are doggedly persistent. Many studies, including our own, find that equally devoted and productive scientists encounter strikingly different treatment depending on their race/ethnicity, gender, sexual identity, and family responsibilities. STEM is thus beset by a paradox: How can a profession that so highly regards merit and objectivity also produce outcomes that are unfair for many scientists and, as we will show, bad for science itself?

To unravel this paradox, this book aims a floodlight on the culture of academic science. Most studies of inequality in STEM focus on illuminating implicit biases about women, people of color, and sexual minorities and documenting unfair behaviors in classrooms and workplaces.[3] Such research is vital for mapping these processes within STEM, yet it leaves unchallenged the notions of scientific merit and excellence themselves.

Our approach is different and unique. In this book, we train our gaze on the widespread, taken-for-granted beliefs within the *professional culture* of STEM. We take as our object of study the very beliefs among STEM faculty about what counts as good science and who counts as excellent scientists. We ask: How is merit conceived of and defined? How fairly is this definition applied? What are the consequences for scientists and for science? Answers to these questions not only illuminate how inequality manifests in STEM disciplines but also shed light on how cultural beliefs and practices around merit and excellence, commonly seen as legitimate and neutral, can reproduce inequality within professional occupations more broadly.

STEM faculty are an ideal population in which to study the core beliefs of STEM culture. These faculty are leading producers of a culture of scientific excellence and strive to live within its tenets. They transmit this culture to their students, who carry it with them out into scientific industries. Academics and the public view the university as a sacred space where basic research (the production of new knowledge about the underlying foundations of phenomena) thrives[4] and where scientific discovery is largely buffered from pressures of politics and profit.[5] Public funds pay for about half of the almost one hundred billion dollars spent each year in the United States on basic research. Much of this research occurs in public universities, and the public is counting on scientists to do their best work.[6]

We examine these beliefs at a top public research university using data from over five hundred STEM professors.[7] Our case university, like many research universities, prides itself on transparency and fairness in faculty recruitment, evaluation,[8] and promotion.[9] Yet at the same time, not everyone has the same chances: Women, members of some racial-ethnic groups, and LGBTQ professionals remain underrepresented and undervalued in their STEM departments. Our study reveals how unequal outcomes can occur alongside earnest commitments to objectivity and excellence.

We show that definitions of merit and excellence in STEM are not the objective, universal concepts they are upheld to be. They are cultural constructs that emerge from historically rooted institutions and are reproduced in the day-to-day interactions of professionals. As cultural constructs, they can reflect and amplify the same biases that plague the broader society.

We analyze *cultural schemas*, or widely shared beliefs, that we argue are core to the definition of merit in STEM. These cultural schemas are cognitive categories that help STEM professionals organize and make sense of their world.[10] They also have moral and emotional dimensions, which make them salient and compelling to scientists.[11] We identify two prominent schemas that anchor cultural beliefs about merit in STEM: the *work devotion schema* and the *schema of scientific excellence*.[12] This book describes these schemas and explains how they uphold various forms of inequality among a population of faculty across STEM disciplines.

Work Devotion Schema

The *work devotion schema* is a cultural mandate that defines work as a calling deserving of undivided allegiance.[13] STEM faculty generally believe that their life's work is their commitment to the mission of pursuing and sharing STEM knowledge.[14] Work-devoted scientists personally identify with their quest for new knowledge and generally accept as valid the expectation of long working hours. Emotionally, work devotion entails a sense of inspiration from their work, sometimes referred to as a "love" or even an "addiction."[15]

Ruben and Kristen, two of the faculty members in our study, will help us illustrate the work devotion schema.[16] Ruben is an early-to-midcareer professor of color in an engineering department. Kristen is a white woman who is a full professor in a biology department. Despite their differences in demographics, discipline, and career stage, their beliefs about the meanings and values of academic science are tightly aligned.

Kristen talks about her work as "just really exciting" and as her "mission." She says that her vocation includes discovery of the ways in which specific genes affect lung development. Ruben reveals a similar devotion to his research when he describes his research on the mechanics of circulatory systems:

I'm passionate about everything. Everything I do, I have to do it to the limit. . . . With research, you become a dreamer. . . . You are even doing something meaningful.

Both Ruben and Kristen take the single-mindedness and long hours of their vocation for granted. Ruben matter-of-factly explains that for him, the typical weekday and the typical weekend day look the same.

Ruben: During the week or during the weekend, it is the same thing. I'm here [on campus] every single day. I'm a night person, so it's pretty [hard] to get up early, but I normally get up at 7:00. And I don't have family. I only have two cats, so they don't need too much attention, so I'm here from 9:00 a.m. to 9:00 p.m.
Interviewer: Okay. Then you go home and sleep?
Ruben: No, then I go home and work on [writing scientific] papers [until] 1:00 to 2:00 in the morning.

Similarly, when we asked Kristen whether she took work home with her on nights and weekends, she responded:

Oh yeah. Always. . . . You can't stop the tide of stuff. . . . I guess I'm kind of, on some level, I just appreciate that it's how it's always going to be.

Most faculty in our study, despite their varied demographic backgrounds, share Ruben and Kristen's devotion to their work and their acceptance of intensive work hours as a necessary part of their calling.

Schema of Scientific Excellence

A second cultural schema that anchors definitions of merit in STEM is what we call the *schema of scientific excellence*. This schema defines certain characteristics as markers of excellence within STEM, and others as tangential or even threatening to excellence. The schema of scientific excellence serves as a cultural yardstick that STEM academics use to measure the competence and worthiness of their colleagues. Those who are seen to have the most valued characteristics are judged as the most meritorious, whereas the competence of those who do not measure up along this yardstick is questioned.

The two qualities that academic scientists generally view as most strongly identified with excellence are creative brilliance and assertive characteristics like competitiveness, self-promotion, and risk-taking. For example, when we asked Kristen what qualities characterize excellence in her field, she mentioned creative intensity, incisive analysis, transformative discovery, and assertively advancing the boundaries of knowledge in one's discipline.

Although Kristen respects those who push forward the boundaries of the field, she also expresses concerns about an academic culture that admires aggressive individualism. She says that her department fosters a "Wild West" culture that rewards scientists who cultivate the persona of a lone cowboy and pay too little attention to the interpersonal skills necessary for the team science and interdisciplinary work that advance pressing social concerns. Yet few colleagues share her skepticism about the schema of scientific excellence.

The schemas of work devotion and scientific excellence are not objective judgments of performance or simple tallies of skill. They are subjective cultural models that help compose a professional meaning system and maintain an unequal status quo.[17] We investigate these cultural schemas in the conceptions of merit in STEM to advance a new approach to a vexing problem: the continued marginalization and underrepresentation of women, LGBTQ persons, and many people of color in STEM. We show how these schemas work quietly in the background to shape interactions between colleagues, justify the distribution of resources, undermine innovation, and reproduce inequality.

Inequalities in STEM

Despite the widespread commitments to meritocracy in STEM, the field is far from providing equal opportunities to equally talented individuals. In some formerly male-dominated fields like medicine and law, women have comprised nearly half of professionals for many years. In contrast, women's representation in STEM degree programs and STEM employment increased in the 1980s and 1990s but generally stagnated after 2000.[18] In some disciplines (e.g., computer science and mathematics), there are proportionally fewer women now than there were two decades ago.[19] Many women in STEM face marginalization and devaluation.[20] The devaluation and disrespect of women, and of gender-nonconforming men, is broadly referred to as gender harassment, which when pervasive or severe, creates damaging consequences for the targeted scientists, their research trajectories, and the enterprise of science.[21] LGBTQ professionals in STEM are also more likely than their non-LGBTQ peers to be targets of negative treatment, including marginalization, career limitations, and professional devaluation.[22]

Compared to their proportion in the US population, white men and Asian men are not underrepresented in STEM.[23] In contrast, the representation of Black, Latinx, and Native American men and women among STEM faculty has remained strikingly low (currently around 8% combined) for several decades.[24] There has also been little progress in the enrollment of underrepresented racial/ethnic minorities in STEM degree programs and STEM employment since the early 2000s.[25] The proportion of women of color among STEM faculty is especially low. Only about 3 percent of employed women STEM professionals identify as Black, Latinx, or Native American.[26] Underrepresented racial/ethnic minority faculty often report experiences of workplace prejudice and isolation.[27]

Asian women are also underrepresented among STEM faculty, compared to their share of the overall population.[28] While Asian men enjoy some of the same privileges of assumed competence as white men in STEM, the experiences of Asian women are different.[29] Asian women face even more pressure than white women to align with norms of passive femininity and are more likely to say that they have to put their heads down and work hard while letting others take the lead.[30]

Our case university lauds its academic excellence and transparency. If equitable practices are in place anywhere in academic science, they should be in place here. Yet we document how marginalization and devaluation still plague STEM departments in this case university.

Further, we find that academic science harbors beliefs and patterns of interaction that can harm innovation. Scientists from every demographic group report cutthroat departmental climates, turf wars, and rewards for self-promotion at the expense of collaboration, which impede scientific advancement.

Why do these inequalities persist despite the best intentions and decades of effort by academic institutions like the one we study? We argue that it is not primarily a problem of "bad apples"—prejudiced individuals who perpetuate bias and engage in discriminatory behaviors. Rather, STEM inequality is fundamentally a problem of the culture of STEM and the conceptions of merit that anchor that culture. As we review below, these cultural schemas are widely shared across STEM faculty, both majority and minority, and serve as powerful but often hidden mechanisms of inequality.

Schemas of Work Devotion and Scientific Excellence Are Hegemonic

Table 1.1 delineates the main contours of the two schemas. Our study shows that the work devotion schema and the schema of scientific excellence are hegemonic in academic STEM culture. Beliefs that are hegemonic have social, cultural, and political dominance in a given context. The term *hegemonic* refers to social understandings and arrangements that are seen as normal, normative, and widely accepted by almost everyone yet benefit a small group at the expense of most others.[31] Across all demographic groups and STEM disciplines, faculty in our study express consensus about what qualities mark excellence in their field and what qualities detract from it. Faculty largely believe that the schemas of work devotion and scientific excellence underpin a fair, meritocratic system of recognition and advancement. They live by these schemas in their own careers, and they use them as the basis for their evaluations of colleagues. Yet as we show, these hegemonic schemas mostly benefit those who already hold the greatest power and privilege in STEM.

It can be challenging to elicit information from study participants about hegemonic ideas as taken for granted as the meritocracy of academic STEM, similar to the proverbial challenge of getting fish to talk about the water in which they swim.[32] One way we try to get leverage on these beliefs is by asking faculty to help us make sense of results from a

Table 1.1 Delineating the Work Devotion Schema and the Schema of Scientific Excellence in Cultural Definitions of Merit in STEM

	Work Devotion Schema	Schema of Scientific Excellence
Description	A shared cultural mandate that defines STEM work as a calling deserving of single-minded devotion, undistracted by other life events (especially childcare).	A constellation of characteristics that serve as a cultural yardstick for measuring up the competence and worthiness of one's professional colleagues and oneself.
Characteristics	Meritorious STEM faculty accept the centrality of STEM work in one's life; moral and emotional identification with one's institution; a sense of transcendent inspiration to do STEM work. *See chapters 2, 3*	Meritorious STEM faculty are expected to have individualistic creative brilliance, and to be assertive and self-promoting leaders. Some scientists also get credit for relational skills. Meritorious faculty conduct research that is "depoliticized," i.e., untainted by political concerns about social equality. *See chapters 2, 4*

research article in the premier journal *Science*, which found evidence of racial inequality in the evaluation and funding of scientists.[33] Specifically, the study examined all the major grant proposals for new research submitted to the National Institutes of Health (NIH) during a seven-year period. Receiving one of these competitive grants can be a game changer, allowing academic scientists to fund major research projects and advance their careers. The *Science* article found that African American academic scientists were 10 percent less likely than white scientists to be awarded a grant after taking into account the scientists' research productivity, education, employer characteristics, prior NIH funding, and other factors.[34]

After we reviewed the findings of the *Science* study with them, many of the professors we interviewed questioned its conclusions, insisting instead that academic STEM was meritocratic. To illustrate, Ruben rejected the accuracy of the study and marshaled three dubious objections to it. First, Ruben held up his anecdotal knowledge of three African American scientists in his field to contradict the study's findings, which were based on an analysis of over 81,000 research proposals.

Interviewer: A research study . . . that was published in *Science* found that African Americans are less likely to be rewarded NIH research awards.
Ruben: That's not right. I have an [NIH] collaborator that's African American, and *he* has two other ones [African American collaborators]. . . . I don't think that's right.

Second, Ruben asserted that the authors of this peer-reviewed, published study probably made statistical errors, such as leaving out important control variables or using the wrong denominator.

Ruben: The statistics are always—[they have] a problem in the denominator. . . .
Interviewer: Okay. So you mentioned that they should control for first language [of the grant applicants].
Ruben: Correct.
Interviewer: And they would get a different picture.
Ruben: Of course.
Interviewer: What do you think that picture would look like?
Ruben: I don't know. But it would be completely different.

Third, and most important, he emphasized his fundamental conviction that NIH awards grants fairly based only on the quality of the science.

I don't think that the grants are awarded based on colors, ethnicities, or original languages. It's just how—*it's just in the science.* (emphasis added)

He and many others we interviewed believe that because scientific evaluation is generally fair, the results of the study must be flawed.[35]

Ruben and the other faculty members in our study are consummate professionals. They have earned positions in a highly competitive university and have dedicated their lives to scientific discovery. Our aim is not to critique their critiques but rather to point out their tendency to hold fast to the belief that science is a meritocracy, even when evidence suggests otherwise. More broadly, our research will show that, like Ruben, many professors' reliance on the schemas of scientific excellence and work devotion can lead them to misperceive and mismeasure the merit of other academic scientists.

Consequences of the Work Devotion Schema

To be a meritorious STEM professor means expressing dedication to one's profession above all other life commitments, but especially caregiving responsibilities. A theme articulated by Ruben, Kristen, and most other faculty we interviewed is that the workdays are long and run without boundaries into personal time and space. The impossibility of handling all of one's responsibilities within a 24-hour day or a 720-hour month and constantly being behind creates an acute sense of stress. Ruben says:

I have a list in front of my refrigerator of things to do, things to write, but it keeps growing. It never, you know, I never get to do those things. . . . It gets busier every month. . . . The lab keeps growing, then I become the bottleneck . . . of the projects, because now postdocs [and grad students] come and ask me, What do I do next? . . . But now everybody has different projects, and then they come to me and [are] like, I don't know, what do you think? I don't know, I don't remember. . . . It becomes more stressful because I'm now the bottleneck.

Kristen loves her job but also finds the many demands on her time and attention to be very stressful. Initially, she describes her dilemma with gallows humor.

The way I joke about it is: Every day, I'm just trying to decide who I will disappoint the least. Because there's always so many things I've neglected.

Yet later in our conversation, far from laughing, she elaborates on the pressure to do her work, apply for grants, and maintain a strong disciplinary reputation in a competitive funding environment where one cannot afford to make enemies. She chokes up as she describes her guilt and anguish—feelings that betray the moral and emotional demands of the work devotion schema.

I feel like I'm always failing at some level. You know, there's always more failures than successes . . . Things I could be doing, and I'm not.

Ruben describes his work-focused life as doable because his live-in companions are two cats. Yet involved parents, particularly mothers, are viewed by their colleagues as struggling to fulfill the work devotion mandate.[36] Women professors report a stigma, an assumption that they fall short of the expectations of single-minded allegiance to science. Mothers are often regarded by colleagues as if they have less dedication and less scholarly productivity compared to men and women without children.[37]

For example, Kristen, who has young children, says:

People do take you less seriously because you're a woman with a family. I think there's a little stigma attached to that in the [discipline].

Our survey results show that faculty who are mothers have similar levels of work devotion and spend just as much time on research as do childless women and men with or without children.[38] Our productivity indices reveal that mothers have similar publication rates, citation counts, and grant dollars as their colleagues in the same departments and advancement levels. To sustain this output, faculty who are mothers have, like Kristen, found "additional layers of help" with childcare and household responsibilities, such as her day care center, babysitter, and housekeeper.

We find that the lens of work devotion distorts recognition of the actual scholarly productivity of mothers. Our quantitative analyses show that after taking into account scholarly productivity, department, and career stage, mothers experience a pay penalty of almost four thousand dollars a year compared with colleagues who are men or women without children.[39] This is striking, given the university's goals of transparency and objectivity in promoting and rewarding faculty. No wonder that many women in our study try to "cover" or deemphasize their motherhood status by planning births during the quieter summer term, avoiding or minimizing the use of family leaves from work, and keeping silent about parental obligations during day-to-day interactions with colleagues.

Motherhood is culturally loaded: It is seen as a uniquely moral, emotional, and time-intensive obligation that violates work devotion. In contrast, some other commitments that interfere with research time, such as consulting for science and technology companies, are not penalized by colleagues in terms of stigma or pay.

The stigma of motherhood not only hurts mothers but also is damaging to STEM departments. We find that faculty—parents and nonparents—who work in departments where they feel there is a stigma against involved parents have lower job satisfaction levels and are more likely to be thinking about leaving their department, compared with faculty in more family-friendly departments.[40]

Consequences of the Schema of Scientific Excellence

Earlier, we explained that the schema of scientific excellence recognizes certain individualistic traits—brilliance and assertive, self-promoting leadership—as the qualities that are most valued in STEM. Faculty give a lower value to the ability to foster relations with others, including empathy and mentorship skills.

We find that scientists' conceptions of how well they live up to these traits do not generally vary by gender, race/ethnicity, or sexual identity. However, the consequences of embodying these excellence traits depend on how an individual's traits are read by others. When faculty who are women, underrepresented racial/ethnic minorities, or LGBTQ individuals are judged by these cultural yardsticks, they are less likely to measure up in the eyes of colleagues.[41]

This cultural devaluation of some groups according to the scientific excellence schema leads to several negative consequences. First and most generally, we find that compared to white men with similar publication rates, faculty of color and white women receive less credit for their research. Previous studies have shown that underrepresented groups generally have to be even more productive than their white men peers to amass the same visibility.[42] Therefore, our findings likely underestimate the devaluation they face.

Second, our study finds that faculty members who do not fully embody assertiveness suffer penalties of reputation and financial reward. Even after scholarly productivity has been taken into account, we find that professors who see themselves as most assertive have larger salaries and are more likely to feel that their research is respected, compared with colleagues who see themselves as less assertive and more relational.[43]

Generally, professional women walk a tightrope of being regarded as assertive enough to be taken seriously yet nice enough to be seen as womanly and likable.[44] Assertive self-promotion is particularly fraught for women of color. We find that compared with white women in our sample, Black and Latinx women faculty are penalized for more assertive self-conceptions, whereas Asian women are penalized for nonassertive self-conceptions.

A third consequence of the scientific excellence schema is that when women demonstrate the qualities of strong mentoring and teaching, they receive less credit than men for these accomplishments; the emotional work and time required are discounted for women, who are assumed to do this naturally. Women may also be criticized more harshly than men when they are not strong in these areas.

Fourth, the notion that the best science and engineering is produced by virtuoso men who act alone to come up with brilliant scientific advances is often inaccurate. Previous studies find that white men are more likely to receive mentoring and collaboration invitations than other groups.[45] Other STEM faculty receive less mentoring help on average, and at the same time they are less likely to be valorized as virtuosos. More broadly, this celebration of individual genius is out of step with the general shift toward team-based science over the last decade.[46]

A fifth consequence is that the excellence of academic scientists who seek to promote diversity in STEM may be downgraded in the eyes of colleagues because these commitments are seen by many as too political for the pure space of scientific investigation. We find that coming under suspicion for politicization is more of a risk for faculty of color, white women, and LGBTQ faculty because their excellence is already less taken-for-granted than that of heterosexual white men. By their very presence, LGBTQ faculty are sometimes seen as bringing what are viewed as uncomfortable issues of sexuality into the supposedly pure realm of scientific inquiry.[47] Black and Latinx faculty are often assumed to care too much about diversity, and they disproportionately carry the load of serving on university committees focused on diversity.[48] At the same time, racial/ethnic minority faculty are often tacitly believed to have unfairly benefitted from their minority status. This leads to what we call the *minority-meritocracy trap*, in which underrepresented professors are often seen as "diversity hires" who advanced through STEM due in part to their minority status rather than their academic excellence.

In sum, this book provides a wealth of evidence showing how the cultural schemas of scientific excellence and work devotion mismeasure and devalue the scientific contributions of underrepresented groups. Table 1.2 summarizes these patterns.

Our book also discusses how the devaluation of talented scientists and their ideas damages scientific innovation.[49] The mandate of work

Table 1.2 How the Schemas of Work Devotion and Scientific Excellence Reproduce Inequality

	Work Devotion Schema	Schema of Scientific Excellence
Description	A shared cultural mandate that defines STEM work as a calling deserving of single-minded devotion, undistracted by other life responsibilities (esp. childcare). *See chapters 2, 3*	A constellation of characteristics that serve as a cultural yardstick for measuring up the competence and worthiness of one's professional colleagues and oneself. *See chapters 2, 4*
How the Schema Reproduces Inequality	Faculty with caregiving responsibilities (esp. mothers) are seen as insufficiently devoted to STEM work and thus less dedicated and successful, despite metrics showing they actually have similar publication rates, impact, grant dollars, devotion, and time spent on research as non-mothers. The schema frames scientists who appear to be spending all their time on science as the most meritorious and deserving of rewards. *See chapters 3, 6*	Broader social biases about which demographic groups are most likely to be brilliant, assertive, relational, and political mean that white heterosexual men are more likely seen to embody this schema than women, sexual minorities, and/or faculty of color. Men, but not women, get credit for relational skills. Black and Latinx women face backlash for assertive characteristics. Asian women experience marginalization for not being assertive enough. Assertive, individualistic "cowboys" are seen as producing the best science; men majority-race, early career scientists may actually receive more informal mentoring than other junior scientists despite the myth of their independence. Scientists believed to be politically engaged are viewed as producing distorted science. *See chapters 4, 5, 6*

devotion—that STEM work requires unending time and undivided allegiance—is not actually a recipe for innovative and significant scientific advances. The celebration of workaholic individualists, who do not take the time to rest, reflect, or care for the next generation, does not necessarily foster the creativity or commitment needed to conceptualize or provide scientific solutions for the challenges facing the world today.[50]

Moreover, our research suggests that academic departments that harbor a stigma against professors who are involved parents may struggle more to retain faculty. Turnover is expensive and disruptive.[51] Recruiting new faculty and getting them up and running with equipment and laboratories can cost universities hundreds of thousands of dollars.[52] Faculty turnover disrupts collaborations and threatens the stability of students and postdoctoral scholars trying to build careers and manage their lives.

Further, we find that most faculty feel they fail to fully live up to expectations of brilliance and assertive leadership, and this sense creates anguish for some. What's more, the mandate to be brilliant but competitive and self-promoting is out of touch with the deeply collaborative work across scientists, disciplines, and generations required to make significant advances in many fields. The schema of scientific excellence rewards scientists who promote their own careers at the expense of collaboration and mentorship, which does not serve the increasingly complex and interdisciplinary world of scientific discovery.

Kristen criticizes the senior men she regards as "cowboys" in her department for failing to mentor younger professors, particularly those who are white women or women and men of color. This lack of collaboration can be seen in Ruben's department, where he has little interaction with the "luminaries" and "rock stars" there. He says, "We see each other in the hall, say hi and bye, that's it." He describes the interactional climate in his department as "difficult" and "very competitive." He explains that the incentive system discourages interaction and collaboration with departmental colleagues.

Ruben: It's unfortunate because . . . I have more collaborations with people in other departments than with people in my department, even though there are people who do similar work to what I do in the department.
Interviewer: Why do you think that is?
Ruben: I guess it's, again, it's the fear of overlap. If we create collaborations, then how are we going to split the contribution? Who is—what is the fraction of contribution of each of one faculty and from the other? . . . The competition with each other is even funny, because we also need grants to do the same studies. . . . So if there are three people that need the grants for the same study section, we are basically competing against each other for funding. And if we do similar work, it's even worse.

Yet Ruben believes that the scientific reward system is fair. He insists that competitiveness in his department is not tied to scientists' race or gender. Rather, he says, it is based purely on the value of the science. He explains:

It is very hostile the way that everybody treats each other in their assessments of their science and assessments of their work, but it doesn't have a body attachment to it. It's just that's the way that is.

The environment may be hostile, he notes, but it's hostile for everyone equally.

Table 1.3 How the Schemas of Work Devotion and Scientific Excellence Are Bad for STEM Professionals and Scientific Innovation

	Work Devotion Schema	Schema of Scientific Excellence
How the Schema Harms All STEM Professionals	The innovation required for scientific responses to major challenges requires reflection, rest, and commitment to the next generation. Yet work devotion demands grueling hours and sacrifices of personal time that leave room for little else in one's life.	Devaluing faculty and ideas that are deemed politicized places limits on the contributions of these scientists and unnecessarily constrains faculty's commitments to other worthy goals (e.g., mentorship, public engagement). Most faculty feel they fail to live up to expectations of brilliance and assertive leadership.
How the Schema Doesn't Serve Science	Departments harboring stigma against parents likely face more expensive and disruptive turnover, which strains departmental resources. Penalties for mothers are not justified by their high rates of productivity and corrode scientific ideals of objectivity and fairness. *See chapters 3, 6*	Schema valorizes individualistic "cowboys" and "rock stars," but scientific innovation often requires deeply collaborative work across departments, disciplines, generations, and diverse identities. Penalties for women, underrepresented minority faculty, and LGBTQ scientists are not justified by patterns in productivity and corrode scientific ideals of objectivity and fairness. Diverse perspectives, often linked to diverse identities, can produce more innovative science but are often marginalized in normative definitions of excellence. *See chapters 4, 5, 6*

In contrast, Kristen says that despite the myth of their independence, majority-race, early career men are more likely than other junior scientists to receive informal mentoring and invitations to collaborate from senior white men, and her statement is backed up by studies.[53] This pattern of senior white men collaborating with other white men not only penalizes underrepresented scientists who are less likely to get invited to collaborate but can also impede scientific discovery. Previous research shows that diverse perspectives, which are often based on diverse identities, improve scientific innovation and problem solving.[54]

In short, we find that these schemas have negative consequences for STEM professionals themselves and for scientific innovation. Table 1.3 summarizes these negative consequences.

The Study

We investigate the cultural definition of merit as it is lived and understood by STEM faculty at a top public research university. Although they are a small proportion of the professional STEM workforce, academic scientists are leading creators and disseminators of STEM professional culture. Faculty at public research universities are charged with advancing basic research, expanding public knowledge about the world, and educating the most talented of the public's children without regard to their gender, race, or sexual identity.

Case-oriented research like ours identifies a small, nonrandom sample and investigates it thoroughly in order to fully understand the complexity of the case.[55] Case-oriented research is not meant to be generalizable; rather, it generates new insight and adds depth and nuance to our understanding of social reality.[56] Our in-depth analysis of this case is made possible by our unique access to university personnel data, including rank, salary, and demographics, for the over five hundred STEM faculty members in our population. We also have our own survey data from over half the population and interview data with eighty-five professors across STEM departments. Because STEM faculty often say that the number and impact of scientific articles are the most objective and valued metrics of productivity, we also constructed a Scholarly Production Indices (SPI) database, which includes publication rates, measures of visibility (citation counts and impact measures), and grant dollars for each professor in our study population.[57] Previous studies show that these metrics are often inflected with bias in ways that tend to inflate the numbers for white men and devalue the work of other groups.[58] Nonetheless, these metrics are widely regarded as measuring productivity, and they usefully hold constant these prized markers of merit across the faculty in our study. We examine whether professors who are most devoted and most embody the characteristics of excellence are actually producing scholarship at higher rates.[59] We find that often they do not.

While our case university is exemplary, it is not idiosyncratic. The schemas we identify may be more or less salient in other institutional contexts, and their effects may be more or less visible there. Yet our site has many similarities to other universities. Our case university is comparable to other highly ranked research institutions in size and student-faculty ratio.[60] The faculty at this institution were trained and professionally socialized at the top research universities in the country, suggesting similarities across universities in these taken-for-granted understandings of merit.[61] Specifically, 81 percent of our survey sample received their PhDs from a university that is currently ranked in the top fifty nationally or globally.[62] Our supplemental analysis of survey data from over seven thousand academic STEM professionals from four-year institutions around the country finds that the schemas of work devotion and scientific excellence are similarly salient among academic STEM professionals across the United States.[63]

As in other universities, faculty from nondominant groups face disadvantages.[64] Women, racial/ethnic minority, and LGBTQ STEM professors at this university are more likely than white men to report chilly climates in their departments.[65] Women are underrepresented in our study population compared to the national population of STEM faculty,[66] but our sample has similar proportions of white, Asian, and underrepresented racial/ethnic minority faculty as other research universities.[67]

In our study, we focused on patterns of inequality along the single and intersecting axes of gender, race/ethnicity, and LGBTQ status.[68] Other social and demographic differences—such as nationality, class, and religion—likely also anchor patterns of inequality connected to the schemas of merit we discuss here. In the interest of bounding our inquiry, we do not focus on those additional axes in our study.[69] These other social differences are important, and we encourage other scholars to investigate them.

Summary of Chapters

The ensuing chapters illustrate the two schemas in detail, describe their resonance among STEM faculty, and explain their consequences for scientists and science itself. Chapter 2 presents the historical, cultural, and social roots of these definitions of merit, drawing on previous scholarship. It also develops our theoretical argument about the broader role of professional cultures in the reproduction of inequality.

The chapters that follow present interview and survey data to vividly portray how these schemas shape the lives of academic scientists today. Chapter 3 analyzes professors' tight adherence to the work devotion schema. It also explains the coercive side of this schema, including its negative consequences for many faculty, particularly for mothers. Chapter 4 presents the four strands of the schema of scientific excellence: creative brilliance, assertive leadership, relational skills, and the devaluation of concerns about diversity. Not everyone benefits equally from measuring up to this schema; we show that there are divergent consequences along the intersecting lines of gender, race/ethnicity, and LGBTQ status.

Chapter 5 shows how the belief in the meritocracy of STEM is widely endorsed by faculty across every disciplinary and demographic background. When asked to explain the tiny proportions of women and Black and Latinx faculty on their campus, professors of all backgrounds blame upstream pipeline issues, point to perceived deficiencies among underrepresented scientists themselves, and raise fears that a focus on diversity compromises scientific excellence.[70] These beliefs and practices ensnare underrepresented faculty in a minority-meritocracy trap. We also describe the explanatory gymnastics faculty perform to justify this warped yardstick as fairly constructed and equitably wielded.

Chapter 6 shows how the schemas of work devotion and scientific excellence share cultural roots and together reinforce a white, heteromasculine, and moralized conception of the scientific calling. We show how many well-intentioned faculty defend what they understand as the purity of scientific excellence and devotion from what they fear are threats from family caregiving, profit, and identity politics. STEM professors from across demographic and disciplinary backgrounds sustain their faith in STEM meritocracy, even in the face of scientifically rigorous counterevidence. The paradox is rooted in a moralized professional culture defended by its many true believers. The more they strive to protect these ideals, the more they reinforce beliefs and interactions that devalue many academic scientists and harm the scientific enterprise.

Conclusion

Our critical perspective on the schemas of scientific excellence and work devotion in this book may be disconcerting, especially for those who have dedicated their careers to these principles. The book's goal is not provocation for its own sake. Yes, these cherished schemas create meaning and can spur scientists on to great work. But our analyses show that they also unfairly disadvantage some groups of faculty, discourage diversity, and impede collaboration and innovation, despite STEM faculty's sincere commitments to objectivity and excellence. Critically reflecting on how scientific merit is defined and measured requires us to step back from deeply held assumptions that have shaped STEM since its earliest days as a profession. These reflections will also open up possibilities for new practices that enable us to fully utilize, respect, and reward the entire human spectrum of talent and to advance science's ability to respond to pressing societal issues with innovative and effective solutions.

TWO

The Cultural Construction of Merit in Academic STEM

This book investigates the cultural foundations of a paradox. STEM professionals revere objectivity and neutrality and believe that they fairly recognize and reward merit. Yet many productive scientists from underrepresented demographic groups report that their work is less valued and respected than that of numerically dominant groups such as white heterosexual men. We show that this problem occurs not simply because universities' hiring and reward processes sometimes fall short of their meritocratic ideals. The problem also lies in the cultural definition of merit within STEM professions.

This chapter delves deeper into the cultural origins of this paradox. It presents our theoretical arguments for how the schemas of work devotion and scientific excellence serve as anchors of the cultural definition of merit in STEM and shows how these schemas have old cultural roots that support and perpetuate gender, racial/ethnic, and LGBTQ inequality in scientific fields. The chapters that follow will engage our survey and interview data to demonstrate how these schemas play out in academic STEM today.

The Paradox

STEM professionals across industry and academia typically assume their fields are meritocracies that reward the best ideas.[1] They believe that most of the time, science, engineering, and math are conducted by disinterested, unbiased individuals whose work is disconnected from the distractions and messiness of culture and politics.[2] They also believe they are able to recognize and reward merit when they see it, with vision unclouded by bias.

Within academic STEM, these ideals of objectivity and neutrality are even more potent.[3] Research universities are viewed as sacred spaces largely buffered from profit concerns, consumer markets, and the vagaries of politics.[4] Research universities seek to foster disinterested, basic science—the foundation for expanded scientific knowledge and social development.[5] Research universities are where STEM work flourishes in what is believed to be its purest form.

Universities, in turn, are expected to recognize and promote the most meritorious research.[6] Such a meritocratic system is broadly acknowledged as better for science, better for students, and better for society. Most faculty believe that the best scholars and the best work rises to the top[7] and that recognition and reward—publications in top journals, grants, awards, positions in top departments—are distributed equitably.

Accordingly, the professors in our sample generally believe that research universities usually operate in a meritocratic fashion. We will show that most of them believe that hiring and promotion practices at their university—and in STEM in general—are fair and unbiased.[8] This university, like other highly rated public institutions in the United States, lauds not only its excellence but also its transparency and fairness in rewarding the best and brightest faculty.

Some faculty pointed to instances where these meritocratic processes were violated. However, these instances were usually portrayed as individual aberrations in an otherwise meritocratic system, perpetrated by a few "bad apples." For example, Peter describes sexism in his department as due to just "one or two" biased faculty:

I know one of our recent female hires pretty well, and I have heard her talk about some of the asinine things that she's heard certain individuals say in faculty meetings that make it clear that they are biased or bigoted or whatever. . . . [So women] have heard *one or two individuals* spout off about it. (emphasis added)

In another department, Emily describes the sexist behavior she attributes to the old guard as no longer common in her department:

One faculty member I know, who has not yet retired, who has made . . . inappropriate advances to young women. . . . Even when he doesn't do anything inappropriate, he just leers at people. And it's, like, "Okay, my eyes are up here." Like, "Don't just stare at my chest when I'm talking to you." . . . And so people just avoid him. . . . But [these kinds of men] are *more the exception these days*, I think. (emphasis added)

Another professor, William, recalled inequities caused by a former department chair who had abused his power. William said that this chair had a pattern of letting departmental politics inappropriately influence his decisions about whether to support assistant professors trying to get tenure. All three examples are interpreted as isolated exceptions to a properly functioning system, rather than factors that undercut faculty's belief in the meritocracy of STEM.

So on the one hand, STEM professors generally believe their fields objectively reward the best ideas regardless of who those ideas come from. But on the other hand, much research, including our own, documents persistent inequalities in career experiences by gender, race/ethnicity, LGBTQ status, and family responsibilities.

Studies have documented the underrepresentation of women and racial/ethnic minority groups in science compared to their representation in the US adult population. Members of these groups are increasingly sparse at higher professional levels.[9] Minoritized racial and ethnic group members, such as Black, Latinx, and Native American faculty, confront racism, discrimination, and exclusion.[10] Many women in STEM, in turn, face sexism, harassment, marginalization, gender discrimination, and motherhood bias.[11] LGBTQ persons in STEM experience similar stereotyping, isolation, and discrimination.[12]

These patterns are found in universities as well as in industry. Even after attaining competitive faculty appointments, many underrepresented racial/ethnic minority women and men, white women, and LGBTQ-identifying persons continue to face marginalization and exclusion from professional and social networks—everyday reminders that they are not fully welcome or respected in their departments.[13]

Our Case University Falls Short as Well

Our data illustrate how some groups of faculty are underrepresented and disadvantaged while other groups, such as heterosexual white men, are systematically advantaged.[14] At this university, underrepresented racial/ethnic minority and women STEM faculty are significantly more likely than their white men colleagues to report experiences of devaluation and disrespect.[15] Moreover, we find that LGBTQ faculty are significantly more likely to experience marginalization and have fewer social and professional networks in their department compared with their non-LGBTQ colleagues.

A common folk theory given to explain the paucity of women and persons of color—both among our sample and in STEM in general—is that there are simply fewer of these individuals in the hirable pool due to upstream problems of poor education, non-elite pedigree, or deficient motivation.[16] The results in this book show the limits of this folk theory: we study unequal outcomes among faculty members whose selection into highly competitive faculty positions and their productivity metrics indicate that they are meritorious. Yet once women, racial/ethnic minority men, and LGBTQ individuals have been appointed to high-status academic positions, many continue to experience more disrespect and marginalization than white heterosexual men.

The paradox of merit is thus: How can a set of professions that so highly values objectivity and fairness in assessments of merit reproduce these unfair outcomes? This book shows that the problem of inequality in academic STEM is not primarily due to university hiring and reward processes sometimes falling short of their meritocratic goals. *We find that the problem lies in the cultural definition of merit itself, which most faculty faithfully uphold and apply.* The dominant definition of merit within the professional culture of STEM is an important but previously underexplored catalyst of social inequality.

In the sections below, we explain how this notion of merit is a part of the professional culture of STEM, a set of meaning systems and practices around professional work that is semiautonomous from the broader society. In the chapters that follow, we analyze how facets of the definition of merit embedded in this professional culture—specifically, the schemas of work devotion and scientific excellence—create and reproduce inequalities. We set the stage by first describing how STEM excellence is an historically rooted and inherently culturally constructed idea.

Historical, Social, and Cultural Foundations of STEM Excellence

Cultural conceptions of what is "good" STEM work, and who are the most meritorious members of these professions, did not somehow emerge naturally from the physical and natural world that scientists investigate. These are socially constructed, historical artifacts. This section makes use of five major insights from science and technology studies (STS) literature, which investigates how science, technology, politics, and culture construct, constrain, and enable one another.

(A) STEM professions as they now exist are the product of cultural and political processes occurring over the last several centuries.[17]

STEM professions, as they are understood in the global economy today, are Western social constructs that emerged out of conflict-ridden historical and political processes that unfolded over centuries.[18] Societies around the world have produced spectacular scientific, technological, and mathematical innovations, such as the structural designs of ancient African and Middle Eastern societies, innovations in mathematical reasoning by Islamic scholars in the second century BCE, botanical and horticultural knowledge in Asia in the Middle Ages, and intricate knowledge of astronomy and tectonics among indigenous peoples of the Americas and Pacific Islands.[19] Yet historically and contemporaneously, knowledge about the natural and physical world from Asia, Africa, and the indigenous communities of the Americas has typically been excluded from what counts as science or engineering in Western terms. For example, colonizing nations encountered indigenous populations in North America with rich and complex knowledge systems about their natural environments—taxonomies, theories, and experimentally derived facts.[20] In some cases, such knowledge was intentionally destroyed by colonizing nations by forced boarding school education for indigenous children and by the intentional demolition of tools and writings in order to better control indigenous populations.[21] Other insights (e.g., South American tribal knowledge about the healing effects of certain rainforest plants) have been appropriated by Western scientists, and the roots of this knowledge in the work of nonwhite persons and non-Western societies have been erased.

Furthermore, STEM fields emerged in the West with the structure and guiding questions they have today not as a logical outgrowth of the protons, microbes, and thermodynamics that serve as the objects of scientific investigation, but through the evolution of cultural meanings given to particular natural phenomena and the perceived worthiness of those phenomena for investments of time and money. For example, modern physics emerged out of astronomical studies conducted in the service of Christian doctrine and the Roman Catholic Church.[22] Aerospace science and technology exists as we know it largely due to capital pumped into national space programs by US and Russian governments during political escalations of the Cold War.[23] And the formalization of engineering training in the 1920s was bolstered by political visions of engineers leading the United States into a utopian, technocratic future.[24]

In other words, cultural beliefs and political power have been at the core of Western scientific and technological endeavors from their very origins. The content and boundaries of what counts as modern STEM knowledge is as much a product of sociopolitical forces of conflict, oppression, and appropriation as the achievements of a community of professional scientists and engineers who work in earnest in the interest of knowledge advancement.[25]

The parameters of what it means to be an "ideal scientist" and to do ideal STEM work are also historically contingent and culturally constructed.[26] As we show in this book, what counts as the contributions most worthy of respect is a collective cultural designation.

(B) The values systems of STEM are Western cultural constructs.

STEM fields today are shaped not only by Western histories of power and politics but also by Western cultural norms and values.[27] For example, the belief that a good scientist is epitomized by individualistic creative brilliance is rooted in Western reverence of the "inspired genius," an individual man receiving divine knowledge "secretly handed on through a sort of apostolic tradition, the lineage including . . . in various versions, Socrates, Aristotle, Jesus, and Aquinas" and Newton.[28] This lineage serves as a cultural touchstone for what science excellence is supposed to look like.

Furthermore, the process of defining "truth" in science is, in part, a collective social process of meaning making that depends on local interactions and norms.[29] The emergence of new scientific facts depends on community consensus about those claims, as well as the collective judgments of peers deemed appropriate to assess the quality of scientific work.[30] Forming this consensus also often creates tension among scientists. Emerging norms around the appropriate manner of dissent could have taken many forms, but the mores of European upper-class polite society during the Enlightenment dictated that dissent in science should be targeted toward the scientific idea rather than the scientists themselves.[31] These beliefs about brilliance and conflict are social constructs that developed in particular historical eras in response to cultural and political processes inside and outside these professions.

(C) Cultural conceptions of "ideal" scientists and engineers presume a hegemonic, heterosexual masculinity.

The Western cultural values shaping STEM include deeply-rooted beliefs about gender.[32] The perception that women do not fully belong in science has roots reaching far back to Platonic and Aristotelian notions of the differentiation between the presumed dominance of men and the presumed compassion and emotionality of women.[33] As science became institutionalized as a profession, the notion of an "ideal scientist" that emerged was one of heroism. The ideal scientist was portrayed in the cultural imagination (among scientists and nonscientists alike) as a hero that "presupposed masculine endurance, competitiveness, physicality, bravery, and grit."[34] Up until World War II, women were culturally imagined as the companions, helpers, or lovers of these scientist-heroes rather than as the heroes themselves.[35]

In recent decades, these overtones of bravery and physicality have diminished. Today, scientists are more willing to collaborate in order to succeed in an era of "big science," and mathematical and analytic prowess have replaced physical grit as the quintessential skillsets of ideal STEM professionals. Nonetheless, this image of the ideal scientist retains a veneer of bravado that is culturally masculine.[36]

The concept of the "ideal engineer" followed a similar historical pattern. Engineering emerged out of craftwork in the early nineteenth century and was explicitly understood as work done by men. As engineering developed into a formal profession in the early to mid-1800s and engineers took center stage in iconic infrastructure projects of the era (e.g., the bridges and skyscrapers that would come to define American skylines), engineers gained stature in the public imagination as rough-and-tumble men who wielded math and science instead of hammers and nails to bring the United States into modernity. For example, engineers were frequently depicted as protagonists in adventure novels of the 1880s. Engineers were "the modern, savvy equivalent to cowboys in westerns who were strong, ambitious men who performed dangerous, important tasks and always got the girl in the end."[37] As with science, the working-class machismo and physicality has faded in cultural understandings of engineers,[38] but hegemonic masculinity runs deep in cultural notions of ideal engineers.

Cultural constructions of the ideal scientist's sexual identity and family status are less well studied. The ideal STEM professional is presumed to be either heterosexual, with a (homemaking) wife and perhaps children at home whom the scientist may or may not see for an evening meal or on the weekends,[39] or so engrossed with his work that he has neither time for nor interest in romance or families.[40] Biographies of gay and lesbian scientists and engineers suggest that nonheterosexuality had often been seen as a threat to STEM work. Gay British mathematician Alan Turing was scorned by the scientific community for his sexuality and was formally prosecuted in 1952 on the basis of anti-sodomy laws. His sexuality was seen as a threat not only to his work but also to the security of Britain. The sexual identity of lesbian astronaut Sally Ride was only revealed by her partner posthumously. Ride took exceptional precautions to ensure that her colleagues and the public did not find out her sexual identity, such as keeping her partner a secret to her otherwise close colleagues, fearing that it would threaten her career as an astronaut and physicist.

(D) Cultural conceptualizations of the ideal STEM professional are racialized.

Cultural stereotypes about the "natural" abilities of different racial and ethnic groups are woven into depictions of ideal scientists. Black, Latinx, and Native American men and women have been engaged in the day-to-day work of the earliest science and engineering laboratories in the United States, but their efforts, like the efforts of white women, were considered support work rather than scientific contributions that deserved recognition.[41] Moreover, scientific advancements were sometimes tested through direct exploitation of peoples and communities of color.[42]

Today, notions of STEM excellence are far from colorblind. Cultural biases about the intellectual inferiority of African Americans, Latinx, and Native Americans for scientific and technological work continue to disadvantage people of color and question their belonging at the forefront of these fields.[43] Asians are more often stereotypically depicted as technically competent at math, science, and engineering as compared with other nonwhite populations, yet they are less frequently seen as having the necessary bravado to be leaders in their STEM fields.[44]

(E) The ideology of depoliticization belies the inherent social construction of STEM.

Finally, a core element of the cultural conception of ideal STEM professionals is the belief that the best STEM work is conducted in a political and cultural vacuum: scientists and engineers are to go about their work equipped with objective equations and tools and to look with great skepticism on people or activities that might break the seal of that vacuum. Recent scholarship has described this as the *ideology of depoliticization* in STEM contexts—the cultural devaluation of diversity and public welfare concerns within engineering and science.[45] Depoliticization asserts that science and engineering are purely technical spaces where "social" and "political" concerns not only can but should be removed from consideration. But, of course, political and cultural concerns are inextricably intertwined with meanings and practices of STEM. Human endeavors are always political and cultural, so these issues can never be disentangled from scientific work.[46] Considerations of inequality and discrimination within STEM are viewed by many as just such politicizing concerns. As we will show, many faculty see the introduction of inequality and diversity concerns in their STEM departments and labs as a threat to the purity of STEM work.

Although many STEM professionals in the last decade have stepped forward to weigh in on politically charged debates around issues of climate change, vaccine uptake, and data privacy, this external engagement with public debates has not changed the salience of depoliticization concerning factors inside the profession, in locations reserved for basic science and engineering work. Raising issues about systemic inequality in STEM departments, we find, is seen by many faculty as a moral breach of the objectivity and neutrality by which STEM professionals are supposed to live.

Because heterosexual white men are perceived as the unmarked, generic category of person in STEM,[47] these men are seen as automatically aligning with the depoliticization ideology. In contrast, women, people of color, and LGBTQ individuals are assumed by some colleagues to be risks to a depoliticized STEM by default. In their very embodiment, these individuals are viewed as likely to raise concerns about diversity and inequality, which challenge the neutrality of STEM.

In short, cultural notions of excellent STEM professionals and excellent STEM work are Western, historically contingent constructs that assume and privilege white, heterosexual, hegemonically masculine men. In opening up scientific merit for investigation, the book is not somehow polluting or politicizing STEM. STEM professions—and their perceptions of excellence—were always already cultural and political. The notions of STEM excellence that we study did not emerge naturally from the subject of investigation but were constructed through historical processes that involved political interests and cultural values. They were, in short, constructed by human beings prone to the social biases of their (and our) time.

Professional Cultures

We take a novel approach to understanding inequality in STEM professions by training our gaze on *professional cultures*. Professional cultures—

especially the cultural definitions of merit within those cultures—can promote, transmit, and disguise social bias. Professional cultures are partially closed off from broader societal meaning systems and are often interpreted as legitimized, neutral belief systems. These cultures emerged as STEM professionalized and harbor the Western, racialized, and gendered values about ideal scientists and ideal STEM work described above. In this section, we dig deeper into the theory of professional cultures to better understand how taken-for-granted beliefs about good science and good scientists can contribute to inequality.

Our focus on professional cultures is distinct from most previous research on inequality in STEM. Such work has focused on societal-level biases about the capabilities, skills, and drive of women, racial/ethnic minority, and LGBTQ individuals that STEM professionals carry with them into STEM workplaces.[48] Such beliefs are implicit and sometimes not fully conscious,[49] and they lead employers and coworkers across the labor force to typically value and reward men over women, white employees over persons of color, and heterosexual, cisgender individuals over LGBTQ-identifying persons.[50]

Our focus on professional cultures is also different from most research that has looked at organizational-level processes of inequality. Such scholars have focused on how biases can be built into the features of organizations such as personnel practices, job structures, and organizational culture and how those biases, in turn, devalue and stymie the work of women and people of color therein.[51]

In contrast to these societal-level biases and organization-specific cultures, professional cultures have largely been overlooked as mechanisms of intraprofession inequality.[52] But what are professional cultures? Professional cultures are systems of meaning, values, symbols, rituals, and interactional norms that are associated with professions and their characteristic tasks.[53] They are distinct from the more local cultures that emerge within specific organizations.[54] Because professionals enjoy considerable autonomy over the activities within their areas of expertise, they often act as partially closed "social collectives" with meanings and values that are semiautonomous from broader societal cultures and structures.[55] Although professions are not as cohesive or demographically homogenous as they were in decades past,[56] they still harbor rich systems of meaning about the professions' tasks, expertise, and ethical commitments. Professional cultures are typically most potent in academia, where professionals are more protected from pressures of monetization and where professional autonomy in the form of academic freedom is the gold standard.[57]

Beliefs about professional purity within these cultures put the highest value on arenas of the profession that are closest to the core of abstract professional knowledge. These "core tasks" are considered most prestigious.[58] In academic STEM, for instance, the core tasks of basic research and technical design are accompanied by more prestige than mentoring or teaching tasks. These value systems are widespread and consequential: they are engrained in professional socialization,[59] and they help buttress the profession's legitimacy in the broader society.[60]

Research has shown that there are three processes—jurisdiction, closure, and professional socialization—that help incubate these profession-specific cultures.[61] Jurisdiction is the set of socially valued tasks (e.g., heart surgery in cardiology, bridge design in civil engineering) over which a profession exerts social, structural, and sometimes legal control. This jurisdiction draws boundaries around what tasks, education, and licensure are the purview of that profession.[62] Professions attempt to guard their jurisdiction against encroachment from state and corporate entities and from other professions.[63] For example, psychiatry must protect its jurisdiction from encroachment by religious leaders, counselors, and neuroscientists, and its ability to prescribe psychiatric drugs. Battles between professions for jurisdiction not only contest a profession's claim of expertise and legitimacy; they are also fought over the ability to determine what competencies and tasks are most valued within a profession's borders.[64]

Jurisdictional boundary-drawing occurs in the context of ongoing blurring and reconfiguring of what "counts" as professional work. For example, interdisciplinary team science has burgeoned in STEM over the last thirty years.[65] These efforts require the integration of techniques and expertise from multiple subfields. They have even spurred the creation of new disciplines, such as nanoengineering and biochemistry. Interdisciplinary team science also tends to be more inclusive of traditionally marginalized scholars such as women and people of color.[66] However, interdisciplinary work is generally viewed as less prestigious in academic departments than more traditional disciplinary work and is often interpreted by academic and tenure promotion committees as less indicative of excellence in one's disciplinary home.[67] Instead of fracturing the coherence of disciplines, interdisciplinarity may actually help stabilize the culture and substance of disciplines through competition and critique.[68]

Closure processes are social and legal barriers that restrict access to the profession to a limited circle of persons deemed eligible as a result of their training, credentialing, hiring, and/or licensure. Closure processes often involve expensive postsecondary degrees or other credential (e.g., professional engineers' exams for engineers, bar exams that vary by state for lawyers, medical boards for doctors).[69] Closure can also require periods of low-paid, temporary employment. For example, some top STEM departments do not even consider hiring new faculty who have not had one or more postdoctoral fellowships after earning their PhD.

Closure is ostensibly designed to ensure the quality of expertise as well as to increase prestige, reduce competition, and boost earnings.[70] By drawing boundaries between insiders and outsiders, closure excludes not only those who lack the expected credentials but also those who seem misaligned with the profession's cultural values.[71] For instance, a study of job talks during campus interviews of finalists for competitive faculty positions found that women were more likely than men to be interrupted when presenting on their original research, making it more difficult for them to bring their presentation to a compelling conclusion that would support their candidacy.[72] Closure selects on certain social and cultural characteristics and helps insulate the profession from internal challenges to its cultural meanings.

Both closure and jurisdiction help professions control how competence is culturally defined and assessed within their borders. Socialization perpetuates these definitions by implicitly and explicitly training new generations into the meaning systems of the profession. Professional education instructs students in the skills needed for competency. It also instills the profession's dominant ideologies and codes of behavior.[73] In STEM undergraduate and graduate education, students learn to take on—and to identify with—the professional cultural values of STEM.[74]

For members of the profession in positions that require the most extensive preparation, this socialization unfolds over an intensive novitiate (i.e., training period). For professors, this often means a decade or more of low-paid, hardworking ascetism, in which novices must demonstrate their command of professional tasks as well as their allegiance to professional norms. This novitiate is partly intended to weed out those who have not developed appropriate dedication to professional norms. After the training period, these beliefs and behaviors are further solidified by practices that socially or legally sanction members who deviate from them.[75]

Jurisdiction, closure, and socialization activities help foster semiautonomous professional cultures, which are fairly consistent across the many jobs and employing organizations within a profession's jurisdiction. Within this protective enclosure, professions create and nurture their own definitions of merit.[76] Professions' definitions of merit are largely unquestioned by outsiders and hold sway in legal regulation of professional activities. Professions are largely left to their own devices to define, assess, and reward what it means to have merit as a member of that profession.

While the definitions of merit stemming from professional cultures are generally accepted as objective judgments of competence and expertise, they are not necessarily neutral or benign. Overlaid upon them are societal beliefs and stereotypes about who is most likely to embody the most valued characteristics and who is likely to be most successful at professional tasks. These definitions may smuggle in, disguise, or amplify stereotypes about women, people of color, and LGBTQ persons in ostensibly legitimate judgments of professional merit. In addition, these beliefs have a moral valiance: nonconformity can be interpreted as a threat to professional excellence. We place these definitions of merit at the center of our investigation. We argue that definitions of merit within professional cultures reproduce inequality because they infuse gender, racial/ethnic, and LGBTQ biases into the yardsticks along which professional competence and worthiness are measured. Cultural conceptions of merit have a moral center of gravity; professional identities include an obligation to faithfully uphold them.

In this book, we focus on two schemas that are central to the definitions of merit within professional cultures: the work devotion schema and the schema of professional excellence. Although the flavor of these schemas varies profession to profession, they likely play a key role in cultural definitions of merit across a wide variety of professional occupations.

What Cultural Schemas Help Constitute Definitions of Merit within Professions?

Cultural schemas are widely shared frameworks for "understanding and evaluating what we know as reality." They develop over time and are largely unquestioned.[77] These schemas are also emotionally and morally charged.[78] They inform and justify particular patterns of interaction, distributions of resources, and institutional and organizational policies.[79]

We identify two prominent schemas within professional cultures that are related to merit: schemas of work devotion and professional excellence. These schemas provide profession members not only with cognitive frameworks but also with moral and emotional commitments that help forge identities and create meaning.

The Work Devotion Schema

The *work devotion schema* is a cultural mandate that defines work as a calling that deserves undivided allegiance.[80] The work devotion schema consists of a number of related elements, including the cognitive acceptance of the centrality of work demands, a moral and emotional identification with the institution or discipline in which one works, inspiration that allows one to transcend the personal limitations of work, and a sense of an emotional high from the challenges of work.[81] The work devotion schema is institutionalized in organizational policies and informal practices, which are set up to reward those seen as devoted and penalize those whose devotion is questioned.[82]

The work devotion schema exists at multiple levels within professional work.[83] Originally conceptualized at the organizational level,[84] the work devotion schema pervades white-collar workplace cultural norms and demands the dedication of employees.[85] The work devotion schema is likely salient within most professional occupations, although the particular flavor of the schema may vary across professions. This schema can also exist at the profession level through its infusion into professional cultures.[86] As we argue, the work devotion schema is potent within the culture of STEM professions, where it takes the form of devotion to a scientific vocation.

Professional Excellence Schemas

As discussed earlier, professions are partially closed social worlds that propagate cultural values that are semiautonomous from other professions and from broader cultural values. Central to these professional cultures are shared beliefs about what it means to be a competent and excellent member of the profession. We term these beliefs *professional excellence schemas*. They include constellations of characteristics that culturally define excellence within particular professions. These constellations can be quite different profession to profession.[87]

Professional excellence schemas serve as cultural yardsticks within each profession that indicate competence and skill. Professionals use these yardsticks to "measure up" the competence and worthiness of newcomers, professional peers, and even themselves. These professional excellence schemas are likely consequential for hiring, promotion, recognition, social networks, and other forms of material and immaterial resources within the profession. They are reinforced through profession-specific interactional spaces (e.g., conferences) and passed down to the next generation through professional socialization.

The constellation of characteristics that are valued in professional excellence schemas may be somewhat arbitrary given the actual tasks and responsibilities that are typical of work in those professions. Conversely, the expertise that is required to be successful in a particular field may not necessarily be valued as a marker of competence. For example, lab management skills are crucial for success among bench scientists, but managerial abilities are not typically included in conceptualizations of excellence in science.

Due in part to the high levels of prestige and autonomy awarded to professions, these professional excellence schemas may be perceived by outsiders as neutral and bias-free judgments of professional skill. The particular constellation of characteristics that are emphasized within professional excellence schemas may be distinct from broader societal understandings of competence within a profession.[88] In this book, we investigate the schema of scientific excellence, the cultural yardstick that STEM faculty use to judge the competence and worthiness of members of their profession.

How Do Work Devotion and Professional Excellence Schemas Play Out in STEM?

Professional Culture of STEM

Like other professions, STEM has its own professional culture. While the particulars of this culture vary by subfield, STEM disciplines have similar intellectual content and come from similar historical backgrounds and thus have substantial overlap in the cultures of the individual disciplines within STEM.[89]

Previous scholarship has documented a variety of elements of the meaning systems, values, and symbols that are part of the professional culture of STEM, including the historical basis of the meanings of a "scientific life,"[90] the rootedness of notions of technological innovation as acts of rugged individualism,[91] and the cultural underpinning of scientific epistemologies.[92]

This literature is important to our conceptualization of merit. We take inspiration from scholars who have opened up the "black box" of STEM to demonstrate the social constructedness of scientific and technological knowledge,[93] merit and evaluation,[94] devotion,[95] scholarly productivity,[96] organization,[97] and epistemologies.[98] However, little systematic attention has been paid to the professional culture of STEM in research on STEM inequality.

Previous research on inequality in STEM has tended to focus on the stereotypes and biases that distort the professional evaluation of women,[99] racial/ethnic minorities,[100] and LGBTQ persons.[101] These stereotypes are interconnected with the Western, white, heteronormative, and hegemonically masculine conceptions of ideal scientists discussed earlier in this chapter. Stereotypes and biases originate in broader societal culture,[102] but the ways they manifest within a professional culture is rarely studied.

Unlike much previous research, our focus is not the gender, racial/ethnic, or LGBTQ biases of the individuals who make up the ranks of academic STEM. Moreover, our analytical goals go beyond documenting the personal experiences of marginalization felt by faculty from marginalized and minoritized groups. These individual-level narratives, though important, provide the beginning, not the end point, of our sociological analysis. We theorize below—and empirically examine in the next three chapters—two schemas that are at the core of the cultural conception of merit in STEM.[103]

Work Devotion in STEM

As noted earlier, the work devotion schema has been studied in other STEM contexts. This scholarship shows that expectations for work devotion are not necessarily inherent in the work but are socially contingent and variable across context and country.[104] For example, a study of computer engineers employed in one large multinational firm found that work hours and intensity varied widely across national contexts, shaping how managers structured work.[105] Workplaces in some of the countries (e.g., India) had intensive work expectations that mirrored those in the United States.[106] But others, like the white-collar workplace in Hungary, had much more flexible work arrangements and little pressure for works to align with the ideal worker norm that dominates US workplaces.[107] This research suggests that the intense pace of STEM work in the United States is not intrinsic to the work itself but is a socially constructed part of organizational and cultural norms about appropriate work time and structure.[108]

Work Devotion in Academic STEM

The schema of work devotion is important in STEM work across all employment sectors,[109] but it is particularly salient within academic STEM. For most STEM faculty, work devotion is a significant part of their personal identity. Previous studies suggest that the discernment of a scientific calling often begins in adolescence.[110]

Work devotion is also a moralized identity. One's dedication to a scientific vocation helps construct a sense of self that is embarked upon as a moral mission.[111] Scientific research, like the earlier religious orders that supported science,[112] is believed to entail a lifelong, passionate, and methodical service to a vocation.[113] Max Weber, an early sociological observer of science, lectured in 1917 on the "scientific vocation" as one of pure, undistracted commitment to the mission of pursuing and teaching scientific knowledge. Those with a vocation pursue scientific knowledge not merely for its technical utility and profitability but also "for its own sake."[114] This moral elevation of pure scientific research is rooted in the explicit religious framing given by sixteenth-century scientists who were part of Christian holy orders[115] and the seventeenth-century cultivation of science by Puritanism as a means for better understanding God's creation and "God Himself."[116] Although the equating of the natural world with divine creation was challenged by Enlightenment thinkers, the understanding that scientists, particularly academic scientists, should be virtuously and singularly dedicated to the pursuit of knowledge has persisted.[117]

The work devotion schema is potent among our sample of STEM faculty in a research-intensive university. They love their jobs, and some say they would do them for free. They routinely take work home with them on nights and weekends. They extol their love for research, excitement from discovery, and appreciation of freedom to chart their own course. Eleven of the eighty-five professors we interviewed had or currently have some involvement in industry and say they prefer the university mission of basic research and teaching over the industry focus on corporate profitability.[118] For example, Bill, a senior professor in an engineering discipline, relished the "freedom" to pursue his own research agenda in academia. He stated,

[In academic STEM] you certainly have much more freedom here to pursue what you're curious about. I don't have a boss in terms of defining the research goals that I focus on, whereas if I'm [in a company,] they have very clearly-defined programmatic goals and objectives and a management chain and hierarchy and all that. I actually worked in industry before I went to graduate school for a few years. And that's exactly what it's like. And I had no desire to go back to that. And so I think the degree of freedom and flexibility that one has in academia is very attractive. It's a unique place where, as a faculty member, you can have stability in your own personal career and combined with the freedom to pursue whatever ideas you wish to pursue.

These beliefs are broadly shared among STEM faculty across several intersectional categories of gender, race/ethnicity, LGBTQ, and parenthood status.[119]

How Does the Work Devotion Schema Contribute to Inequality in STEM?

This devotion demands all the time and energy that one is able to give.

Historically, the apostles of science were assumed to be men undistracted by other life responsibilities. In 1917, Max Weber took for granted that academic scientists would be men. Journalistic accounts in the 1920s and 1930s reinforced the notion that "women's relationship to genius was as caretaker of the bodily needs of those men who had achieved it, since women were too distracted by domesticity to achieve genius themselves." This was the fate of Albert Einstein's first wife, Mileva Maric, who relinquished her own scientific career to care for Albert and their children.[120] A 1953 study of elite men scientists illustrated that the most devoted scientists gave their allegiance to their work while resisting their wives' requests that they be home regularly for dinner. Women were generally assumed to lack the single-mindedness and stamina required to do the best science.[121]

In our study of twenty-first-century scientists, some men and many women confront challenges in balancing their scientific vocations with other life responsibilities such as caregiving. However, we will show that these professors are as equally as work devoted and productive on average as those without caregiving responsibilities.

Yet that does not mean that all STEM faculty are culturally perceived to be work devoted by their colleagues. The family devotion schema is a morally laden schema that demands parents'—especially mothers'—full dedication to their children.[122] The family devotion schema is culturally incompatible with work devotion. STEM professionals with caregiving responsibilities—particularly mothers with young or school-age children—may be seen by colleagues as less work devoted, and thus less meritorious, than their colleagues even if they are equally as productive and committed.[123] Professors who use university policies for family accommodation, or those who are presumed to need these policies, may be subject to a "flexibility stigma,"[124] which devalues their scientific contributions.

Schema of Scientific Excellence

We empirically identify a *schema of scientific excellence* that defines a set of characteristics as markers of excellence within academic STEM disciplines. Faculty who embody the most valued sets of characteristics are seen as the most meritorious. The professional competence of those who are not seen to measure up along these characteristics is at risk of being questioned. This schema is not an objective judgment of performance or a simple tally of human capital; it is a subjective cultural yardstick that is deeply engrained with the professional meaning systems of STEM.

In our data, we delineate four groups of characteristics that make up the schema of scientific excellence. First, faculty members most strongly identify scientific excellence with innovative, pathbreaking, creative brilliance. This notion of brilliance is rooted in earlier Western traditions of genius discussed above.[125]

Another set of characteristics that are broadly venerated are assertive traits, including competitiveness, self-promotion, strong leadership, and risk-taking. Faculty report that their STEM disciplines puts a somewhat lower value on relational qualities—empathy, being a good teacher, mentoring, and being skilled at interpersonal relationships. A devalued characteristic is diversity commitments, which are seen to risk politicizing STEM.

The schema of scientific excellence is articulated similarly across demographic groups and STEM disciplines. The creative brilliance and assertive qualities are recognized by all groups as the most valued markers of excellence. All groups rank the relational qualities somewhat lower, on average, and tend to consider overt commitments to diversity and social justice as inconsistent with disciplinary schemas of excellence. Taken together, these characteristics delineate the schema of scientific excellence that most faculty believe define merit in their discipline.

How Does the Schema of Scientific Excellence Contribute to Inequality?

The schema of scientific excellence reproduces inequality through several processes. First, the characteristics that are most valued in professional excellence schemas are most often associated with heterosexual white and Asian men.[126] These men are the "unmarked category" in STEM: once they reach the faculty ranks, they are typically presumed to be excellent and devoted until proven otherwise. Women, underrepresented racial/ethnic minorities, and LGBTQ faculty have to keep their excellence and devotion on display and disarm colleagues' fears that they will politicize their STEM environments with concerns about inequality and diversity.

The scientific excellence characteristics of creative brilliance and assertive leadership are more often associated with men than women in

STEM.[127] Relational characteristics are more often associated with women. However, women are not rewarded for them because they align women more closely with (devalued) hegemonic femininity.[128] In this way, common race and gender stereotypes get mapped onto the characteristics in this schema.[129] In other words, these biases become second order: they are deployed through cultural judgments of professional excellence.

White and Asian heterosexual men faculty in our study are generally rewarded for displaying assertive leadership, whereas women—especially Latinx and Black women—are often penalized for it.[130] In addition, underrepresented faculty are more likely to be seen as deficient in these valued characteristics and experience isolation in their professional settings.[131] Moreover, STEM faculty, especially faculty of color, who emphasize diversity commitments feel as though they are excluded from social networks. Finally, we find that these traits matter even after scholarly productivity is taken into account. Our analyses show how the schema of scientific excellence disadvantages women, Black and Latinx men, and LGBTQ faculty *net of* their productivity.[132]

In sum, these two schemas help constitute the cultural meaning of merit in STEM.[133] They are hegemonic and widely shared across all types of faculty. They define the most honored way of being an academic scientist in this particular time and place. These schemas are not objective judgments of performance or a simple tally of human capital; they are subjective cultural models deeply integrated into professional meaning systems.[134] Yet as we will show in the chapters that follow, STEM academics with the most valued sets of characteristics and who best display work devotion are seen as the most meritorious.

THREE

The Work Devotion Schema and Its Consequences

Science and engineering faculty at the university we study epitomize devotion to work and see this devotion as an integral part of merit in STEM. Faculty say that they love their work, and even those with young children dedicate most of their waking hours to their profession. For instance, Michael, a father, states,[1]

I take work home with me all the time. I really love my work. I feel lucky to be able to do this job. If I were independently wealthy, I'd be perfectly happy to pay for the opportunity to have this job. . . . The part that I like best is discovering things that no one on this planet knew before.

Similarly, Yolanda, a mother, says,

[I feel] highly motivated to work, yeah. I think that's the love of science, and that kind of thing. . . . It's not a big deal for me . . . to work twenty-four seven, 365 days out of the year. It's what I want to do, so it's never really felt like a job to me. . . . I also feel really lucky that I found it.

Donna, who hopes to have children soon, states,

I love the freedom and the creativity. I see a lot of big challenges, and it is fun too. I think there's constantly new things coming up . . . lots of interesting possibilities and collaborations all of the time.

Francisco, a father, remarks,

So I am definitely one of those people dedicated to the work. . . . With faculty life . . . there's no boundaries. It's not like you finish your work at 5:00 p.m. and go home.

This chapter studies the meaning of the *work devotion schema* and its personal and social consequences for STEM faculty. To preview our results, our interviews reveal a passion and dedication with which many professors pursue their scientific calling. Our survey data show that those who are most ardently devoted to work also tend to be the most productive, professionally integrated, satisfied with their university, and the least likely to intend to leave.

Fully conforming to the work devotion schema requires long hours and steadfast determination, which even the most dedicated scientists can struggle to achieve.[2] The schema also devalues the time faculty spend on family caregiving.[3] Our analysis of survey data reveals that many faculty members report that parents of young children, especially mothers, who openly engage in family caregiving are viewed in their department as less committed to their careers.[4] Our interview data put flesh on the bones of these quantitative models. We find that many professors, even those with children themselves, generally accept the perception that mothers are less hardworking and less productive than other colleagues in their department.

Professors' assumptions that faculty with caregiving responsibilities are less meritorious are contradicted by our data. When we measure self-reported work devotion and work effort, we find that parents of young children are, on average, more likely to personally embrace work devotion than other professors. In addition, mothers work just as many hours as fathers. Mothers and fathers work fewer total hours than their childless colleagues but spend the same amounts of time on their research as do childless faculty members. Further, analysis of our Scholarly Production Indices (SPI) database shows that mothers are equally successful at winning research grants and have equal or higher publishing rates than childless colleagues in their departments and at similar ranks.

Even so, there is a pervasive cultural belief among STEM faculty that mothers are less devoted to work than their colleagues. Mothers incur much of the cost of this belief: on average, mothers are paid less than other colleagues with similar levels of productivity and grant funding. But there are also collective costs: in departments where stigma against family caregiving is most common, all department members—parents and nonparents—tend to be less satisfied with their jobs and more likely to have plans to leave the university.

The Work Devotion Schema

In many professional workplaces, the *schema of work devotion* is a powerful cultural frame that promotes the belief that work demands and deserves undivided allegiance.[5] The work devotion schema is present within many professional occupations,[6] and its manifestation likely varies across different professional cultures. In STEM, work devotion is salient across employment sectors.[7] It is potent within academic STEM, where it takes the form of devotion to a scientific vocation.[8] Yet the extent to which individual STEM faculty actually adhere to this schema is an empirical question.[9]

We measure professors' personal adherence to work devotion in our survey with a multidimensional work dedication scale (see figure 3.1).[10] This scale measures the facets of work devotion found in previous qualitative work:[11] cognitive acceptance of the legitimacy of putting a great deal of extra effort into research beyond departmental expectations, moral identification with and emotional investment in departmental and disciplinary values, and a sense of inspiration from colleagues and students. (The appendix provides detailed information on scale operationalization and analytic strategy.)

We find that work devotion is generally accepted by the professors we study across all demographic backgrounds.[12] Faculty have similarly high levels of attachment to this schema regardless of gender, race/ethnicity, and sexual identity. Adherence also does not vary systematically by department or career stage. Figure 3.2 presents means on the work devotion measure along several intersectional categories of gender, race/ethnicity, LGBTQ, and parenthood status.[13] Mothers and fathers of children under sixteen are just as likely as other STEM faculty to personally embrace work devotion expectations. Similarly, underrepresented racial/ethnic minority women and men faculty are just as likely as white and Asian women and men to embrace work devotion. In other analyses, we find that parents of children aged six or younger are actually more likely to personally embrace work devotion than other faculty.[14] Thus, work devotion is hegemonic: it is part of the professional culture of academic STEM overall, not just a belief common to certain groups of faculty.[15]

Most of the faculty in our sample derive personal enjoyment out of this devotion. For example, John, a mathematician without children, says he often chooses the "pleasure" of working nights and weekends if he has a research problem on his mind. He explains,

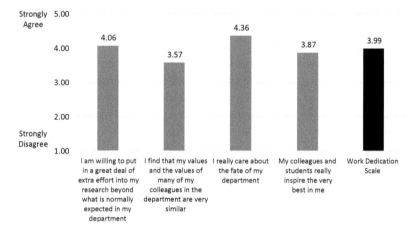

3.1 *Average Values on Work Dedication Measures and the Work Dedication Scale*
Average values on work dedication scale measures, and mean value on the work dedication scale (an average of the four measures). See the appendix for detailed item wording.

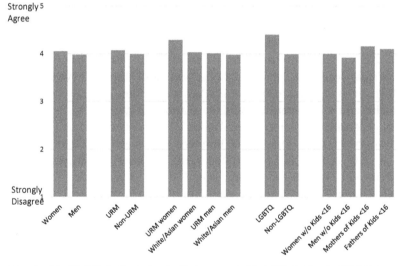

3.2 *Predicted Work Dedication by Gender, Underrepresented Racial/Ethnic Minority (URM) Status, LGBTQ Status, and Parenthood Status*
Predicted values on the work dedication scale by gender, URM status, gender-by-URM status, LGBTQ status, and gender-by-parenthood of child under sixteen (net of variation by department, academic rank, and other career measures). Values are produced from OLS regression models with demographics and interaction terms; all other control variables were held at the mean. None of these demographic differences are statistically significant.

I can solve problems at all times. There is a great pleasure in that, actually, in cutting through a mathematical problem and seeing the light. And you can take that pleasure at any time.

Others are equally enthusiastic about teaching and mentoring. For example, Minzhu, a father, explains that he is most passionate about "work[ing] with my students on discovering something new. So that's very satisfying. And also to see how my students have turned out. Usually they turn out very well." Similarly, Amanda, a mother, says,

I enjoy the process of discovery. I enjoy figuring out how . . . systems work. I really enjoy interacting with students. I actually really enjoy teaching. So yeah, all of it. It all kind of fits, it works for me. It makes me feel like I'm doing something good with my life.

Another father, Ramesh, remarks that like himself, his friends would "do what they're doing even if they didn't get paid because [they] really care about [their research] subject. For me, it's . . . exploring, being the first one to ever see something. . . . It's exciting."

Some faculty members analogize the joyful excitement of discovery to an addict's high. Michael, whom we met at the beginning of this chapter, says laughingly, "The excitement of that process is tremendous for me. And I'm an addict." Joseph, another father, describes his engagement with research as a "passion . . . in the form of desire for intellectual discovery. Once you make some discovery that just turns you on, you kind of get greedy for it and addicted to that."[16]

Given the value that is placed on work devotion in STEM, what are the benefits for individual professors who embrace this schema? What happens when one's work devotion is questioned by colleagues? The next section addresses the consequences of the work devotion schema for the STEM faculty in our study.

Positive Correlates and Consequences of the Work Devotion Schema

Previous studies have argued that personal acceptance of the work devotion schema is both a cause and a consequence of professional success. For academic scientists, the socialization into work devotion helps ensure that the most dedicated scientists persevere in relatively low-paid graduate school and postdoctoral programs, despite the long odds of landing a tenure-track job at a top university. As Francisco explains,

Faculty typically love what they do, and they have survived a filtering system. It's really harsh. You need, like, you know, hundreds of thousands of people to generate one faculty, right? You go through that process, and typically you love [what you do enough] for you to continue to do that. . . . It's a very long process.

For those who have succeeded in getting faculty positions at the university we study, their earlier dedication is rewarded with participation in an elite scholarly community and the ability to attract the best students. Kimberly explains some of the distinctive aspects of her department,

The quality of the people you can hire is very good. What's different here maybe than other places is that . . . the expectations are very high, so to be good here, to hold your own here, you need to do very good stuff, you need to publish very good papers, you need to get good funding, I mean just to be on par with our peers. And so the expectations are high, but the infrastructure—and not just physical infrastructure, lots of places have that, but the human infrastructure— . . . the intellectual infrastructure is great here.

Kimberly also explains that her department's "graduate program is one of the top in the country, . . . so you have the opportunity to work with some really good younger people."

The survey results similarly show that individual faculty members continue to reap professional dividends by embracing work devotion. Compared to their peers in similar departments and of similar ranks and demographic backgrounds, we find that faculty who have high levels of dedication also have higher salaries, publish more articles per year on average, and are more satisfied with their jobs. Those who are the most work devoted also are less likely to say they plan to leave academia for industry.[17]

In our study, faculty who most ardently embrace work devotion are less likely to report personal experiences of marginalization and are more likely to believe their department colleagues view them as highly productive.[18] Of course, work devotion and experiences of respect and inclusion are likely co-constructed: if faculty members feel marginalized or that their research is not respected, this likely impacts the extent to which they are devoted to their work. Nonetheless, these results suggest that individual embrace of work devotion has positive consequences for many professors.

Negative Correlates and Consequences of the Work Devotion Schema

Alongside these positive outcomes, we also find that expectations of work devotion can lead to long hours, stress, attenuated personal relationships, and the sense of never being able to measure up to the standards of the department.[19] These challenges confront many faculty regardless of whether they have children.

Work without End

Recall Ruben from chapter 1, a professor without children, who describes himself as intensely devoted to his work. Like many faculty we interviewed, Ruben works long hours, including nights and weekends. He works on campus all day and then goes home to work on papers until one or two in the morning. He has been successful in obtaining research funding, which has led in turn to more projects, more graduate students and postdoctoral scholars, and more stress. Yet he says his productivity is only average for his department: "I guess mine is probably within the average. The problem is, in my department we have like rock stars." He describes these luminaries as "really successful" and possessing true "dedication." He says further, "They are really good, and they just do it all day, all night, all the time. . . . They never stop [working]."

Stigmatizing Parents

The work devotion schema fosters a *flexibility stigma* that devalues employees who openly acknowledge their personal and family obligations.[20] Flexibility stigma refers to the normative penalties that attach to those who seek (or are presumed to need) flexible work arrangements in order to manage family responsibilities. Because they fear that using formal policies aimed at work/life balance will trigger this flexibility stigma and lead to career setbacks, many who need such policies avoid using them.[21] Workers who need flexible schedule arrangements for family or personal reasons are often stigmatized because they violate their workplace's norms about being a devoted, ideal worker.[22]

Compared to the typical US workplace, the professors in our study already reflect the ideal worker norm. Most are dedicated to their work and work far more than forty hours per week. As previous research has shown, many new parents, mothers and fathers alike, leave full-time

STEM employment for jobs elsewhere after having children.[23] The parents in our sample have stayed in academic STEM full-time after becoming parents. Although the university offers a policy allowing faculty with family responsibilities to adopt a part-time tenure-track schedule for a time, none of the faculty in our study have taken advantage of it, and its use is virtually unheard of among their colleagues.

Some freedom to schedule when and where they do their work is already built into the job for many faculty.[24] Even faculty who are in charge of large laboratories enjoy daily, weekly, and monthly schedule control, and they frequently use graduate students, postdoctoral scholars, and professional laboratory managers to broker the day-to-day tasks of their experiments. In addition, the teaching load at the university we study is generally low: faculty teach a median of two eleven-week courses each year. Respondents recognize that they have considerable autonomy: over 70 percent of faculty in our sample agree that they have "a lot of control" over their balance of personal and work lives.[25]

Yet we find that flexibility stigma is directed against faculty who are open about family obligations, even as they continue to work intensively in full-time positions. Drawing on our survey data and qualitative interviews, we find that a professor's choice to use work-life balance policies such as temporary leaves for the purpose of family caregiving—and even the choice to have children in the first place—is viewed as violating the moral expectations of work devotion in academic STEM.[26]

Our survey taps flexibility stigma by asking faculty if there are negative consequences for making use of work-life balance policies and whether there are commonly held beliefs in their departments that mothers and fathers are seen as less committed to their careers than nonparents (see table 3.1 and the appendix). We use regression models to examine which faculty are most likely to report experiencing a flexibility stigma (table 3.2). We find that women are more likely than men to be aware of this kind of stigma, as are parents of young children compared to colleagues without children.

Given the race to win grants and stay aloft in national and international rankings, is the stigma against those with family commitments, particularly mothers, justified in the meritocratic system at an elite university? Do mothers have less scientific merit than others? We now consider a series of questions in this vein.

Are mothers less able to dedicate the necessary time and energy to their scientific work as their colleagues? First, we note that mothers of children under age sixteen spend more time on an average weekday and weekend doing childcare than comparable fathers do, even when controlling for

Table 3.1 Means and Standard Errors of Dependent and Independent Measures ($N = 266$)

	Mean	Std. Error
Flexibility Stigma Measures		
Flexibility Stigma Scale (1 = Strongly Disagree [SD] to 5 = Strongly Agree [SA])	2.125	.05
Fathers considered less committed (1 = SD to 5 = SA)	1.754	.06
Mothers considered less committed (1 = SD to 5 = SA)	2.129	.07
Negative consequences for using arrangements for work-life balance (1 = SD to 5 = SA)	2.522	.07
Consequences Measures		
Considered leaving academia for industry (1 = SD to 5 = SA)	1.669	.07
Intend to remain at institution for remainder of career (1 = SD to 5 = SA)	3.888	.08
Satisfaction with experiences at institution (1 = Very Dissatisfied to 5 = Very Satisfied)	4.050	.07
Work-life balance scale (1 = SD to 5 = SA)	2.808	.07
Dedication Scale	3.988	.04
Willing to put in extra effort (1 = SD to 5 = SA)	4.064	.07
Values are very similar to colleagues (1 = SD to 5 = SA)	3.574	.07
Care about the fate of the department (1 = SD to 5 = SA)	4.360	.05
Colleagues and student inspire the best in me (1 = SD to 5 = SA)	3.867	.06
Productivity		
Log(Avg. grant dollars per year)	11.746	.23
Log(Avg. articles published per year)	1.300	.05
Demographics and Work and Family Circumstances		
Woman (yes = 1)	.237	.03
URM indicator (yes = 1)	.083	.02
LGBTQ indicator (yes = 1)	.020	.01
Married or partnered (yes = 1)	.904	.02
Respondent has child over 18 years (yes = 1)	.310	.03
Respondent has child from 16 to 18 years (ye s =1)	.092	.02
Respondent has child from 7 to 15 years (yes = 1)	.260	.03
Respondent has child from 3 to 6 years (yes = 1)	.162	.03
Respondent has child under 3 years	.122	.02
Academic step (step 0–30)	18.346	.65
Assistant Professor (yes = 1)	.192	.02
Associate Professor (yes = 1)	.154	.02
Full Professor (yes = 1)	.590	.03
Teaching Professor (yes = 1)	.064	.02
Log(Salary)	11.659	.02
Hours worked per week	58.100	.82
Received retention offer? (yes = 1)	.079	.02
Respondent is in a dual academic career couple (yes = 1)	.332	.03
Respondent has used a formal work-life program (yes = 1)	.139	.02
Hours spent per week on research	20.218	.82
Hours spent on childcare on weekdays (parents of children under 16 only)	3.400	.19
Hours spent on childcare on weekends (parents of children under 16 only)	3.210	.20
Personal experiences of marginalization	2.290	.06
Chemistry	.120	.02
Computer science	.105	.02
Math	.068	.02
Physics	.075	.02
Biology specialty 1	.071	.02
Biology specialty 2	.064	.02
Biology specialty 3	.023	.01

continues

Table 3.1 (*continued*)

	Mean	Std. Error
Engineering specialty 1	.034	.01
Engineering specialty 2	.019	.01
Engineering specialty 3	.086	.02
Engineering specialty 4	.090	.02
Engineering specialty 5	.045	.01
Engineering specialty 6	.045	.01
Multidisciplinary department	.117	.02

Table 3.2 OLS Regression Predicting Respondents' Reports of Flexibility Stigma in Their Departments with Demographics, Family, and Work Circumstances ($N = 266$)

	Coeff.	Std. Error	
Woman	.462	.134	**
Underrepresented racial/ethnic minority	.253	.185	
LGBTQ	.856	.450	†
Married or partnered	−.166	.195	
Parent of child over 18 years	−.091	.155	
Parent of child from 16 to 18 years	.288	.188	
Parent of child from 7 to 15 years	.123	.135	
Parent of child from 3 to 6 years	.083	.150	
Parent of child under 3 years	.514	.176	**
Academic step	.004	.012	
Teaching Professor	.554	.285	†
Log(Salary)	.075	.339	
Hours worked per week	−.002	.005	
Received retention offer	−.064	.245	
Respondent is in a dual academic career couple	−.038	.126	
Respondent has used a formal work-life program	−.179	.172	
Chemistry	−.269	.220	
Computer science	-.320	.209	
Math	−.285	.226	
Physics	.335	.241	
Biology specialty 1	−.271	.238	
Biology specialty 2	−.110	.245	
Biology specialty 3	−.496	.351	
Engineering specialty 1	−.416	.337	
Engineering specialty 2	−.129	.366	
Engineering specialty 3	−.271	.222	
Engineering specialty 4	−.106	.212	
Engineering specialty 5	−.452	.277	
Engineering specialty 6	−.621	.264	*
Constant	1.381	3.733	
F-value	40.220		
Adjusted R-square	.174		

Note: *** $p < .001$; ** $p < .01$; * $p < .05$; † $p < .10$. The multidisciplinary STEM department is the reference category for department.

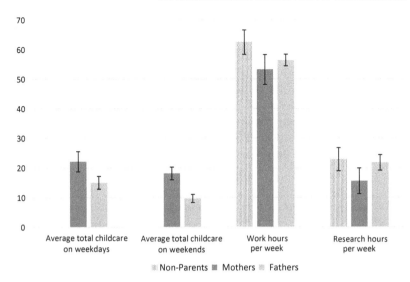

3.3 *Mean Hours Spent on Childcare on Weekdays and Weekends, on Total Work per Week, and on Research per Week, by Parenthood Status of Children Under Sixteen*
Bars indicate 95 percent confidence intervals. Two survey questions captured the amount of time respondents spend on childcare. The first question asked respondents how much time on the average weekday they spend on childcare as their primary activity (less than thirty minutes, thirty to sixty minutes, one to two hours, three to five hours, six hours or more). To create the "average weekday childcare" measure above, we center-coded these value ranges and then multiplied the value by five (to account for time spent on childcare across all weekdays). The second survey question asked respondents how much time they spend on the average weekend on childcare as their primary activity (less than one hour, one to three hours, four to ten hours, eleven to twenty hours, twenty-one or more hours). We center-coded these value ranges to create the "average weekend childcare" measure above. Mothers spend significantly more time on weekday and weekend childcare than fathers but do not spend less time on total work hours or on research hours than either fathers or nonparents.

demographics, department, and faculty rank.[27] This finding reflects gendered societal expectations that motherhood is a more time-intensive responsibility than fatherhood.[28] Yet despite spending more time on childcare, mothers in our study report, on average, the same number of total work hours and the same number of hours dedicated to their research as do fathers (see figure 3.3).[29] Our qualitative interviews, discussed later, show how many faculty mothers burn the candle at both ends in order to be present for their children and focused on their research.

Even though they work similar hours as fathers, are mothers perhaps less personally dedicated to their work? No. Our dedication scale indicates that mothers and fathers of children under sixteen are, on average, equally likely to personally embrace work devotion as other faculty (see figure 3.2).

Is mothers' personal embrace of work devotion reflected in their scholarly production? To investigate this question, we draw on our Scholarly Production Indices (SPI) database, which contains scholarly output and visibility for each faculty member (see the appendix for details). We also collected information on grant awards from a university database that tracks funding awarded to each faculty member. Because differences in productivity could presumably accumulate over time, the categories "mothers" and "fathers" in this analysis include people who have children of any age. We find that faculty members of similar ages, depart-

Table 3.3 OLS Regression Predicting Log Average Articles Published per Year Using Demographics, Job, Research Time, and Motherhood Status ($N = 266$)

		Coeff.	Std. Error	Sig.
Individual Characteristics				
	Underrepresented racial/ethnic minority	−.154	.150	
	LGBTQ	−.140	.281	
	Married/partnered	.187	.165	
	Father	−.263	.133	†
	Childless woman	−.247	.175	
	Mother	.440	.217	*
	Teaching Professor	−1.879	.244	***
	Step	−.001	.005	
Department Variables				
	Engineering specialty 1	.333	.241	
	Engineering specialty 2	.813	.169	***
	Engineering specialty 3	.701	.169	***
	Engineering specialty 4	−.084	.223	
	Engineering specialty 5	.448	.214	*
	Biology specialty 1	−.214	.182	
	Biology specialty 2	−.250	.193	
	Biology specialty 3	.476	.286	†
	Chemistry	.260	.158	†
	Computer science	.497	.164	**
	Ecology	−.071	.306	
	Math	−.452	.191	*
	Physics	.662	.175	***
Research				
	Hours spent on research per week	.004	.003	
Constant		1.138	.224	***
F-Value		11.170		
Adjusted R-squared		.487		

Note: *** $p < .001$; ** $p < .01$; * $p < .05$; † $p < .10$. The multidisciplinary STEM department is the reference category for department. "Mother" represents the women × parenthood interaction term; "father" represents the non-interacted coefficient for parenthood status; "childless woman" represents the non-interacted coefficient for woman. Childless men are the reference category for gender-parenthood status. Because productivity differentials accumulate gradually over time, motherhood and fatherhood status indicate whether respondents have children of any age, rather than just children of the youngest ages.

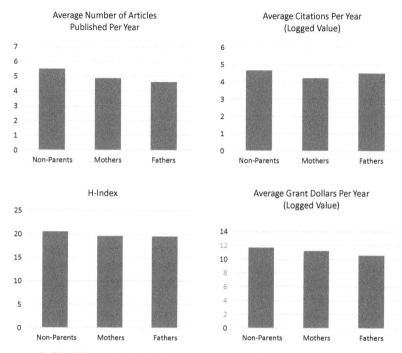

3.4 *Predicted Values on Productivity Measures by Parenthood Status of Children of Any Age*
Predicted values by parenthood status produced from OLS regressions predicting
ln(average articles per year), transformed in the figure above to non-logged values for
clarity; ln(average citations per year); H-index; and ln(average grant dollars per year).
Models included an interaction term between gender and parenthood status to produce
predicted values for mothers and fathers. To account for differentials in publications,
visibility, or grants that may accumulate over time as a result of care responsibilities, we
indicate motherhood or fatherhood status of respondents who have children of any age.
All other control variables (e.g., department, step, teaching faculty indicator) were held at
the mean. Mothers have significantly higher average articles per year than fathers, net of
controls (see table 3.3).

ments, and academic levels receive similar average extramural funding
dollars per year, regardless of their gender or parenthood status.

More important, we find that mothers are just as productive as their
colleagues or even more so.[30] Mothers of children of any age in our sample have similar scholarly article production and impact compared with
other faculty in the same departments and at similar stages of advancement. On one measure—the log average yearly number of articles published over their careers—mothers were actually more productive than
otherwise similar colleagues (table 3.3).[31]

Figure 3.4 presents the data visually, comparing the productivity of
mothers and fathers to that of their childless colleagues, as measured by

average articles per year, citations per year, grant dollars per year, and H-index (an indicator of visibility in their discipline).

Professional women with young children rely on the school system and paid or unpaid caregivers to educate and care for their children. But even with these institutional resources, many mothers we interviewed were pushed to the limit to handle their family obligations while also moving their careers forward. That they have maintained levels of scholarly productivity equal to nonparents and fathers in the face of their productivity being questioned is remarkable.

Our data were collected prior to the COVID-19 pandemic, when taken-for-granted resources of in-person schools, daycares, and other caregivers evaporated seemingly overnight in 2020. Before the pandemic, mothers were already doing more for children on average than fathers were. The disappearance of crucial institutional resources during the pandemic required mothers in many families to spend even more time raising their children, from supervising online education to providing after-school care, because friends and adults in other households were no longer seen as safe companions or caregivers. Publication rates of many faculty mothers have been temporarily negatively affected by this disappearance of care resources in the community.[32] We expect that their productivity will return to pre-pandemic levels after the nation recovers. Yet there may be long-term damage of the pandemic on mothers' careers, especially for faculty on the tenure clock. The gendered effects of the pandemic lay bare the uneven burdens of care that faculty mothers shoulder compared to fathers and childless peers.

Many Faculty Assume a Moral Tension between Motherhood and Academic Science

Our survey results and interview data both point to the intense hours worked by mothers, fathers, and nonparents alike. Despite spending more time per week caring for their children, mothers spent just as much time on work and on research as fathers. Yet many faculty hold broader assumptions that mothers are less committed to their STEM work and stigmatize those who use work-life accommodations. How does the mistaken belief that mothers are less productive on average—and therefore less worthy—persist, despite academic STEM's commitment to transparency and meritocracy, and the lack of difference in actual productivity between mothers and nonmothers?

Our interviews reveal some of the meaning behind these quantitative findings.[33] Many faculty members assume that it is natural for mothers of young children to be less productive than they were in their childless years, and they expect mothers to fall behind their colleagues as a result of their caregiving responsibilities. These beliefs are undergirded by the schema of family devotion, a broad cultural understanding that children are fragile and precious and that they deserve their mother's devoted care.[34] Many faculty hold the implicit assumption that mothers are compelled by family devotion, despite knowing mothers who dedicate long hours to scientific research, publishing, and other university duties. This perspective is voiced by both men and women with a range of family situations.

Avoiding or Delaying Motherhood

Some childless women seem relieved to be able to focus exclusively on the vocation of science and to opt out of the cultural expectations of family devotion. For instance, Angela, a senior professor without children, talks about her "three full-time jobs": running her lab and writing up findings, applying for grants, and being an attentive mentor and teacher. She proudly shows off photographs of generations of her students and their children. She believes that it is unusual for mothers to be willing to dedicate all the time that a high-level research university requires, due to their commitments to their present or future children. She elaborates:

You know, it is a sixty- to eighty-hour-a-week job, and so I don't think we should ever expect [the ratio of women and men STEM faculty] to be at a 50/50. I think we should only ever expect to be at about 25/75, to be honest with you, because, you know, most women prioritize their children at a somewhat higher level . . . and don't want a sixty- to eighty-hour-a-week job, you know. So I've had a number of female grad students and postdocs who have chosen, for example, to go to smaller universities.

Astrid, a senior professor without children, discusses how her child-free status is a "good thing" because it gives her and her academic husband uninterrupted time to work:

And one of the good things [is] . . . we don't have kids. . . . That means we can work a lot more than someone who has younger kids. And given both our personalities, we do work a lot more. . . . When one of us is just overwhelmed and goes into, we call it, "trekking in Nepal" mode. That means if you wouldn't get in touch with me if I were in Nepal, then don't contact me. We get that, and don't feel left out. . . . [Science] is something we are both very compelled by, and we share it. . . . If there is a conflict between work and personal stuff, the work trumps everything. . . . That's [something] we understand.

Other women wish to become parents but fear that motherhood will damage their careers. For instance, Devika, an assistant professor, says she is worried about the "stress" of having children when she is already so "pressed for time" in her work.

Several women report that they delayed childbearing until after tenure.[35] Yet Donna, who had been advised by senior colleagues to delay childbearing until after tenure, is almost forty and is no longer willing to wait. However, she is finding it more difficult to become pregnant than she had anticipated, in part because it is hard for her and her academic husband to find time to spend together. If even conceiving a child is hard to schedule, she worries, how will they manage the time demands of childrearing?

Most of the academic scientists we study are not troubled by needing daily or weekly schedule flexibility or worried about having enough face time in the department. Instead, their fears about the potential stigma of parenthood center on maintaining—and displaying for their colleagues—a consistently high level of productivity as they face an up-or-out timetable for promotion from assistant professor to associate professor with tenure, followed by a lockstep ladder for further promotions.

Mothers and Fathers

Mothers in our survey work similar hours per week as fathers yet spend more time caring for children. The interviews reveal that fathers are less likely than mothers to talk about juggling or scheduling work around family life or other nonwork obligations, and when they do discuss work-family issues, it is in a more relaxed, less anguished way than we hear from mothers. For example, Jason discusses day-care arrangements for his toddler and his baby as a less-than-ideal but tolerable cost of the privilege of being an academic scientist. On the one hand, he states that he and his wife, another professor, "try to structure things so that [their children are] not being raised by somebody else." On the other hand, he explains,

[My two-year old] is in full-time daycare, and our younger child—he's only five months old—and he's in daycare three days a week. Is that what one would dream of? Maybe not. But it's where we are.

When asked whether he ever feels a lack of work-family balance, he laughs and says yes, but he is in this job because he is "incredibly self-motivated."

Like Jason, Yolanda also has a baby and a preschooler. But her tone is less lighthearted and more grim.

I feel like I work twenty-four seven. . . . Every weekend, every night, I feel pretty much constantly on call. . . . The last thing I do in bed is I'm checking my emails, and the first thing I do is checking my emails and that kind of thing, and then working on science. . . .

The nanny comes at 9:00. . . . I get into the office right around 10:00 every day. . . . I leave at 7:00 at night, and by the time I get home, both of my daughters are usually sleeping; my husband is home. So I am with the kids in the morning, I see them for a couple hours in the morning, he sees them for about fifteen to thirty minutes before they go to sleep, and then we . . . wake up and do it again.

Consistent with other research on full-time employed mothers,[36] some mothers in our study try to be actively involved in their children's lives after school, which allows them to fulfill some of the cultural expectations of family devotion. They pay for this dual devotion by working long hours after their children are asleep. As Shannon says,

My schedule now is pretty challenging because it's my decision, because I want to be with my kids and take them to the activities and things, so usually after they go to sleep, I'm on the computer. I pretty much average three or four hours a night of sleep. . . . So it's difficult.

The dominant perspective among faculty we interviewed is that being both a mother and a productive scholar is a challenging—and sometimes impossible—combination. Many simply believe that women "are not as productive" when their children are young. For example, in response to a question about whether her department is welcoming to women, Amanda, a mother, states,

[There is] a tiny bit of impatience that happens when women are at that stage where they're really spending a lot of time with their kids and not putting as much effort into their research. . . . But there's only two junior women and no senior women at all in my group, so it ends up being male faculty that have this concern that we might not be as productive as we need to be in order to get to tenure. And they *want* us to get to tenure. They want us to succeed. So I think that while it generally is pretty welcoming, I think that there does end up being a little tension certainly around core family issues.

When asked whether the same worry comes up around men with young children, Amanda answers,

A little less so, because when I think about the young male faculty that have kids, I think that it *pulls them away* less than it has *pulled away* the women.

Fathers and mothers of young and school-age children juggle multiple obligations. Yet we find a gender difference in how they experience this balancing act. The fathers who say they are preoccupied by work while they are at home do not express anguish. Some emphasize this work focus as a virtuous indication of their personal work devotion. Francisco reports that he expects his family to accommodate his work devotion.

So I am definitely one of those people that are dedicated to the work. . . . My family has learned how to live with this; they are very good about it. My wife and my daughter, like, you know, the first question my daughter asks is, "Are you busy now?" Like they know that I can be just sitting, but I'm thinking about what I have to do at work.

Another father, Brian, also works at home most nights. He describes himself and his husband as career-focused professionals who share the job of raising their young children with an "excellent nanny." When we asked him whether his personal or family responsibilities were affected by his work, he responded,

Not really. I feel extremely lucky that I am allowed or able with my partner to afford extensive domestic help through a nanny. If I didn't have that, the answer would be unequivocally yes. Because I have an excellent nanny at home that I trust and is just wonderful, I feel like I can devote a lot of time to my career aspirations still, and feel like I'm participating appropriately in family life.

In contrast to fathers, mothers of young and school-age children are likely to explain that they are pulled away from their research because of their families. For example, Emily remarks,

I find science fun when I feel like I'm at the top of my field. Not just . . . doing something mildly interesting in the corner, but it's very exciting to feel like I'm leading the field and doing things that are on kind of the cutting edge of science. And that requires a lot of time and energy to stay on the cutting edge, and that's very hard to do with kids.

Further, these mothers express a sense of anguish missing in the interviews with fathers. Emily goes on to say,

I often feel stressed at home when I'm with my kids, that I should be working or that I haven't gotten enough work done. And there's a level of anxiety there which is not ideally how I would like to behave with my kids.

Shannon echoes these concerns:

Even like at night time, if my kid's like, "Mom, just lay with me before I go to sleep," I'm always like anxious because I'm like, "I can't. I have work to do." So I don't always like to say that, but it's stressing me out, and then they pick up on [my stress].

Kristen, whom we met in chapter 1, explained that she has "additional layers of help" including a day-care center, babysitter, and housekeeper. Nonetheless, she feels "the intrusion of really specific guilt" that she doesn't do more with her children: "There's never enough time for those guys. Yeah. It's hard."

These mothers express distress about failing to be fully present for their children during their limited hours with them. At the same time, they staunchly defend their work dedication. Shannon says that she and one other departmental colleague are mothers of young children and that they both have "stellar research" careers.

[My colleague with kids and I] are both not sleeping. I mean we're sending emails at 3:00 in the morning to each other. It takes a certain person to be able to do it.

Yet in contrast to the career success many mothers experience, a broader belief in STEM departments persists that mothers' careers falter because they are juggling a competing moral commitment to their families. This belief is especially striking among the respondents who are members of heterosexual, dual-academic couples. The women we interviewed in these couples tend to discuss the challenge of juggling career and caregiving. The men tend to emphasize the challenge *for their wives* of juggling work devotion with a moralized commitment to caregiving.

For example, Mark states that his wife, another STEM professor, worries more than he does about the quality of their children's day-care center.

I think you very rarely find that a day care will be up to the same standards [as care at home], but I think it should come reasonably close. . . . I mean, otherwise it becomes very difficult—*probably more for my wife*—but it becomes very difficult to work if you are not having high-quality day care at the same time. . . . Because you start asking yourself, "Wouldn't it be better to stay home with your children?"

Mark acknowledges that he is experiencing some feelings of guilt but that his wife has those feelings more frequently.

Joseph, also married to an academic scientist, says,

[Balancing work and parenting is a] challenge, and my wife is also a faculty member [here], *so she is also having trouble balancing as well, probably much more so than me*. . . . I just think it's mostly in the realm of perception of what she should be doing, so she *might feel a bit more guilty about neglecting our toddler*, if she does. . . . I think she is actually feeling the *competing tensions* for her time a lot more than I am, and I can imagine that that's typical for most women as opposed to men. (emphasis added)

Joseph believes that his wife feels guiltier than he does about not spending time with their toddler and that this lack of time is framed, for her, as "neglecting" the child. His report of his own and his wife's experiences aligns with a broader social pattern. Guilt is a response to a moralized set of obligations: mothers are typically more likely than fathers to be assigned the responsibility for family devotion,[37] and mothers are more likely than fathers to feel guilty when work interferes with family time.[38]

Reflecting further, Joseph attributes the experience of his wife and other academic women he knows to a natural and perhaps inevitable set of difficulties women face in maintaining cutting-edge scientific research and scholarship once they become mothers. He continues:

It is really hard for women to actually get back into . . . the job and carrying out science. . . . Just the day-to-day aspects of keeping a laboratory going, even just thinking about things in a way that you have to [keep] up with current discoveries in the field, so you have to know what other people around the globe have done as well, and so just getting back into the grind and thinking about science is very difficult once you are away for a while.

This perspective, shaped by the work devotion schema, justifies mothers' presumed professional slowdown as an insufficient ability to run a laboratory, keep up with the field, and even to think about science in a creative and sustained way.

Managing Stigma

Our quantitative data show that making use of family accommodation policies such as childbearing leave and reduced teaching loads can be perceived as evidence of dwindling career commitment. This belief is vividly expressed in the qualitative data. Donna, who worries about her ability to conceive a child, describes departmental perceptions that faculty who take family leave or stop the tenure clock are "not doing well from a career perspective." Similarly, Melissa, a mother of young children, notes that if someone uses a family accommodation policy such as taking a family leave or stopping the tenure clock in her department, "it causes other people to lower their expectations of your productivity."

Some fathers also covered their family caregiving. For example, Nicholas said, "I'm very careful about what I say to people [about my family] at work. . . . You have to be very careful about what people know about the way you spend your time. The assumption is that you should *[be] doing just this job.*" Brian, a father with a same-gender spouse, states that watching department reactions to a colleague who took a childbearing leave for each of her children gave him pause. He says further,

And I know that the Chair and the department leadership were just like "*Really?* [Another leave?] *Again?*" And it did set sort of a negative taste in people's mouths for a while. I have not personally taken any time off at this point yet due to my family situation. And I partly do that, to be completely frank, because I don't want to be perceived as one of the people who can't balance family and work.

Given this stigma, it's understandable that many parents avoid family accommodation policies and programs on campus. We present an extended segment of our interview with Minzhu, a former chair of a department with over sixty faculty.

Interviewer [I]: How do the faculty in your department respond when someone has or adopts a child and wants to take some kind of family leave?
Minzhu [M]: I don't remember whether we've had such a situation, actually.
I: It's not something that comes up very often?
M: No. Certainly not when I was chair. And now I'm not chair, so actually I don't know. Some people take leaves, but I don't know for what reason. Usually people take leaves because they started a company, and that's the only reason I know. I'm not

aware of adopting a child or having a child [as a reason someone took a leave]. . . .
They just have to explain to the chair, and the dean approves it. . . . It's not as
though they have to explain to the whole department. . . .

I: I see. Okay. Is that something that happens fairly often? People taking time away to
work on a company or something?

M: I don't know what you mean by "often." But certainly there are cases where I'm
aware, maybe four or five at least, in the past . . . since I came here.

I: Do you think if word got out that someone left to care for a child, took time off to
care for a child, that that would be treated differently than someone leaving to
start a company?

M: I don't have an example of a child leave, so I cannot say.

Whether or not women use policies like family leaves, the stigma can
still adhere to motherhood itself. Some mothers try to sidestep this
stigma and its accompanying assumptions of lower productivity by simply never mentioning the fact that they have children. As Jessica says,
"People make judgements. . . . I keep my personal life sheltered because
it just undermines your professionalism." Many mothers "pass" as nonparents in their department and reveal their family situations only to a
few trusted academic friends.[39] William confirms the success of this con-
cealment, saying, "Most faculty don't talk about their kids. I couldn't
tell you who has kids and who doesn't."

Jessica's story is remarkable. She had given birth shortly before join-
ing our case university. Then she gradually learned that her baby daughter had special needs. Her child required additional support, including
attending several medical appointments each month. In Jessica's words,
"It was really pretty insane." However, she says she ensures that her colleagues remain unaware of her family obligations and never misses her
professional responsibilities.

I never told them. . . . I'd say, "I have an off-campus appointment." I just never let
people know. I was always available when people wanted me here. I never missed
anything. I tried to rearrange my schedule around whatever was necessary on campus.

She maintains the devoted worker ideal by leveraging the flexibility in
her day-to-day schedule and by relying on a secret squad of helpers. She
says that she has to "support this army of people"—including a nanny, a
housekeeper, and a gardener—"to help me with my daughter to allow me
to go to work." She goes on to say, "I just farmed out everything. I know a
lot of people say, 'I can't afford to do that.' I couldn't afford *not* to do it."

Hoping One's Career Reputation Survives a Pregnancy

If professors become pregnant, their imminent motherhood can become less of a secret. Expectant mothers try to manage this issue in a variety of ways. These include trying to time their births for the summer months, delaying pregnancy until after their academic files for tenure and promotion have been turned in, and limiting the time they spend on family leave.

As an example of the limiting time strategy, recall Yolanda, the mother of a baby and a toddler. She declined to take most of the leave that was available to her because she had large research grants to manage. She explains, "I worked up until six hours—I worked until basically my water broke." After the delivery, while still in the hospital, she began taking conference calls and answering work emails.

Yolanda explains, with evident relief, that her career reputation "survived" intact. However, she also acknowledged that by privileging the cultural expectations of work devotion over those of family devotion, she may have lost something irreplaceable.

We survived, and it was totally fine, which was great, and now everything is great—but it's a very precious time when you have a baby. It's a very special time, and I feel like maybe I got a little bit ripped off on it.

Despite the efforts of many women faculty with children to hide or minimize their identity as mothers, many mothers pay a price for symbolically violating the work devotion schema. In Jessica's words, motherhood is perceived to undermine their professionalism.

Mothers' scientific endeavors are devalued in more concrete, monetary ways. We find that on average, mothers of children of any age suffer an earnings penalty compared to colleagues in their department at similar levels of advancement and with similar levels of actual scholarly production (see table 3.4 for results and the appendix for details).[40]

Figure 3.5 depicts the magnitude of this motherhood salary penalty by showing predicted values of annual earnings for various groups, including the same controls as in table 3.4. Within the same department and academic level, the gender gap in earnings is small. Men earn about $563 more per year than women, on average. However, the earnings gap between fathers and mothers is seven times larger. Again controlling for department, academic level, and productivity, fathers earned on average

Table 3.4 OLS Regression Model Predicting Log Salary Using Demographics, Job, Productivity, and Motherhood and Fatherhood Status (N = 266)

		Coefficient	Std. Error	Sig.
Individual Characteristics				
	Underrepresented racial/ethnic minority	.051	.035	
	LGBTQ	−.085	.071	
	Married/partnered	.033	.036	
	Father	.035	.033	
	Childless woman	.078	.042	†
	Mother	−.103	.051	*
	Teaching Professor	.319	.058	***
	Step	.028	.001	***
Department Variables				
	Engineering specialty 1	.119	.057	*
	Engineering specialty 2	.022	.043	
	Engineering specialty 3	.025	.042	
	Engineering specialty 4	.045	.052	
	Engineering specialty 5	−.031	.051	
	Biology specialty 1	.084	.043	†
	Biology specialty 2	.005	.045	
	Biology specialty 3	.123	.069	†
	Chemistry	.008	.037	
	Computer science	.072	.039	†
	Ecology	.078	.073	
	Math	.027	.045	
	Physics	−.030	.043	
Productivity				
	Log average articles per year	.067	.016	***
Constant		10.947	.050	***
F-Value		40.220		
Adjusted R-squared		.775		

Note: *** $p < .001$; ** $p < .01$; * $p < .05$; † $p < .10$. The multidisciplinary STEM department is the reference category for department. "Mother" represents the women × parenthood interaction term; "father" represents the non-interacted coefficient for parenthood status; "childless woman" represents the non-interacted coefficient for woman. Childless men are the reference category for gender-parenthood status. Because salary differentials accumulate gradually over time, motherhood and fatherhood status indicate whether respondents have children of any age, rather than just children of the youngest ages.

$3,833 more than their otherwise similar colleagues who are mothers.[41] This difference is statistically significant.

The magnitude of this motherhood pay gap is striking, given the homogeneity of the population (all STEM, full-time, tenured or tenure-track professors at one university). Two-thirds of the women and three-quarters of the men in our sample are parents, so the motherhood wage penalty potentially affects most faculty women, whereas the fatherhood bonus potentially affects most men.

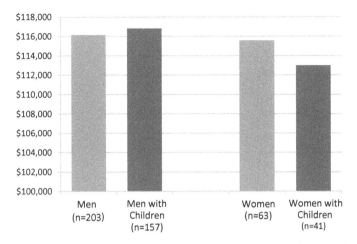

3.5 *Predicted Salary by Gender and Parenthood Status, Net of Department and Demographic Measures (N = 266)*
Predicted annual salary by gender and parenthood status, produced from the OLS regression model depicted in table 3.4 and transformed into non-logged dollar values. All other control variables (department, rank, teaching faculty indicator, URM status, LGBTQ status, weekly work hours, partner status) were held at the mean.

In sum, the work devotion mandate that science requires undivided commitment leads mothers to be viewed as less committed and less deserving of respect and advancement that their faculty colleagues. The implicit cultural assumption that mothers are less worthy is reflected in their lower average pay. This stigma against mothers persists despite the fact that mothers, on average, devote similar hours to research, earn similar grant dollars, and have equal or superior publishing rates compared with otherwise similar colleagues who are not mothers.[42]

In addition to the singular costs to mothers of being viewed as less productive, we also examine the consequences of flexibility stigma for departments generally. Analysis of our survey data shows that faculty who report flexibility stigma in their departments have lower job satisfaction and are less likely to plan to stay in their current jobs than their peers who do not experience flexibility stigma (see table 3.5).[43]

In particular, faculty who see flexibility stigma in their departments are more likely to consider leaving academia for industry, are less likely to intend to remain at their institution for the rest of their careers, and are significantly less satisfied with their experiences at the university overall (see figure 3.6).[44]

Table 3.5 OLS Regression Models Predicting Persistence Intentions and Job Satisfaction with Flexibility Stigma and Controls ($N = 266$)

	Leave for Industry			Remain at Institution			Satisfaction at Institution		
	Coeff.	Std. Err.		Coeff.	Std. Err.		Coeff.	Std. Err.	
Flexibility Stigma in Department	**.630**	**.234**	**	**−.375**	**.211**	†	**−.764**	**.200**	***
Woman	−.909	.401	*	.479	.366		−.236	.342	
Underrepresented racial/ethnic minority	−.530	.542		.134	.484		−.299	.458	
LGBTQ indicator	.545	.945		.130	.994		.417	.876	
Married or partnered	.443	.588		−.027	.524		−.785	.492	
Parent of child over 18 years	−.011	.436		1.215	.412	**	−.095	.380	
Parent of child from 16 to 18 years	.732	.566		−.733	.500		−.841	.481	†
Parent of child from 7 to 15 years	−.266	.379		.277	.324		.066	.333	
Parent of child from 3 to 6 years	−.325	.431		.128	.424		.334	.376	
Parent of child under 3 years	−.745	.493		−.443	.443		.350	.460	
Academic step	−.040	.034		−.004	.030		−.010	.029	
Teaching Professor	−1.050	.804		.480	.843		1.075	.692	
Log(Salary)	−.010	1.104		2.105	.969	*	1.298	.872	
Hours worked per week	−.001	.013		−.012	.013		.002	.012	
Received retention offer	−.740	.759		−.135	.595		.288	.488	
Respondent is in a dual academic career couple	.109	.365		−.607	.345	†	.071	.330	
Respondent has used a formal work-life program	.874	.447		−.124	.441		.122	.443	
Chemistry	−.022	.621		−.953	.563	†	−.650	.504	
Computer science	1.946	.567	**	−1.799	.597	**	−.114	.530	
Math	.215	.710		−1.152	.724		−.977	.590	†
Physics	−.019	.662		−.784	.682		−.109	.588	
Biology specialty 1	.454	.719		−1.270	.662	†	−1.100	.584	*
Biology specialty 2	1.402	.619	*	−1.858	.623	**	−.716	.571	
Biology specialty 3	.872	1.040		−1.123	.948		−.897	.878	
Engineering specialty 1	1.806	1.170		−2.761	.933	**	−1.862	.787	*
Engineering specialty 2	--	--		−.402	.900		−.546	.950	
Engineering specialty 3	.791	.628		−1.983	.593	**	−1.290	.538	*
Engineering specialty 4	.536	.627		−1.329	.577	*	−1.014	.543	†
Engineering specialty 5	1.508	.774		−.383	.821		−1.495	.736	*
Engineering specialty 6	.876	.776		−1.215	.824		.401	743	
Constant									
/cut1	1.544	12.133		18.819	10.773	†	8.414	9.607	
/cut2	3.071	12.125		19.353	10.760	†	10.005	9.600	
/cut3	4.000	12.140		20.949	10.756	†	10.299	9.599	
/cut4	5.689	12.121		22.717	10.764	*	12.702	9.613	
F-value	1.17			2.05		**	1.45		†

Note: Adapted from table 3 of Cech and Blair-Loy (2014). *** $p < .001$; ** $p < .01$; * $p < .05$; † $p < .10$. The multidisciplinary STEM department is the reference category for department.

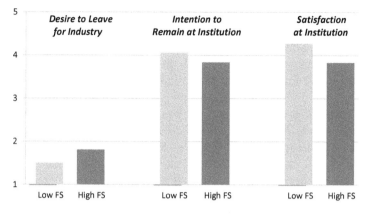

3.6 *Predicted Values on Three Outcome Measures, by Low (First Quartile) and High (Third Quartile) Reported Levels of Flexibility Stigma (FS)*
Adapted from figure 1 in Cech and Blair-Loy (2014). This figure represents the predicted probabilities on each of the three outcome measures by low (lighter bar; first quartile, 1.667) and high (darker bar; third quartile, 2.667) flexibility stigma scores. Explanatory variables from table 3.5 (including gender, race, sexual identity, family status, hours worked per week, advancement level, income, and academic department) were used for probability prediction; the values of all other variables were held at the mean.

Conclusion

This chapter has demonstrated the reverberating impact of the work devotion schema, which holds that science, as a vocation, requires singular commitment and dedication. The professors in our study generally feel enlivened by their work and by advancing the boundaries of scientific knowledge. The work devotion mandate is broadly accepted and hegemonic. Adherence to it does not systematically vary by gender, race/ethnicity, or LGBTQ status, and it does not vary intersectionally within these groups. Parents and nonparents alike embrace work devotion; parents of children under age six embrace it even more tightly. Those who adhere most closely to the work devotion schema enjoy a number of benefits, including, on average, higher salaries, greater productivity, higher job satisfaction, and greater integration into the social and professional life of their departments.

Because work devotion is central to the definition of what it means to be meritorious in science, those who are seen as lacking this marker of merit are devalued. However, *which* behaviors are threatening to work devotion is highly arbitrary: caregiving responsibilities are considered deleterious to work devotion, but other nonresearch activities, such as consulting or administrative responsibilities, are not. Although all STEM faculty feel pressure to demonstrate their work devotion, this cultural schema disadvantages some faculty more than others.

Many professors believe that mothers—more than fathers—are naturally and inevitably pulled away from devotion to work by a competing, moralized commitment to childrearing. Unlike fathers, mothers are framed as less capable of handling the day-to-day requirements of running a laboratory, pushing the boundaries of their disciplines, and even thinking scientifically in a sustained and creative way. These biases, rooted in the work devotion schema, justify mothers' career slowdowns and penalties and support unfair and inaccurate assumptions that mothers are less productive. These biases are likely also behind the fact that mothers experience a significant pay penalty compared to colleagues at similar points in their careers and with similar levels of productivity.

Despite this widespread cultural devaluation and material disadvantage, our quantitative results show that mothers are just as meritorious—just as work devoted and equally or more productive—than their colleagues in the same department and at the same job level.

Faculty do not know how most of their colleagues spend their days; they generally expect their colleagues to use their autonomy and schedule flexibility wisely to advance their research, mentor graduate students, and teach. Faculty assume that the proof is in the pudding; time well spent will be evident in the quantity and impact of scholarship and will be assessed in the biennial or triennial personnel reviews. In short, they feel that they know scientific merit when they see it. Most faculty assume that men and women without children who have won faculty appointments at the top university studied here are assumed to be devoted and effective scientific researchers.

In contrast, there is an implicit assumption that mothers are *not* using their autonomy in the service of work devotion. Absent a detailed knowledge of how their colleagues spend their time, faculty generally fill in the cognitive gaps by assuming that mothers, struggling with the competing moral claims of work devotion and family devotion, are unable to maintain a creative and sustained scientific research profile. These assumptions are held by many, including men married to women professors and including faculty mothers themselves.[45] The gap between beliefs about mothers and mothers' actual productivity demonstrates how the work devotion schema defines merit in ways that reinforce inequality, despite evidence to the contrary.

To cope with assumptions that mothers cannot also be stellar scientists, some mothers in our sample "pass" as scientists whose parenting responsibilities never encroach on their work time. However, by doing so, they deprive themselves of access to campus resources designed to help with family responsibilities, thereby reinforcing the stigma associated with using these resources. By hiding or downplaying a central feature of their nonwork lives, mothers take on additional cognitive and emotional labor, potentially face social isolation (both external and self-imposed), and possibly miss out on developing informal connections with colleagues that are integral to fostering mentoring and advocacy relationships.[46] Some respondents also regret feeling like they have to sacrifice "very precious time" with their young children to live up to these work devotion expectations.

The institutionalization of the work devotion schema comes with collective costs for entire departments. Like a toxin in the cultural environment, the presence of flexibility stigma impacts far more than individual parents.[47] We find that it reduces job satisfaction and plans to stay for all members of the affected department. We now turn to chapter 4, which presents the contours of another schema that (mis)measures merit: the schema of scientific excellence.

FOUR

Mismeasuring Merit: The Schema of Scientific Excellence as a Yardstick of Merit

This chapter asks, How do scientists understand excellence in STEM? Are the characteristics that convey excellence equally likely to be recognized and rewarded among all faculty?

We begin by elucidating four strands that are central to the cultural *schema of scientific excellence* in academia. Our interview data reveal consensus across faculty that the ideal STEM faculty member exudes creative brilliance—the ability to combine new discoveries with systematic scientific thinking in ways that drive novel understanding at the boundaries of one's discipline. This is the most highly valued strand of the schema of scientific excellence. We then use interview and survey data to identify three additional strands. First among these is assertive leadership, which includes competitiveness, self-promotion, and risk-taking. Many professors assume that assertive behaviors enhance one's brilliance and attract attention to one's contributions in their scientific community. We also identify a set of relational qualities associated with scientific excellence, including having interpersonal skills and being a good mentor. These attributes allow scientists to equip and motivate their teams to push their research forward. Finally, we find that a commitment to advancing diversity is devalued by many STEM faculty and can undermine one's reputation for scientific excellence. According to the schema, considerations of diversity distort the goals of scientific inquiry and should be kept separate from STEM academic research. Across demographic and disciplinary differences, faculty generally expressed consensus that these four qualities demonstrate excellence in STEM.

After describing these four strands, this chapter assesses the degree to which faculty personally identify with them—the extent to which these characteristics are part of faculty's self-conceptions.[1] We find that faculty's self-conceptions along these characteristics are highly similar across demographic groups and disciplines. Yet while most agree on what the ideal professional in their field looks like, most also see themselves as deficient. Although most professors we interviewed praise brilliance as denoting excellence in their discipline, less than a third describe themselves as brilliant. Similarly, most see assertiveness as a cultural marker of merit but view themselves as falling short of the assertive ideal. At the same time, many faculty see themselves as more relationally skilled and more committed to the promotion of diversity than the "typical" excellent member of their STEM discipline.

To further unpack the operation of the scientific excellence schema, we examine how it plays out in the lives of Kristen, the biologist we met in chapter 1, and Dan, a physical scientist. Their perspectives exemplify how merit is typically conceived (and misconceived) by the smart, well-meaning faculty in our sample.

Dan and Kristen's stories open the door to questions about the scientific excellence schema—in particular, whether the schema in fact measures a propensity to make excellent contributions to science. Counter to the schema's assumptions, we find that the factors culturally assumed to be markers of excellence are not necessarily connected to actual productivity or scholarly visibility.[2] Even so, we find that adhering to the schema, and embodying its most valued characteristics, translates into real monetary and social benefit. Faculty with more assertive self-conceptions, for example, take home higher salaries and report receiving more respect for their research, even though on average they are no more productive than their colleagues. Even more, the qualities the schema valorizes are not equally available to all groups or recognized when they are present. The schema of scientific excellence is, in other words, a warped yardstick. It exaggerates the worth of majority group faculty while devaluing the scientific contributions of many of their women, Latinx, Black, and/or LGBTQ colleagues.

How Faculty Define Scientific Excellence

Legends and Demigods: Creative Brilliance

Michael's statement quoted at the beginning of chapter 3 illustrated his work devotion. But it also shows his commitment to discovery:

I take work home with me all the time. I really love my work. I feel lucky to be able to do this job. If I were independently wealthy, I'd be perfectly happy to pay for the opportunity to have this job. . . . *The part that I like best is discovering things that no one on this planet knew before.* (emphasis added)

Most of the faculty we interviewed associated scientific discovery with creative brilliance and saw it as particularly highly valued in their field.[3] Across the board, they described this form of excellence as a vivid scientific imagination that is harnessed to produce groundbreaking discoveries:

Ling: I sit on two departments, [and] they generally agree, they do see that what's really outstanding is defined as groundbreaking discoveries.

John: There are some who are demigods and legends and are fantastically imaginative, and real ground-breakers. . . . [My specialty] lends itself to imagination, and there are [quite] a few brilliant ideas out there.

Jill: There's no doubt that research is what is most important. I would say mostly people would say that the important aspect of valuable research is that it be novel, creative, original, and having a large impact on the work that is done subsequent to that. . . . That's pretty uncontroversial.

Members of different disciplines sounded their own riffs on this dominant theme. As a biologist, Michael said that "excellence" in his field consists of the following:

Creativity of experimental design. Imagination in designing experiments to answer questions about the way the world works, or in this case the way the [immune] system works. The rigor with which one answers a particular question.

Kevin, a mathematician, reported that "proving hard theorems is the main criterion" of excellence. Computer scientists described excellence as developing elegant systems, and for experimental scientists it was developing innovative research designs that point to new answers to longstanding puzzles. Jessica, an engineering professor, thought that an excellent professor must master the fundamentals of the discipline and then go beyond them by creating new knowledge and discovering fresh approaches to enduring disciplinary questions.

In any engineering field, there's a traditional set of knowledge. So having a deep understanding of that basic knowledge is definitely [part of excellence]. . . . People would look for that, I think, in somebody that they would say is excellent. But also . . . people want [a professor] to be creative also, and creating new knowledge.

More broadly, the professors we interviewed felt that brilliantly creative yet rigorous science is that which brings humanity closer to greater "truth" about the world. For instance, Amy, a biologist, stated,

Speaking as a scientist, that creativity is probably the number one thing. And also being able to describe whatever happens in a matter that really reflects the truth.

Similarly, Andrew, a mathematician said that the most excellent discoveries are objective, crystalline, and long-lasting. The proof of a theorem, he said, "is true now, and it'll be true in a hundred years."

Most of the faculty we interviewed (88 percent) pointed to creative brilliance as an important component of how their disciplines view excellence. Yet only about a third (36 percent) identified their own creative brilliance as something they celebrate with confidence. For instance, when we asked Christopher what he enjoyed most about his work, he talked about the joy of creating new molecules in his laboratory.

Seeing my own ideas and the ideas of my students come to life. That's the best part. People think of science as very sort of systematic, . . . but chemistry is [also] very creative. Especially when you do what we do [in my lab], which is make molecules. So you sort of envision things and why they might be interesting or might be fun to make, so you do it. And then when it works and does what you think it did, or maybe does something even more unexpected, then that's very gratifying.

Among the assistant and associate professor levels, the proportion of faculty we interviewed who hail their own creative brilliance are similar by gender and by race. However, among the full professors—faculty who have the most status and longest research records—men are more likely than women to talk about and identify with their own creativity and brilliance.[4]

Assertiveness

Assertiveness is also widely held as a marker of scientific excellence in STEM disciplines. This valued strand is a collection of several related traits: competitiveness, self-promotion, strong leadership, and risk-taking.[5] Most of the faculty we interviewed agreed that the typical successful person in their discipline embodies these characteristics, especially competitiveness and self-promotion. As these professors saw it, an ideal scientist takes risks in their scholarship to explore uncharted territory, competes aggressively with other scientists to have the best ideas first, confidently promotes their findings, and serves as an intellectual leader in their field.[6] These assertive qualities were similarly valued by faculty across different specialties of STEM and all demographic groups as a marker of excellence in the discipline.[7]

Several faculty explained that the assertive strand of the scientific excellence schema is so highly valued because it develops, communicates, and promotes the fruits of a brilliant research program. For example, Jennifer noted that alongside "high-quality" and "innovative" science, actively promoting one's argument in publications, conferences, and conversations is important for being perceived as excellent.

[How would my field characterize excellence?] I would say high-quality science. Innovative thought. Externally, the journals you publish in. Clear thinking at conferences. Willingness to speak up and argue for your point.

Heather described the typical successful member of her physical sciences department as having a "competitive gene." Most faculty, like Jennifer and Heather, accepted assertiveness as a straightforward component of scientific excellence. However, a few respondents, such as Jason and Amy, reflected more critically on whether assertiveness is actually a reliable marker of excellence. Jason suggested that scientific creativity is more likely to be noticed as such by others if it is confidently and aggressively promoted:

In academic hiring, and so on, we tend to be very driven by these kinds of personality traits, how confident does the person sound. . . . I know a lot of people who are just incredibly bright and have done a lot of very creative work [but get less credit for it. Others] tend to be the ones that often take the credit even though they may not have necessarily done the work or whatnot. . . . So it's kind of like that, and people like this tend to be more sort of—self-promoting is the wrong term, but it means what I am alluding to . . . visible is the right euphemism for it, while the others [just do their research].

As Jason's statement suggests, assertive self-promotion is not necessarily linked to the actual way scientific discoveries unfold.

Amy, a woman of color, similarly described self-promotion as an absurd requirement of the discipline, disconnected from the quality of the scientific work.

Interviewer: So you think self-promotion is really necessary to kind of excel in this discipline?

Amy: Definitely. I feel that I don't like it, but when I talk to certain [colleagues], the first thing I say is how great I am. And that's ridiculous to me. (*Laughs*) Why am I doing this? But that's the only way that they recognize you and even recognize that you are there. . . . I really don't like that.

To be perceived as excellent scientists—or to be noticed at all—STEM faculty often need to announce their brilliance through a bullhorn.

Using our survey data, we can systematically compare the ways that faculty evaluate their own personal traits compared to the cultural schemas of excellence prevalent in their disciplines.[8] Although most professors recognize that assertive qualities are broadly believed to be markers of scientific excellence, we find that on average, all demographic groups view themselves as less assertive than the scientific ideal. Faculty's assessments of their own assertiveness are remarkably similar across the sample; they do not systematically vary by gender, by race/ethnicity, or by LGBTQ status.[9] We discuss later in the chapter whether everyone is given equal credit for having this assertiveness.

Relational Qualities

Alongside creative brilliance and assertiveness, a third strand of scientific excellence is a set of relational qualities, including empathy, being a good mentor, and being skilled at interpersonal relationships. Although relational qualities are typically seen as positive markers of excellence, respondents reported that their disciplines give less value to these characteristics than to brilliance and assertiveness.[10] Professors' opinions about the importance of these relational qualities do not differ notably across STEM disciplines (see figure A.2).

In interviews, several professors emphasized the importance of interpersonal skills and graduate student mentoring alongside creative brilliance, as in the case of Kelly, who listed "working well with people" alongside "creativity, productivity, communication skills, [and] inquisitiveness" as hallmarks of scientific excellence. Some emphasized that the ability to manage, motivate, and mentor younger researchers and facilitate effective collaborative relationships with colleagues is key to developing and promoting the research that stems from the pathbreaking ideas of the lead researcher. As Charles put it, in addition to brilliance, "excellence also involves being able to transfer your skills and your knowledge to students." Similarly, Joseph described the interplay of creative brilliance and good people skills:

> Most people might argue that basic smarts is the most important characteristic. . . . [But also], the ability to manage people really is a huge aspect of getting ahead. . . . So certainly the good people managers are the ones that are most successful. . . . You'd hope that there is a healthy balance between those two things so to have the imagination to be able to go forward with a certain set of pursuits or experiments and to actually work with graduate students.

In the course of this comment, Joseph touched on multiple strands of the schema: excellent science happens when the lead scientist has "imagination" (creative brilliance), the ability to assertively push the science forward, and interpersonal skills to mentor the students and postdocs working in their labs.

Respondents generally see themselves as possessing strong relational characteristics. Women are slightly more likely to identify with this trait than men are. Although this gender difference is statistically significant, it is substantively small.[11] There are no significant differences by race/ethnicity or LGBTQ status in the likelihood of seeing oneself as relational.[12] Neither are there intersectional racial differences among men and women.[13] Importantly, all groups see themselves as more relational than they see the typical successful person in their discipline.

Devaluing Diversity Promotion

Respondents reported that the promotion of diversity is the least important quality in their disciplines' schema of scientific excellence. Most respondents disagreed that caring about diversity is a marker of excellence in their field, so this is generally a devalued trait. There is little variation on this measure by STEM discipline, except that those in biological sciences are slightly more likely to value diversity promotion as part of excellence in their field than faculty in other disciplines.[14]

This devaluation of diversity commitments is related to STEM fields' widespread embrace of *depoliticization*. Depoliticization is the belief that STEM is an objective space that can, and should, be stripped of social, cultural, and political concerns related to the diversity of scientists.[15] Faculty who openly express their commitment to advancing diversity in their departments or disciplines are at risk of having their excellence thrown into question because they violate this norm of depoliticization.

Even faculty who say they care about diversity among STEM faculty and students reveal that commitments to increasing diversity are seen as less important than—and even a potential threat to—research excellence. For example, Melissa described departmental discussions about race and gender diversity in hiring and promotion:

It's hard to also balance, like, what are this person's contributions going to be in the area of mentoring, acting as a role model, teaching, and those kind of things, as opposed to *are you willing to sacrifice on research*? And I think the attitude is that we shouldn't ever sacrifice on research quality. (emphasis added)

Similarly, Amy stated that when her departmental colleagues discuss the need to increase diversity, the consensus is, "Well, yeah, of course that's important, but the more important thing is science," as though more diverse candidate pools must always trade off research quality.

Although faculty were aware that the schema of scientific excellence in their discipline devalues diversity commitments, respondents from all backgrounds generally reported personally valuing diversity. Although women have slightly stronger personal commitments to diversity promotion than men, there are no racial/ethnic or LGBTQ status differences on this measure, nor intersectional variation in the gender difference by race or LGBTQ status.[16]

This cultural conception of what scientific excellence entails is not idiosyncratic to STEM faculty at this particular university. Our supplemental analysis of STEM Inclusion Study data from STEM professionals in four-year universities across the US finds the same patterns in the relative value put on the four strands of the schema of scientific excellence (see the appendix).[17]

Manifesting Excellence

Our analysis of the survey data above indicates widespread agreement among faculty about the markers of excellence in STEM, even as their assessments of their own characteristics diverge from these markers. There is also agreement that individual faculty must continually work hard to demonstrate to colleagues that they are brilliant enough, assertive enough, appropriately relational, and not too distracted by diversity to live up to the expectations of excellence in their disciplines.

We now turn from a discussion of the general contours of the scientific excellence schema to an analysis of how these strands play out in faculty members' day-to-day lives. In other words, who is seen to embody the characteristics of excellence, and whose excellence is misrecognized? To help explain these processes, we turn to the cases of Dan and Kristen. Both are highly regarded professors devoted to their careers. Each describes how they strive to manifest scientific excellence. They try to demonstrate their research brilliance by taking risks with new ideas, pursuing evidence with intensity, and promoting their findings to the broader discipline. They assume that these practices will bear fruit in grants and publications, which will in turn translate into career advancements and strong collegial relationships of mutual respect.

Dan is a professor in the physical sciences. He is a rising star in his field, an engaged teacher, and a caring member of his immediate and extended family. He describes himself as a passionate scientist who works days, nights, and weekends. He runs a large research group, meets frequently with graduate students and postdocs, constantly writes papers and grant proposals, and travels frequently to present research. His words echo the work-devoted scientists in chapter 3.

So, I work all the time, all day long, every day. . . . I do have down time, but I work a lot. I'm always working and thinking. This job consumes most of my life.

When asked about what it takes to be seen as excellent in his field, Dan explained that in addition to being "extremely bright" and "very creative," scientists must also display a focused aggressiveness if they hope to implement and make visible their brilliant ideas.

You have to be focused and focus on the job. . . . [Also] you have to be extremely bright, very creative . . . aggressive in terms of getting things done, getting money, aggressive in getting people to respond to your wishes, especially your students, and having people, you know, work well for you.

When asked whether most members of his discipline would agree with him, he responded, "Yeah. I mean, a lot of the job is focus and discipline, and you're pushing and pushing the boundaries of the field."

Dan said that his department holds these standards of assertive, hard-driving brilliance.

> [In my department,] there is a ton of absolutely first-rate people in the field, in research, extremely smart, extremely bright, extremely intense and hard-driving, without the unnecessary egos and . . . meanness that you may find in other . . . top programs in the country, which I spent lots of time in.

Yet he and his departmental colleagues also value collegiality:

> You have to be a good citizen, so that means you have to do—for the department you have to get along with people, you have to just be a good colleague and a helpful, supportive colleague.

These remarks show the intertwining of multiple strands of the schema of scientific excellence: creative brilliance advanced by assertiveness ("hard-driving," "intense") and reinforced by relational qualities ("without unnecessary egos and . . . meanness"). The "extremely bright" members of his department are willing to be interpersonally supportive of colleagues they view as excellent.

Dan listed some of his accomplishments, including several well-placed articles, multiple nationally competitive awards, and constant invitations to travel, speak, and promote his work.

> [My lab has] had a good amount of research success, so I've had a lot of invitations to go places, and so for instance in . . . this past year, you know, I was probably traveling every two weeks.

> [I've won an] unusual number of awards at this stage in the career . . . and difficult ones to get, which have lots of national competition. And I've been not successful in just getting like one or two but like [several]. And so I think that because of that my department is very, you know, extremely supportive.

His final sentence showcases his understanding that his department is collegially supportive because of the external validation of his excellence by his scientific community.

We hear similar themes in an interview with Kristen, a star biologist. Kristen has earned accelerated promotions since she was recruited to the university. Like Dan, Kristen described herself as devoted to scientific inquiry. She runs a large research lab and mentors undergraduates, graduate students, and junior faculty. Unlike Dan, Kristen has young children.

Because her husband is generally home evenings and weekends, she said, "I always take work home." She traveled as many days as possible to promote her research. When asked what she enjoyed most about her work, she described how she leads her lab in creative discoveries within the context of collaborative science.

> I think science is just really exciting. . . . I like the discovery aspect of it, the idea that you can see something that just nobody has appreciated before. . . . I really like the idea that we do the science as a community of researchers. My peers, my other faculty peers. I really like sharing that excitement with them and the other people in my lab. So I [like] the fact that it's a discovery-based agenda and that it's collaborative.

When asked about what characterizes excellence in her field, Kristen, like Dan, coupled innovative creativity with assertiveness. She described this in terms of creative, incisive thinkers.

Recall Kristen's description of "clear metrics of excellence" that launched chapter 1. Like Dan, Kristen couples innovative creativity with "pushing things forward and in an aggressive way." By "pushing things," Kristen means pushing ideas, graduate students, postdocs, network members, grant proposals, and article submissions—all aimed toward the goal of fulfilling her discovery mission. Like Dan, Kristen stated that creative ideas are only fully recognized as creative once they are assertively propelled forward to achieve "concrete milestones."

> [In] advancing my research, I have my particular projects. . . . My mission there is to move those projects forward, and you can really mark the progress toward that by publications or grants awarded, . . . [by] concrete milestones.

Like Dan, Kristen emphasized the importance of advertising one's work through disciplinary networks and travel. In order to garner awards and publications, brilliant scientific work needs to be aggressively promoted not only in written submissions to journals and grant agencies but also in informal networks throughout the discipline.

> It's essential. To do well, you have to force yourself to push yourself into these networks, whether you really feel like it or not.

Kristen described these networks as critical for getting informal peer reviews on initial drafts.

Both Kristen and Dan saw excellence as defined by a focused, incisive creativity that is aggressively promoted throughout the discipline. They took for granted the broader assumption that scientific worth is measured by external milestones, such as awards and publications. Department colleagues may not have shared Dan or Kristen's research specialty but could count up their papers and grant dollars, and Dan and Kristen could circulate news of their accomplishments in casual conversations. Both professors felt rewarded by their departments in the form of promotions and respect because they are seen as achieving these milestones.

Yet Kristen seems to find it more arduous than Dan to push herself into disciplinary networks. Perhaps, she mused, this is due to her gender and her childrearing responsibilities. She explained that although she was not actively excluded from disciplinary networks, she found gaining inclusion in a male-dominated discipline far from "natural and easy."

I'd rather just do my own thing. But you have to . . . stay in the loop, and so I actually have to make a schedule [to call people]. I have to force myself, which I bet to other people it's just very natural and no big deal. I don't know if it's just me personally or sort of gender politics or things like that. . . . The colleagues who I really try to emulate, I know they're spending a lot more time on the phone, a lot more time on [video calls] and such than I am. . . . I don't feel that it's natural and easy to be included. I have to make a specific effort.[18]

In addition, Kristen faced the challenge of balancing work and family. Unlike Dan, who had no young children, Kristen needed to juggle her travel with her family responsibilities:

I choose to do travel that I feel is important for my career. You greatly endanger your career if you don't travel a certain amount. It's definitely something [my husband and I] are always negotiating, how much can I travel.

The demands of the schema of scientific excellence are heavy. Like Dan, Kristen felt "very successful" but also that she was not doing enough.

When asked how the department views her research productivity, she responded,

They probably view it more positively. Yeah, I think so, because I have money [from grants], you know. But I'm worried about keeping that money, so I keep the papers coming. Actually, my department has been really—has really rewarded me very nicely. They accelerated my promotion. . . . They have really treated me like someone whose work they really value.

Echoing concerns of the mothers quoted in the previous chapter, Kristen believed that her scientific contributions would be more highly valued if she were not a woman and a mother:

I definitely had people take me less seriously, is the simplest way to put it. . . . The family status and woman thing go hand in hand. . . . People do take you less seriously because you're a woman with a family. I think there's a little stigma attached to that in the [discipline] at large. I think here [in the department], it's just maybe people they don't expect to find you here as often. They make certain assumptions about what your work life is like.

Dan and Kristen also had different perspectives on collaboration. Dan believed his department expects and rewards supportive collegiality, consistent with the strand of relational skills. In contrast, although Kristen personally values collaboration, she felt that her department cultivates a "Wild West" culture of aggressive individuality. Her phrase underscores the gendered connotations of the assertive strand of scientific excellence: a sometimes contradictory set of expectations that requires scholars to push themselves into valuable social networks while also cultivating the persona of a lone cowboy or superstar "rocketing to the top." Kristen reports on the language her senior colleagues use during faculty recruitment:

[The university has] a Wild West kind of attitude. I don't think it's nurturing. The style of the campus is [not that] we're growing and watering these wonderful plants of our junior faculty. . . . People actually use that specific Wild West phrase in talking about it, like in a positive [way]. "I think you could be a pioneer here. You want to get something done, you come here and it can happen."

[During recruitment, these are] the terms senior faculty use: "We want the very best, the pioneers, the superstars, you know—the people who are rocketing to the top, and you know they'll come here and they'll thrive."

Because of this Wild West culture, Kristen said, serious mentoring of junior colleagues is regarded as "an altruistic act" and is not rewarded in personnel reviews. She argued that this ideology does not fit the realities of the scientific enterprise, which requires collaboration and peer review. She believed that the careers of junior colleagues are harmed by senior faculty's reluctance to mentor them, such as providing comments on initial drafts of their proposals and papers.

(Mis)Conceiving Excellence

The case studies of Dan and Kristen raise a new set of questions about the schema of scientific excellence: Are those who embody the characteristics of the excellence schema actually the most productive scientists? Are there other benefits for aligning with this schema, even if there's no productivity bonus? If so, do faculty with different demographic backgrounds and identities all share equally in those benefits when they adhere to the schema? In this section, we investigate broader patterns of misrecognition of bias across different demographic groups, comparing women and men, racially minoritized faculty and white and Asian faculty, and LGBTQ and non-LGBTQ faculty with similar self-conceptions and productivity.

Are Faculty with the Most Valued Traits More Productive?

This section examines data from our survey and from our Scholarly Production Indices (SPI) database to identify the consequences for individuals who are assertive and self-promoting. If these ideal traits are actual markers of excellence, then the faculty who embody them should be the most meritorious. Because faculty overwhelmingly think that proof of merit is in the quantity and quality of scientific publications, we measure whether faculty's self-conceptions of having assertive and relational traits, and downplaying diversity concerns, are linked to their actual scholarly production.

Contrary to cultural beliefs among faculty about these markers of scientific excellence, professors who see themselves as embodying the valued assertive and relational characteristics do not, on average, write more scholarly articles or produce research with greater visibility in terms of citations or H-index. Further, we find that those who see themselves as personally committed to diversity, a devalued trait within the culture of academic science, have just the same rate of scholarly productivity as their colleagues (see figure 4.1).

Are There Social and Monetary Benefits to These Valued Traits?

Although those who embody the most valued traits of scientific excellence are not any more productive than their colleagues, do the faculty who have those traits receive any other benefits? Or is the cultural value

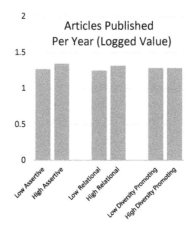

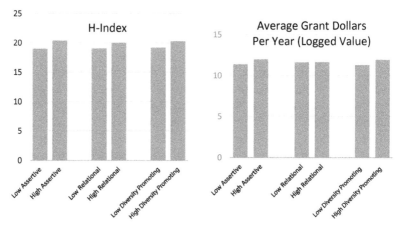

4.1 *Scholarly Productivity Measures, by High and Low Values on Assertive, Relational, and Diversity-Promoting Self-Conceptions*

Bar charts represent predicted values that were produced by running OLS regression models predicting each outcome with the self-conception measures (included one at a time), gender, LGBTQ status, URM status, department, teaching faculty indicator, and step. "Low" values on each characteristic represent the 25 percent quartile on each measure (Assertive: 3.25; Relational: 3.667; Politicizing: 3.00), and the "high" values on each characteristic represent the 75 percent quartile on each measure (Assertive: 4.25; Relational: 4.33; Diversity Promoting: 5.00). All other variables in the model are held at their mean values. None of the self-conception measures were significant predictors of the three productivity measures above.

placed on these traits simply a harmless idiosyncrasy of academic STEM culture, with no tangible social or monetary benefit? Here, we examine whether faculty enjoy benefits when they exhibit assertive and relational traits, or whether they experience penalties for diversity commitments, despite the fact that these traits are not linked to productivity.

We find that although assertive faculty do not produce more work, they do enjoy reputational and financial rewards.[19] For two similar professors with the same scholarly productivity (in the form of average articles published per year), the one with the more assertive self-conception will have a higher salary than their colleague. We find that there are reputational benefits too: holding constant demographic, discipline, and career stage variation, assertive faculty enjoy greater feelings of being respected in their department as well as in their discipline and are more likely to feel they "fit in" with their professional peers and department colleagues, net of their productivity (see figure 4.2).[20] Those who perceive themselves as relational are also more likely than otherwise similar colleagues to perceive that their research is respected in their department and that they fit in with colleagues in their department and their discipline.

On the flip side, holding constant productivity and demographic characteristics, faculty who are more personally committed to diversity face a reputational penalty: they feel that they have to work harder to be seen as legitimate scholars in their departments (see figure 4.2). In other words, for two professors at the same advancement stage, in the same department, and with the same publication track record, the one who is committed to promoting diversity feels they have to work harder to earn the same respect for their STEM work as a colleague who is less personally committed to diversity.

In sum, the professors we study believe that faculty with the qualities of creative brilliance, assertive self-promotion, and the interpersonal skills to manage complex research programs and mentor students manifest scientific excellence and deserve respect and full inclusion in academic life. In fact, professors who regard themselves as assertive and self-promoting do not produce scholarship of greater visibility or higher impact. Nonetheless, they are generally paid more and earn more respect.

Uneven Benefits and Penalties

Does everyone who exudes these markers of scientific excellence have equal access to the attendant rewards? We find that this is not the case. As we show later in this chapter, underrepresented academic scientists face more skepticism about their innate brilliance. White and Asian heterosexual men are generally rewarded for displaying assertive leadership, whereas women—especially Latinx and Black women—are penalized for it. Further, interpersonal skills generally benefit men but can cost women respect and professional integration. And some faculty are seen by their colleagues as overly committed to diversity, simply by their membership

Annual Salary (Log Value)

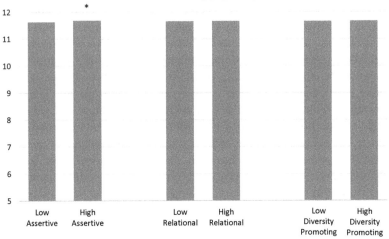

Have to Work Harder than Colleagues in Department
to Be Perceived as Legitimate Scholar

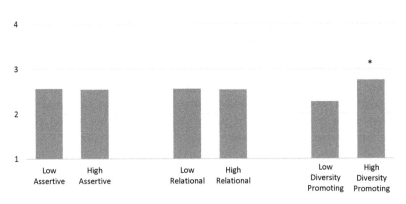

4.2 *Reward and Respect Measures, by High and Low Values on the Self-Conception Measures*
Bar charts represent predicted values produced by running OLS regression models
predicting each outcome measure with the self-conception measures (included one at
a time), log average articles per year, gender, LGBTQ status, URM status, department,
teaching faculty indicator, and step. "Low" values on each characteristic represent the
25 percent quartile on each measure, and the "high" values on each characteristic represent the 75 percent quartile on each measure (see fig. 4.1 note). All other values in the
model are controlled for by being held at the mean. Asterisks indicate the significance of
the self-conception measure in each regression model (two-tailed tests), net of controls.

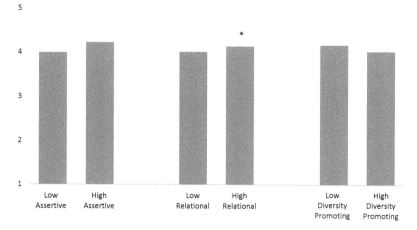

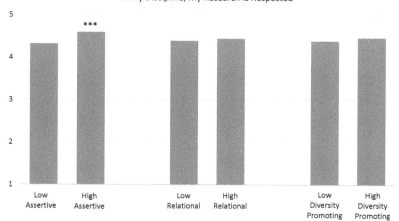

4.2 (*continued*)

in a devalued demographic category. Despite the assumption that the standard of scientific excellence is universal and can apply to anyone, not every professor reaps the same benefits and rewards from living up to the schema's ideals.

Unequal Assumptions of Creative Brilliance

Overall, underrepresented groups experience less professional respect and are more frequently excluded by colleagues. Even among those with

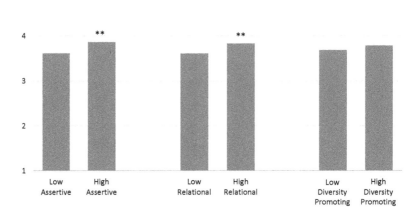

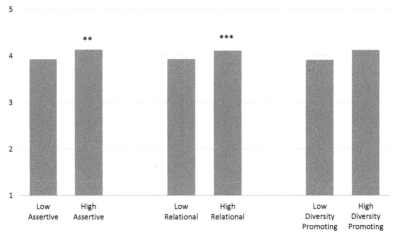

4.2 (continued)

the most highly cited work published in top journals, Black and Latinx men as well as women across all racial/ethnic categories experience less professional respect from colleagues compared to white and Asian men in the same department and at the same career stages and level of productivity.[21] In the name of research excellence, some white and Asian men are overvalued for their contributions. This is largely because assertive, creative brilliance is implicitly associated with white masculinity (see chap. 2). The default assumption is that women and other under-represented groups are less competent and less excellent than the white male "standard." In contrast to their white and Asian men colleagues, women and Black and Latinx faculty of all genders are not assumed to be creatively brilliant simply because they have been recruited to a top STEM department. They have to "prove it" over and over again.

These patterns are evident in our survey data. Compared to men who are similar by department, step, demographics, and research productivity, women are significantly more likely to report that they have to "prove it again"—that they have to work harder than their colleagues in both their departments and their disciplines to be perceived as a legitimate scholar.[22] Further, compared to men at the same job level, in the same department, and with the same scholarly productivity, women are less likely to feel that their research is respected in their departments.[23]

Unequal Rewards for Assertiveness

The ideal STEM professor is expected to be an assertive, competitive, self-promoting leader. In our survey data, faculty only reap the full recognition and reward for assertive self-promotion if they are white or Asian men.[24]

We find some evidence that when departments value assertiveness in hiring new faculty, they are less likely to hire women. Heather, who earlier described her most successful colleagues as having a "competitive gene," elaborated on how this expectation filters out many women and some men who don't share this trait.

And the women in the department, . . . the reason they've been successful at this is because they have largely the male competitive characteristics, and so they compete directly, head-to-head with the males and can do okay.

That means that the male faculty say, "See? We have women. And they're just like us. . . . They look just like us but in skirts." [Laughs] And that isn't allowing for the full range of women who are out there, because not all women scientists behave like male scientists. And not all male scientists actually behave like males, either.

Furthermore, while white and Asian heterosexual men are generally rewarded for displaying assertiveness, this expectation can be a no-win situation for women, who risk backlash for violating cultural expectations of femininity.[25] According to Angela, a white full professor, being assertive is a balancing act; through her day-to-day interactions, she senses that her men colleagues often felt "like their toes are being stepped on."

A big source of stress that I have actually is managing interactions with my colleagues. . . . I think that men have a way of interacting with other men that they don't really like to have to interact with successful women. . . . I don't mess around. I try to get stuff done because I don't have a lot of time, and so I feel like they feel like their toes are being stepped on all the time. . . . And I think they wouldn't feel that way if it was another guy who was doing that to them, but because I'm a woman, they don't expect that from me, and so then they, you know, they just react very negatively.

Angela added that the problem of being seen as too assertive is a "common" challenge faced by female academic scientists: "I've talked to several of my women professional friends about this, and they all have the same issues."

As we discuss in the introductory chapter, it is important to understand how these patterns may play out intersectionally, with different consequences for faculty who are situated in different places across the multiple demographic axes we study.[26] For instance, although professional women generally have to walk the "tightrope" of seeming assertive enough to be competent yet not so assertive as to be seen as unfeminine and therefore unlikable, this balancing act is particularly perilous for women of color.[27] Our survey data show that Latinx and Black women with assertive self-conceptions are particularly penalized when compared with white women. Specifically, assertive Black and Latinx women are less likely than assertive white women to feel that their work is respected in their department and more likely to report that they must work harder than others in their departments and their disciplines to be perceived as legitimate scholars.[28] In contrast, Asian women are more likely than white women to be penalized for a lack of assertiveness. Asian women, who are often stereotyped as passive and submissive,[29] receive more respect for their research in their departments and disciplines when they have more assertive self-conceptions, compared to white women and to Asian women with less assertive self-conceptions.[30]

Unequal Rewards for Relational Traits

For women academic scientists, it is bad enough to be seen as incompetent. Being valued primarily for warmth is even worse. Gender essentialism—beliefs about the "essential nature" of women and men—are foundational to the devaluation of women STEM faculty.[31] Women across racial categories are typically assumed to be inherently more empathetic and relational than men. This is the basis of gendered expectations that women perform emotional labor in their workplaces, such as the empathic mentoring of underperforming students and the "office housework" of committee service drudgery. In the United States, women are assumed to be naturally empathic and nurturing, so they often don't receive credit for developing and exercising these skills on the job.[32]

The relational strand of the schema of scientific excellence includes empathy, mentoring, and the interpersonal skills needed to manage a research team. But these traits among women can undercut others' perception that they are serious scientists.

For example, Lisa described two of her senior men colleagues demeaning women candidates for faculty jobs, even when their credentials—such as well-cited publications and glowing recommendations from experts in their field—indicated that they were brilliant scientists.

[Her colleagues] make statements that women are irrational. . . . Even if you bring them extremely qualified women with extremely [laudatory] recommendations.

Further, she reported, in the faculty meetings where the job candidates were discussed, these senior men ignored the women's professional accomplishments and commented instead on their interpersonal warmth.

I mean, whatever candidate would be excellent . . . and [faculty ask them] "How do you like her?" [They answer,] "Oh, she's a nice girl," in a sense not addressing the scientific part of the person.

In this example, perceiving a woman candidate as warm ("a nice girl") diminished her scientific accomplishments and her adult personhood.

This finding is echoed in our broader survey results. Men receive benefits for being relational, but women do not receive those same benefits.[33] Women professors who are more relational are less likely to feel they fit in with others in their discipline and are less likely to feel that their work is respected, compared with other women and compared with men.[34]

These survey results indicate the subtle ways that essentialized expectations of women as empathetic and relational may be used against them. This is the basis of gendered expectations that women perform emotional labor in their workplaces. In a masculine-dominated professional space like STEM, these essentialized expectations that women are inherently relational may disadvantage women faculty—who are seen as not sufficiently serious or objective.

Marginalization

Social integration within one's STEM departments and disciplines increases a faculty member's access to new knowledge and opportunities for collaboration, which boosts research productivity. Kristen described her colleague networks as critical for getting informal peer reviews on initial drafts, arguing that having specialists read one's work before submission greatly increases the chance of a positive decision from reviewers.

I think that how good your grant is depends on how many people read your grant carefully and gave you feedback. Assuming those things like same productivity, that the science is good, the person is good. So then how good [the grant proposal is] really depends on how many people gave you input, because this is like a crowdsourcing thing. It's the attitude the grant leader takes, and you can't see that yourself when you're writing it.

Kristen believes professional integration and respect is just as important to the productivity of a scholar as the innovativeness of the science.

However, underrepresented groups—women of all racial/ethnic groups, Black and Latinx men, and LGBTQ faculty—are more likely than other colleagues to experience marginalization and isolation in their departments and disciplines, even when they embody the most valued markers of excellence. This marginalization does not just make workplaces more socially unpleasant for some faculty; it can actually make it more difficult for them to do their work. Susan, a white full professor quoted earlier, captured this dynamic when she explained her experiences of isolation:

I have tried to be on committees involving my expertise at [my department] from the day I got here, and . . . I've had the doors slammed in my face so quietly that I don't even know they're slammed. . . . [They think] I'm strange and weird, and it makes me not want to be there. So I wind up spending more time in my [other] office [at a research center]. . . . And the reality is they've created a highly uncomfortable environment for me that makes me feel that I could be more productive when I'm emotionally comfortable in other places on campus.

Assumption of (Devalued) Diversity Commitments

Overall, faculty who express commitments to diversity feel like they encounter additional hurdles in proving their excellence. Those who see themselves as embracing commitments to diversity are more likely to say they have to work harder to be perceived as a legitimate scholar, compared with similar colleagues (at the same department, job level, and productivity level) without this commitment (see fig. 4.2). Women of color are particularly penalized for diversity commitments compared to white women. Black and Latinx women with strong diversity commitments report less respect in their home departments, compared with white women and Black and Latinx women with less strong diversity commitments.[35] Asian women with strong diversity commitments report less respect for their research in their discipline, compared with otherwise similar white women and Asian women with lower diversity commitments.[36]

Some faculty—women of all races, racially minoritized men, and LGBTQ faculty—are automatically presumed by their colleagues to have deep commitments to diversity and social welfare that come at the expense of their responsibility for producing objective science.

LGBTQ Faculty Experiences

An important and underexplored question is the extent to which LGBTQ STEM faculty experience devaluation. Studies of broader populations document that LGBTQ persons are often subject to disparaging attitudes and prejudice (also called heterosexism), as well as common assumptions about the naturalness and appropriateness of a strict male/female binary and heterosexual relationships (also called heteronormativity).[37] Research on STEM fields shows that LGBTQ persons are more likely than equally qualified non-LGBTQ peers to experience harassment, exclusion, professional devaluation, and fewer career opportunities.[38]

We heard some reports from non-LGBTQ faculty about comments they overheard from faculty colleagues suggesting the presence of heterosexism and heteronormativity in their departments. For instance, Jill, who identifies as a straight cisgender woman, told the story of a senior colleague who expressed their concern when she moved into a house in a LGBTQ-identified neighborhood, saying, "'Oh, you live in [Midtown]? . . . That's terrible. It's full of *those people'* . . . referring to homosexuals. [The colleague] thought it was terrible living there just because of all the homosexuals." Another non-LGBTQ professor, Emily, said that her colleagues were "still kind of homophobic in ways that don't come up directly."

Susan, another straight cisgender woman, described a situation where a student in her department was transitioning genders. Susan reported with sadness that a faculty administrator had expressed anger about the student's transition, saying the administrator "did not want the student anywhere near [the faculty administrator's] office" and that they were uncomfortable with the possibility that their child "might come to campus randomly and encounter this student."

Our interviews suggest that explicit expressions of heterosexism and heteronormativity are relatively rare. Most LGBTQ respondents did not report encountering overt LGBTQ-related prejudices. For example, Arjun said, "I don't think I have ever received negative feedback" for identifying as LGBTQ. Brian stated, "I don't feel like I've been treated differently in any active way." John concurred:

I've never been aware of any [instances of open hostility] . . . my homosexuality is pretty much known in the department. I have never gotten up on a soap box . . . but I speak of it freely in private and in personal conversations, where there is a natural reason to mention it. . . . So I don't think that all of my colleagues know that I am gay, but I think most do. . . . [They] don't give a damn.

Even though interviewees reported that expressions of overt heterosexism are rare, our survey results reveal more subtle LGBTQ disadvantages: LGBTQ faculty are significantly less likely to feel they "fit in" with others in their department and are significantly more likely than their colleagues to feel that they have to work harder in their discipline to be perceived as a legitimate scholar.[39] Further, LGBTQ faculty are more likely than their colleagues to report that they separate their personal lives from their professional lives.[40] These differences remain net of productivity, department, career stage, and other demographic characteristics.

Some LGBTQ faculty feel pressure to "pass" as non-LGBTQ or to "cover" or downplay their status to be seen by colleagues as serious, committed STEM faculty. One gay faculty member recalled his anxiousness that his sexual identity would be revealed during his on-campus interview. Even after landing this competitive job and establishing himself on campus, he said that he remained "concerned that I am being viewed as too flamboyant or frivolous [by colleagues]. . . . I don't feel any discrimination, but I don't necessarily feel that I was being included in their networks."

Other LGBTQ faculty expressed similar concerns that their LGBTQ status is an obstacle to integrating into the social networks of their departments. Eric said, "I tend to be reticent in a lot of ways about my personal life," and he sometimes felt "excluded from the informal networks in [his] department." Similarly, Brian, who said earlier that he did not initiate conversations about his same-gender partner and family, explained that he had a "cordial but not a social relationship" with most of his colleagues.

Kelly chose to keep her LGBTQ status hidden from her work colleagues to avoid straining her professional relationships. She said that this decision was not motivated by overt hostility but rather by the "clueless" nature of her predominately heterosexual men colleagues.

It's hard. . . . Working with a lot of men it just doesn't feel like . . . it's never appealing to just come out as lesbian. Also, because already they find me very bitchy and crazy. My personal and my sexual life is so out of the mainstream of [my field], and nobody asks.

We will explore these issues further in the next chapter.

Hegemonic Beliefs, Divergent Rewards

This chapter has shown that there is strong consensus among the faculty we study about what characterizes an excellent scientist, mathematician, or engineer. Most professors believe there is such a thing as a clear metric of excellence. Across gender, race/ethnicity, and sexual identity, and across the intersections of these identities, faculty adhere similarly strongly to this vision. There is also near consensus on how well professors feel they live up to the assertiveness dimension of the scientific excellence schema. The schema of scientific excellence is thus hegemonic: it is a culturally dominant understanding, endorsed by both the professors the schema privileges and by those it marginalizes.[41]

This culture of scientific merit resides within a competitive academic labor market, in which the expanding numbers of new PhDs and postdoctoral fellows are met with a stagnant number of tenure-track faculty positions. The professors in our study are among the small proportion of STEM PhDs who have won the prize of faculty appointments at a top research-intensive university. Their close embrace of the cultural definitions of merit may help them legitimize their own success.[42]

Yet we find that many underrepresented faculty who adhere tightly to these ideals and exemplify the same valued traits as their peers are not as rewarded for their alignment with the schema of scientific excellence. Women across racial/ethnic categories and Black and Latinx men do not benefit the same way from assertive and relational characteristics as white and Asian heterosexual men within the same departments and career stages and with the same levels of productivity. Our intersectional analyses reveal the complex and arbitrary ways in which these characteristics do or do not get rewarded. Black and Latinx women face respect and inclusion penalties compared to white women when they are assertive, and Asian women are penalized when they are not. Such patterns mirror ubiquitous social stereotypes about women of color: Black women are often stereotyped as pushy or angry and Latinx women as too emotional or strong-willed, while Asian women are often stereotyped as overly passive.[43]

We show that the seemingly straight and true yardstick of the scientific excellence schema is warped by gender, racial, and heteronormative biases built into the very idea of excellence. The recognition of traits of excellence and the rewards for those traits are not objective or neutral. Although our analyses reveal that women of all races, Black and Latinx men, and LGBTQ persons are as productive and visible as their white and Asian heterosexual male colleagues, on average they do not receive the same benefit for assertive or relational traits. Instead, these benefits are allocated along well-trod social stereotypes.

White and Asian heterosexual men are more likely to be given automatic credit for their brilliance and assertive leadership, and they benefit further if they are seen as skilled in mentoring and interpersonal relations. In contrast, equally productive faculty who are Black, Latinx, women of any race, and/or LGBTQ feel less well-respected and integrated into their professional communities, even when they embody these same valued characteristics. Across faculty in general, professors with more assertive self-conceptions are not more scientifically prolific than their colleagues, yet on average they do earn higher incomes. The next chapter will show how most faculty members—majority and minority alike—nonetheless regard the scientific excellence schema as fair and defend it from critique in ways that exacerbate inequalities among STEM faculty.

FIVE

Defending the Schema of Scientific Excellence, Defending Inequality

Chapter 4 showed that although the schema of scientific excellence is believed to be an objective yardstick, it undervalues the scientific contributions of women, people of color, and LGBTQ faculty. This chapter shows how this yardstick is defended as straight and true by faculty and is used selectively to help justify patterns of inequality in STEM departments and disciplines. This process is not the doing of a few misguided professors with old-fashioned biases but rather a taken-for-granted part of the *professional culture* of academic STEM.

We begin this chapter by presenting evidence of the ubiquity of the belief that academic STEM is meritocratic. We then show how professors defend this belief, even in the face of evidence to the contrary. When asked to account for the tiny proportion of women and Latinx and Black faculty on their campus, professors of all demographic backgrounds blame pipeline issues that reduce the number of candidates or point to the deficiencies they perceive among underrepresented group members themselves. When presented with peer-reviewed statistics that robustly document unequal treatment of underrepresented academic scientists, many professors question the validity of the statistics and present their own anecdotes as counterevidence.

Faculty members often double down on the schema of scientific excellence, which defines concerns about diversity as at best distracting from and at worst polluting excellence. They argue that STEM should be a depoliticized space, sequestered from such concerns. Further, the very presence of faculty who are Black, Latinx, women, or LGBTQ is seen by some to raise "political" matters of identity in the otherwise "pure" space of science. These beliefs manifest day-to-day in how majority faculty sometimes treat their minoritized colleagues, fostering awkward and marginalizing interactions. This sets up what we call a *minority-meritocracy trap* and reinforces the notion that minority colleagues do not measure up. Many faculty members defend the schema of scientific excellence and divert responsibility for underrepresentation and inequality away from their departments, their disciplines, and themselves.

Widely Held Beliefs Justifying Meritocracy

We find a widespread conviction among STEM professors in our study that departments and the university fairly assess and reward scientific merit.

Beliefs about Promotion

At major research universities like the one we study, the most coveted job for academic research-oriented recent PhDs is an assistant professor position on the tenure track. About eight years after the completion of the PhD, an assistant professor faces an intensive review for promotion to associate professor with tenure.[1] The quantity and impact of research publications over the career arc are the central criteria for advancement. Other criteria include satisfactory teaching and adequate administrative service to the university and discipline.

This intensive evaluation by multiple individuals—outside experts in the field, departmental colleagues, and several levels of senior university administration—is designed to produce a comprehensive and fair evaluation. The review yields an up-or-out decision: professors who are not favorably reviewed for promotion and tenure must leave the university.

The next major milestones are promotion to full professor and, years down the line, promotion to distinguished professor. At each of these ranks, advancement criteria include meeting benchmarks in research, teaching, and service, but research contributions are weighted most heavily at each stage.

Most professors in our study believe that tenure and promotion decisions at this university are meritocratic. According to Jessica, a full professor, the tenure review process of junior colleagues in her department is transparent and universalistic.

So basically the criteria for tenure [here is] exactly the same as in any other [research-intensive] department. Which is that [faculty] publish in the best journals. . . . So they're still looking at the impact factor of the publication, and how many journal publications, how much money you're bringing in, so your productivity and your ability to get funds. And of course, then, teaching and service.

Faculty also generally assess the evaluation processes leading to the promotion to full professor and to distinguished professor as equitable. According to Gabi, a distinguished professor, the evaluation process of his record has been fair. Gabi's annual publication rate is very high. He said, "I just did my work. There's nobody else [in the department] who does quite what I do. But I think what I do has been valued, evidently."

Between the major milestone reviews leading to the associate, full, or distinguished professor ranks, faculty undergo smaller step evaluations every two or three years. These smaller reviews are internal to the campus; they do not solicit letters from outside experts. They depend significantly upon colleagues' assessments of the professor, with approval by a higher-level administrator. A successful internal review advances the professor one rung up the within-rank career ladder and signals the likelihood of a timely promotion at the next milestone. An extraordinarily successful internal review will accelerate the professor up two rungs. These step increases are also the primary vehicle for salary raises.

From the perspective of Angela, a full professor, these smaller reviews are also "very fair."

I think our department is very fair because when we go up for our reviews every [two to three] years. . . . You put together your package and it gets evaluated by a committee [and the department]. And they're very fair. So you know, when that process occurs, I feel like I get evaluated fairly.

These understandings are reflected in our survey data. Figure 5.1 shows that over 90 percent of the faculty we studied believe that tenure requirements at this university are reasonable. Over 85 percent agree that they understand the criteria for achieving promotions.[2] Eighty-three percent of faculty somewhat or strongly agree that tenure is primarily based on excellence rather than politics or demographics.[3] Reflecting

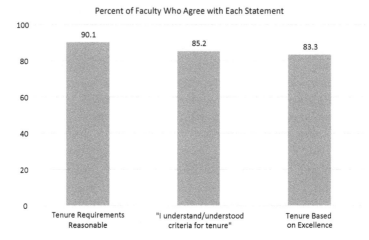

Percent of Faculty Who Agree with Each Statement

Note: The figure includes only tenure-track assistant professors and associate and full professors who received tenure at the case university.

5.1   *Faculty Assessments of the Fairness of the Tenure Process at Case University (Percent Who Somewhat or Strongly Agree)*

the near consensus on these points, the assessments of the fairness of the tenure process do not significantly vary by gender or LGBTQ identity. Responses are also largely similar by race; the only difference is that Black and Latinx faculty are somewhat less likely than white and Asian faculty (81.8 percent versus 90.6 percent) to report that tenure is based on excellence rather than politics or demographics.

Beliefs about Hiring

In addition to seeing promotion and tenure decisions in their units as fair and transparent, most faculty members in our study are also certain that hiring decisions are fair. When recruiting new colleagues, professors express confidence that they can fairly and accurately judge scientific excellence, undistorted by considerations of scientists' demographic background or identity.

Mateo, a former academic administrator and tenured professor of color, makes an even stronger statement. He says that he and his colleagues are so exclusively focused on objectively judging a candidate's scientific quality that they do not even think about demographic identities such as race, gender, and sexual identity; such qualities "wouldn't cross our mind." He further states,

I don't think we would even want to know in selecting a candidate what they are [demographically]. . . . I think we look for qualities as a scientist first . . . because we tend to be very objective about what the person is doing or producing. We read their papers; we don't particularly say, Oh, this is a paper by [for instance] a bisexual. *No one would think about it.* It's a biologist. . . . Anyway I think that if a bisexual, gay, or lesbian candidate comes up, we would never even inquire, *it wouldn't cross our mind.* (emphasis added)

Melissa, a white professor, also maintains that her department in the engineering school generally chooses the "best" candidate regardless of demographic background.

I do feel like, especially engineers, being sort of more analytical and data driven, my observation is that they will look at the CVs and pick the best candidate, regardless of ethnicity or gender.

Similarly, Dan praises his department for holding up research excellence as the most important criterion in faculty hiring.

When we go to hire people into my department, the number one criterion is research excellence. . . . The best person gets the job, and if the best person is underrepresented, they get the job.

Attempting to illustrate his point, Dan explains that his department recently hired a Latinx professor.

You know we hired a kid [in the last few years], Mexican-American guy. [He] went to [a top-ranked department for his PhD], and the kid's incredible. But he's Mexican. It just didn't matter. We don't care about that. He was the best guy, so he got the job.

Although Dan seeks to praise his new colleague, his reference to him as a "kid" suggests that he views this new professor through a paternalistic lens.

In short, most faculty we interviewed are confident that they as individuals, and their departments and disciplines in the aggregate, recognize and reward excellence regardless of demographic characteristics. In their eyes, STEM is a properly functioning meritocracy. They are confident in the fairness of the scientific excellence yardstick and their ability to recognize excellence when they see it.

To gain additional leverage on how these faculty understand STEM as a meritocracy, we presented them with two pieces of evidence demonstrating patterns of underrepresentation and bias in STEM. We then asked them to explain these patterns. Such an approach makes the paradox at the center of our book explicit to our respondents: How can STEM be properly meritocratic in the face of evidence that women and people of color are underrepresented and devalued? These interview questions allowed us to observe faculty's meaning making as they attempted to explain—or explain away—these factors.

Why So Few?

It is likely no surprise to faculty that women and people of color are underrepresented among STEM faculty ranks compared with their representation nationally. However, many may not be aware of how this underrepresentation pans out in their own university.

First, we asked faculty to help us understand why, among STEM faculty at this university, less than 15 percent are women (of any race) and less than 6 percent are underrepresented racial and ethnic minorities (i.e., Latinx, Black, and Native American). Our goal was to understand if and how faculty would draw on their cultural understandings of excellence to account for these statistics. If STEM is fair, and STEM excellence is equitably measured, then how would they explain these patterns of underrepresentation?

Rather than raise questions about the fairness of evaluation procedures in their STEM departments and disciplines, most of the professors we talked to reaffirmed their conviction—voiced earlier by Mateo, Melissa, Dan, and others—that assessments depend purely on the academic "merits" and "research excellence" of the scientists themselves. For that to hold true, professors had to pin responsibility for these demographic patterns elsewhere. Many faculty members explained that the underrepresentation of women and people of color is justified by upstream "pipeline" or "pedigree" issues. Others argued that their departments were actually already sufficiently diverse.

"Pipeline Issues" and "Pedigree Issues"

A common explanation of the underrepresentation of women and people of color at this university was that there were very few qualified minorities in the applicant pools for graduate school programs and for faculty positions to begin with. This limited supply is seen as a "pipeline issue."[4]

For example, Calvin, a tenured professor of color, cites small numbers of underrepresented graduate students and faculty in the pipeline that his department recruits from. He explains:

We get our students from the top ten schools, and in some years there is not a plethora of people of color. . . . Sometimes the numbers are as small as one or two, and in some years there are none.

Others explain that pipeline issues are caused by upstream conditions of racialized socioeconomic inequality in the United States. Illustrative of this is a twofold explanation advanced by Christopher, a white full professor. First, he posits, underrepresented racial/ethnic minorities are more likely than whites to be from lower-income backgrounds. Second, he reasons, science is not framed as an upwardly mobile career option.

Most of the applicants [for graduate school] we get are white or Asian males. . . . With minorities, there's some sort of pipeline issue that [goes] back to the collegiate or high school level or earlier. Probably it's because on average they're socioeconomically more disadvantaged . . .

If kids don't have, like, parents that are scientists, or the school doesn't have a lot of [STEM] activities at a young age, I don't know that science ever comes to the forefront as something that is . . . a way out or a way to a better life. The way to a better life is to become a successful business person or a lawyer or whatever, but I don't think science is seen as that.

Bill, the white full professor who has chaired campus-wide personnel policy committees, agrees with Christopher that the pipeline issues for racial minorities are rooted in racialized economic inequality and educational disparities. He puts the origin of the pipeline issues for women as starting in elementary school.

I think it's got to be cultural, that young girls are—somehow get the message that they're not as good in math. I mean, my niece, for god's sake, is in fourth grade. Even though on these tests and things she does extraordinarily well, she has somehow convinced herself that she's not any good in mathematics, . . . So at the end of the day, I have to think it's something in our culture that gets this message to girls long before they even become women, that gee, you're not really—this is not your talent. You should do something else.

Bill thinks this is unfortunate but well beyond anything that his department or discipline is able to address. He thinks that his department fulfills its obligations to make race- and gender-blind decisions.

Really the only thing that anybody cares about is what are the merits of the candidate. Period. And my view is that's the way it should be.

Although women and Black, Latinx, and Native American persons are underrepresented in the population of scholars who earn PhDs every year compared to their representation in the population of the United States overall, there are many more scholars who graduate with PhDs in STEM fields from these groups than are represented among the assistant professor ranks.[5] Thus, the "pipeline issue" serves more as an explanatory crutch than an accurate empirical representation of the potential diversity of the hiring pool.

A variant of the pipeline issue is the "pedigree issue." Heather, a white professor, defines pedigree as a scientist's intellectual origins, including their graduate school and former advisor.

If [faculty applicants] didn't come from Berkeley, Harvard, Princeton, Yale—you know, the handful of schools—they won't look at you.

She then implies that underrepresented scientists in her discipline disproportionately attend graduate school in lower-ranked departments, which she believes explains their absence in her department. For example, she states,

And there's a lot of women who aren't—they don't have that competitive gene, or they didn't know that you need to go to one of those [top ten] places to be on your pedigree in order to be looked at.

She thinks that the dearth of competitive and qualified women and racial minority candidates from top departments is unfortunate, yet she believes that the expectation for elite pedigree is applied fairly and consistently to all faculty job applicants.

There's still the pedigree issue, because everybody on our faculty has a degree from a top ten place somewhere.

We heard an echo of this sentiment earlier in Dan's protestation that the

"Mexican kid" hired by his department had attended a top-ranked PhD program in the United States.

The Belief That Departments Do Not Actually Have an Underrepresentation Problem

A related approach many faculty use to make sense of the underrepresentation in their ranks is to maintain that their units already have a fair proportion of the suitable minority faculty available in the broader pool. For example, Perry, a white full professor in a large department, explains that the virtual absence of Black and Latinx faculty in his unit fairly reflects the near absence of what he believes are competent minorities in the candidate pool.

> We don't have any. [Laughter] . . . Well, no, we do have a few, but—we're talking [the] physical sciences. . . . The statistics that are always quoted, and I believe this, are that there are very, very few people *who are actually qualified* who are racial minorities. (emphasis added)

Perry presumably thinks that most racial minorities with STEM PhDs lack the pedigree or other credentials that would make them "actually qualified."

Other faculty responded by insisting (contrary to the actual demographic representation) that their departments are actually diverse. To illustrate, Ramesh, a professor of South Asian descent, ticked off the names of women his department has hired in recent years.[6]

> We hired Hoa, an Asian woman. And we just hired Jean, the wife of one of our faculty members. And we just hired also as a lecturer, someone who I think is the wife of one of our faculty members too . . . and we have Saanvi.

He identified two of the four women as "the wife of one of our faculty members," perhaps implying that they were trailing spouses. One of the wives is an unnamed lecturer, a lower status position than that of her husband. Ramesh explicitly stated that one of the women is Asian, presumably offering an example of a colleague adding racial diversity as well as gender diversity (although, as we note, Asian faculty are not demographically underrepresented in STEM fields in the United States or at our case university).

In his response to our question about the small proportion of Black, Latinx, and Native American STEM faculty on campus, Bill diverts the question by saying that the university's numbers look good compared to the past and compared to other countries.

Those are actually better numbers than they used to be, I think. It's interesting because I look, I have research collaborations and colleagues from around the world. And . . . if I look in France and Spain, actually the Mediterranean countries, even Italy to some degree, in my field at least, there's better representation of women [here] than there is from those countries. . . . And then when I go to Asia—Korea, Japan, China—it makes us look good. [Laughs]

Further, Bill complains that the statistics are based on definitions of underrepresented minority that are confusing and undercount the actual diversity of the campus.

And this, frankly, I find quite annoying. Well, what counts? I mean, we have many, a number of faculty from Pakistan, India, that sort of [thing]. Well, does that count? No.

In these interpretations, professors emphasize the insufficient supply or the deficient quality of underrepresented academics, or they protest the idea that these groups are underrepresented at all.[7] Even if the faculty see biased structural or cultural processes that restrict the supply of Black and Latinx men and women of every racial background from entering STEM, those issues are earlier in the causal chain than they feel they or their department have any responsibility to help rectify.

"We Would *Welcome Them"*

Brian provides another example of views we heard several times: their department's composition reflects the qualified applicant pool, and his department would be welcoming if minority faculty were hired.

Interviewer: Do you think your department is welcoming toward underrepresented minorities?

Brian: I think so, I think so. . . . There's been active recruitment, and when such recruitment has failed, it ultimately just comes down to the candidate pool. It's just not available in our field. . . . It's very hard to identify excellent candidates. . . . We have no . . . [corrects himself] We have I guess one ethnic minority that we just hired last year, or at least the way [our university] characterizes it.

Gabi concurs that his department would be welcoming if minority faculty were present in recruiting pools.

Gabi: There are no—I don't even know what to call them—underrepresented minorities there. . . . But I think [the department] *would* be welcoming. . . . The pools are . . . very sparse.

Interviewer: So what does the modal person look like in these pools? Say, for an assistant professor position?

Gabi: White male. Or Asian male, or Indian—I mean East Asian male, Indian male. . . . Very few other groups.

Gabi defends this proportion of 0 percent underrepresented racial minorities in his department in two ways. First, he says it is consistent with the faculty applicant pool. Second, like Bill, he thinks that the university's definition of who counts as underrepresented does not make a lot of sense.[8] As a European-origin, white Latinx professor, Gabi notes that he is sometimes counted as "underrepresented," which doesn't fit his own sense of identity. He states that other individuals (such as a woman colleague from India) who are not counted as underrepresented do in fact add diversity.

There certainly are no Hispanics unless you count me as a Hispanic, which I sometimes am counted as. . . . The [unit] is varied; there are women, there are women of different origins, there are people with backgrounds from, I don't know, India, which is not an underrepresented group. . . . [So there's] some diversity there. So, yeah, I think there's a lot of welcoming.

Initially in the interview, Gabi seems to share the view of Christopher, Heather, and Perry that the paucity of Black and Latinx STEM faculty on campus is based on upstream supply problems that their department are not responsible for. But later, Gabi observes that despite similar challenges, other top-ranked departments somehow manage to recruit higher proportions of underrepresented scientists to their faculty.

Zhangyong, a full professor, believes that his department works hard to encourage women and underrepresented racial minorities to apply and treats them fairly in the recruitment process.

I've sat on search committee[s] before, and we do make an effort to try to recruit women. I think the general attitude, you know people's sense, is we want to get more women. But we still don't have enough.

He is puzzled by how his large department continues to hire so few underrepresented new colleagues, despite good intentions.

Based on what I know and talking to other people, we don't have anyone really biased against women or minorities. . . . I feel we welcome them; but still, we don't have that many in the department. . . . I don't know why.

Similarly, Dan, who above praised his department's focus on research excellence as the "number one criterion" for hiring new faculty, is bemused by the fact that no women have been hired in his subfield in recent years.

And so for whatever reasons . . . I don't know. I mean it's just that the candidates that— when those searches are there, the candidates that have risen to the top have tended to be men, which I don't, you know, but it's definitely not a discriminatory thing, and it's not to say that there's not, you know, great female candidates in that field. It just hasn't happened.

Gabi, Zhangyong, and Dan seem well-intentioned but mystified. They don't believe that individual colleagues harbor bias or animus. And because the cultural schema of scientific excellence is so deeply taken for granted and widely accepted, they cannot see how it might be subtly defining some faculty candidates as less excellent than others. These pipeline and pedigree explanations are powerful cultural frames that excuse the faculty and their departments from taking significant action to rectify underrepresentation.

How Do Professors Account for Evidence of Unequal Treatment Once Underrepresented Persons Get Faculty Appointments?

A second research-backed factual scenario shifted the professors we interviewed beyond accounts of why they believed so few underrepresented professors were hired in their departments and asked them to reflect on possible barriers for people who have already successfully reached the faculty ranks. As we previewed in chapter 1, we presented faculty with findings from a research article published in an unimpeachable source— the flagship scientific journal *Science*[9]—that raises serious questions about the fairness of the evaluation of scientists and their research. Specifically, we asked,

A study published in *Science* found that African American scientists were less likely than white scientists to be awarded actual NIH [National Institutes of Health] grants to fund their research, even with the same productivity levels. What do you think about that?

The *Science* article's authors included Donna Ginther, a famed economist, and Raynard Kington, who served as deputy director and acting director of the NIH. The article analyzed data from over 81,000 major (R01) NIH grant proposal submissions, prestigious and competitive grants that, if awarded, would provide the lifeblood of a scientist's research enterprise. The article documented that Black scientists were 10 percent less likely than white scientists to be awarded these prestigious grants, even when many factors that could also affect proposal success were controlled for (such as the proposers' educational background, previous grant awards, research productivity, and employer characteristics).[10]

These results confront the widespread belief that merit in science is fairly recognized and rewarded. We aimed to understand if and how faculty would draw on their cultural understandings of merit to respond to the article's critique of the fairness of the evaluation of grant proposals. As before, seeing how faculty respond reveals a great deal about their understanding of how merit is perceived and applied in STEM.

In chapter 1, we discussed how Ruben, a professor of color, rejected the results of the *Science* article in part because he was personally acquainted with three Black scientists who were NIH grant recipients. Like many other professors we interviewed, Ruben assumed the results must be flawed, because he was convinced that science operates fairly.

Christopher, a white full professor and frequent NIH grant evaluator, was already familiar with the article. He said the study was "a big thing. [The senior author] was Raynard Kington, the former deputy director of NIH." To illustrate further, we consider Christopher's response at length.

Interviewer: So what do you think was the cause of that? How does that happen?
Christopher: I have no idea. I mean honestly. I told you I'm reviewing eight grants for the NIH this week. It's just like trying to hire somebody. There is no ethnic information on that application at all. That I recall. None that's revealed to us. And if it is, obviously I don't look at it, because I don't know that it's there. It's totally blind, so you'd have to be *presumptive* of what the person's ethnicity was based on the name. And if anything, the only ones I would be able to guess were Asians. . . . You know, their names are distinctive. There's no way I could tell from those applications who's African American or not. Except for the people I know. . . . So at the end of the day, *I have no friggin' idea*. I really don't know. Because I don't see that information [about the applicant's race/ethnicity]. (emphasis added)

Christopher says that the reviews could not have been racially biased because the proposer's race and ethnicity were not listed on the application. He states that the evaluation of proposal quality is based solely on the scientific excellence of the proposal. He discounts any mismeasuring of excellence that could creep in because some of the applicants' race (and gender) can be surmised through names or through reviewers' prior knowledge of the applicants.

The thought [of race or gender] *never even crosses my mind.* . . . And I don't think any of the other twenty people [reviewers] in that [National Institutes of Health] room give a crap about that. *They just care about the science.* . . . It's nothing but the science. It's all about "Is this grant good? Is it going to have an impact? Is it going to teach us something? Is it going to . . . promote the discipline?" . . . Never in a back room in the deepest, darkest corner have I ever heard anybody say anything about the gender of a candidate—which, okay, that you can tell from a name sometimes—and certainly not the ethnicity. *I've never heard it even once* in reviewing grants for a decade now. (emphasis added)

Christopher rejects the results of the *Science* study because in his ten years of evaluating NIH grants, the race or gender of the proposal writer "never even crosses my mind" and was never overtly discussed. Like Ruben, Christopher is convinced that the evaluation of grant proposals is about "nothing but the science." He also maintains that other evaluators on the many review panels he has served on would also have refused to explicitly consider race or gender, even if those demographics could be inferred by applicants' names.[11]

The evaluation of NIH and other large, prestigious grant proposals are high-stakes events. Given the necessity of funding for STEM research labs,[12] the investment that reviewers make in evaluating grant proposals, and the weight that these prestigious grants have in faculty promotion reviews, it is paramount to Christopher that evaluations be merit-based. His belief in a fair assessment of scientific excellence trumps a serious consideration that the findings in the *Science* article are real.

Keeping Science Pure: Bracketing Diversity Considerations from Scientific Work

Like Christopher, many of the faculty we interviewed experienced an acute disconnect between their fundamental belief that STEM is meritocratic and the scientific demonstration of systemic racial bias that we presented them with during the interview. Instead of reevaluating their understanding of STEM as meritocratic—something consistent with the norms of objectivity and rigor that are core to the scientific method—faculty often provided their own anecdotal experience as counterevidence to cast doubt on the results of the study, or dismissed the results outright. A common ideology within the professional culture of STEM—depoliticization—helps us understand this type of response. *Depoliticization* is the belief that science and engineering are purely technical spaces where "social" and "political" concerns like inequality or identity not only can be but should be removed from consideration.[13] Such concerns threaten to pollute what is otherwise considered the objective, bias-free operation of STEM within the academy.[14]

We earlier saw the manifestation of this ideology in the devaluation of diversity commitments in the schema of scientific excellence. Here, we explore the broader implications of depoliticization for how excellence is assessed in STEM. As we note below, even taking note of a scientist's race, gender, or LGBTQ status is seen as potentially polluting the evaluation of good science. Their faith in a depoliticized science helps account for why many of the analytical, evidence-respecting professors we talked to believe they are able to ignore the race and gender signifiers commonly embedded in names, their personal knowledge of the scientist, or information easily accessible online.[15]

In contrast, a few professors report that their departments and search committees *do see* race and gender, but only during the weeks in which job openings are advertised and aggregate statistics on the applicant pool are collected. These professors are aware of historic inequities and chronic underrepresentation of certain groups in their units. As an antidote, they follow university guidelines to actively recruit and consider women and Black and Latinx men.

But by the time the applicant pool is set and the search committee sits down to evaluate individual candidates, these professors say that race and gender become invisible and irrelevant to the evaluation of candidate records. They argue that thinking any further about a candidate's demographic background, or the way they or their colleagues might be biased toward or against certain applicants, would violate the scientific excellence schema's prohibition against allowing social and political concerns to contaminate scientific evaluation.

For example, Bill, the white full professor who has chaired campus-level personnel policy committees, states that although many demographic groups are underrepresented on campus, search committees "bend over backwards" to give those groups full consideration. At the same time, he says that outreach and job advertisement efforts do not interfere with the hiring decisions he believes are color- and gender-blind.

I know [that] on search committees, that we actively seek out female candidates for positions and sort of bend over backwards to say okay, does this person really fit kind of what we're looking for? . . . But at the end of the day, I think *the decision as to who to hire has nothing to do with what's the gender or what's the ethnicity.* It's like, Is this a really good person? (emphasis added)

His faith in the schema of scientific excellence gives him confidence that his and his colleagues' awareness of a candidate's race and gender can magically disappear so faculty can fairly and objectively assess whether "this is a really good" scientist.

Academic scientists are accountable to the schema of scientific excellence, which offers disembodied markers of scientific merit and defines consideration of demographics and diversity as a violation. Faculty such as Gabi and Zhangyong are seeking tools to implement changes to the demography of their departments. Yet they are constrained by depoliticization commitments, which define as polluting any serious engagement with evidence suggesting that academic STEM is not meritocratic. Depoliticization also defines racial, ethnic, gender, and other identities as irrelevant and potentially polluting to the objective evaluation of science. Further, the experiences of LGBTQ faculty illuminate how depoliticization can silence LGBTQ persons in the name of keeping science "pure."

Maintaining Invisibility: Experiences of LGBTQ STEM Faculty

At least formally, persons who identify as LGBTQ are welcomed at this university. Near the center of campus sits a generously funded LGBTQ community center with talented staff, engaged students, and LGBTQ and allied faculty affiliates. And broadly, STEM faculty in our study reject the notion that personal identity, such as sexual identity and gender expression, has any place in judgments about scientific worth. Recall how Mateo, a full professor and former academic administrator, says that the evaluation of scientific papers is objective because, for example, "no one would ever think about" whether the paper was written by a sexual minority.

However, compared to non-LGBTQ colleagues, LGBTQ faculty are more likely to feel devalued and unwelcome and are more likely to report keeping their personal and professional lives separate.[16] These differences remain net of productivity, department, rank, and other demographic characteristics.[17] These seemingly contradictory findings make more sense when we see them as stemming from depoliticization, which frames even taking note of a scientist's race, gender, or LGBTQ status as potentially contaminating the fairness and objectivity of STEM.[18]

The frequent invisibility of LGBTQ status means that it is often acts as a different kind of difference than gender or racial/ethnic categories, which tend to be more visible.[19] LGBTQ faculty who worry about potential bias in their workplaces may not reveal their status, or they tell only a few trusted colleagues. For example, Eric is relieved that his colleagues are "socially aware" enough not to voice any negative views they may have about LGBTQ persons.

And I think certainly most people are smart, cognizant, socially aware enough that if they know of an LBGT faculty member, they just don't say anything even if they have certain beliefs that might be counter.

Many non-LGBTQ faculty we interviewed claim that they do not know any LGBTQ professors in their units. These views are held by faculty who took great pains to express to the interviewer that they "had no problem with" LGBTQ persons. Consider Susan, who ponders with surprise the fact that she is not aware of any LGBTQ faculty in her large department, despite her openness about her sexual minority family member.

I don't know any LGBT [faculty]. That's interesting, because I'm very open about the fact that my sister is gay. And anybody who would be gay or a lesbian could easily come to me and identify themselves as such and know that there would be like no judgment, no second thought, at all. And even so, nobody's ever identified themselves to me that way.

As another example, Gabi noted,

There are a fair number of people who are single, but I have no idea about their sexual orientation. I just simply don't know. If they are gay or lesbian or whatever, they certainly don't show it or talk about it or bring it forth. So that has never, I don't think ever in my department. . . . I don't ever remember seeing a gay or lesbian. . . . They're not present in any visible way.

Consider also the instance of Kevin, a white heterosexual man and full professor, who says that "nobody cares" about sexual orientation.

Interviewer: Do you think the department is welcoming to the LGBTQ faculty?

Kevin: I have never heard that discussed, so as far as I know nobody cares. Your sexual orientation is not part of your work [in physics], *so there's no reason for that to come up.* There are a few people in the department I would guess might be gay, but I don't know really. We've never discussed it at all. (emphasis added)

Yet not knowing the LGBTQ status of colleagues is not the same thing as welcoming LGBTQ colleagues. Some descriptive statements that this topic never comes up slide into prescriptive statements that discussions and expressions of LGBTQ status *should never come up* in the workplace. For example, Perry, another heterosexual professor, said,

I don't think of them [LGBTQ faculty] as any different from the rest of the faculty, and I don't think most of the other people of the faculty do. But there's another issue . . . there are the [LGBTQ] people who are just out there in your face because that's how they've figured out how to do it . . . it's sort of like, "Hey, I'm gay, and you need to know this!" *And I really don't feel I need to know this in a professional context.* It's not an issue for me, but I don't need to be reminded of it every day necessarily. (emphasis added)

Some LGBTQ faculty also say they don't know of any other LGBTQ faculty in their units. For example, Arjun said,

There isn't anyone else who is gay or lesbian identified, quite oddly enough, in the entire division, which has over seventy faculty; there is no one that I know of who is out.

He puzzled further over the paucity of openly LGBTQ graduate students in his division.

And I actually confirmed this because I spoke with [an association of LGBTQ-identified graduate students]. . . . And I said, I was wondering, do you guys know of anyone who is LBGT in [life sciences]? And [no one said they knew anyone]. . . . So it is very odd and it leads me to think . . . [that] for some reason, they feel an inability to come out. . . . And I don't know why that would be, unless there is a kind of culture that makes that difficult.

Most of the LGBTQ-identifying faculty we interviewed explained that even though they are not completely closeted, they keep their LGBTQ status close to their chest. This tendency is not surprising, given the assumptions among many of their faculty colleagues that it is best if topics of sexual identity or gender expression do not come up. For instance, in his department, Brian does not bring up topics related to his sexual identity, husband, or family life.

I am not actively out to a lot of colleagues, meaning I don't go up and introduce myself as an LGBT-identifying person to a faculty member. And to those people, I don't talk about family either.

Perhaps partially connected to Brian's silence on his personal and family life, he feels that is own research output is highly productive and highly valued by the department. Another gay man, Eric, wonders whether his professional relationships would suffer if he were less "reticent" about discussing his personal life. While musing on the absence of actively out LGBTQ faculty in his unit, Eric ponders,

But would someone not come out because they feel like somehow the climate was uncomfortable in our department? I couldn't say. It wouldn't shock me to find that someone feels that way. And that maybe they would feel it was somehow more comfortable for them to just keep their private life separate and sort of not bring this in some way to work at all.

LGBTQ status requires engaging in status management—determining when and whether to reveal one's LGBTQ status to one's colleagues and mentees, and when to make that status salient in informal conversations.[20] These decisions about deemphasizing, covering, or revealing sexual identity and family relationships are exhausting and can reduce professional integration and increase isolation. Simply speaking about one's same-gender partner can seem like an "in your face" airing of diversity concerns in ways that lead their colleagues to question LGBTQ faculty's commitments to scientific excellence.

By promoting depoliticization and its bracketing of issues about gender, race, and LGBTQ status as tangential to real STEM work, faculty can bypass conversations about diversity and inclusion in their departments. As a result, depoliticization may increase isolation among marginalized and minoritized group members and help prop up the unequal status quo.

Faculty Critiques of How the Scientific Excellence Schema Is Used

We have seen that most faculty responded to our question about why there are so few women and underrepresented racial/ethnic minority STEM faculty on campus in ways that defended their departments and disciplines as fair meritocracies. In contrast, a few faculty members critiqued the belief that judgments about scientific excellence are based solely on academic merit.

Earlier in this chapter, Jessica, a full professor, described the tenure and promotion process of junior colleagues in her department as fair and transparent. Like Heather, Jessica sees pedigree—including the academic scientist's PhD granting institution and former advisors—as indicators of merit, alongside the number of papers published "in the best journals."

But later, when asked about the small numbers of women and even smaller numbers of Latinx and Black faculty in STEM departments on campus, Jessica responded that academic scientists tend to mismeasure true scientific excellence.

There's this belief that we have to be excellent here. There's a *big* [emphasis] on excellence. I mean, I think it's appropriate. *But I think it's exclusive.* . . . Because I think people still do not believe that women or minorities are as excellent as, kind of, traditional white men who are in these fields. . . .

So if you took a man and a woman, and they both have these same credentials, I still think, on this campus, the fact that you're a woman . . . people would perceive you as not as excellent. . . . Partly because, I think, because you don't *look* like you're excellent. You're not . . . you don't . . . even though you have all these credentials, you're not . . . what *looks* like excellent. (emphasis added)

Defenders of a fair evaluation system on campus, such as Melissa, Mateo, and Bill, assert that colleagues do not care about or think about the race, gender, and sexual identity of academic scientists whose work they judge; they claim that these demographic characteristics do not cross their minds. In contrast, Jessica suggests that what is actually missing from people's minds is a cultural definition of excellence that includes scientists of every racial and gender identity with credentials deserving of full credit for their accomplishments.

Some critics said they had been true believers in the meritocracy of their profession until recently, when they experienced scales falling from their eyes. For example, Antonio, a Latinx tenured professor, was reflecting on his recent service on faculty recruitment committees.

I have to be honest with you, like, you know, I thought the system was as fair as it gets until very recently. Then I've seen [in faculty recruitment] . . . I've been stunned by the collective disregard [for awareness of bias]. . . . So, bias against women, against African Americans, or, you know, Hispanics and so on. It's completely unfounded. Like, just out of a feeling, like, you know, a person [on our search committee] will have a five-minute conversation with someone [during their job interview] and decide [against them], and this is considered to be a good justification for, like, shutting down a person that has a fantastic record.

Sarah, a white full professor in a different department, also reported gradually realizing that departmental decisions around hiring and promotion did not live up to meritocratic ideals. This misconception of merit became more obvious to her over time as she looked back on the career trajectories of underrepresented scientists who had previously applied to her department and been rejected. She says that her department has systematically failed to recognize the brilliance of minority and women job candidates, who then went on to build dazzling careers at other universities.

There was an outstanding Black candidate who got turned down [by us] and was then hired by a more prestigious university, a higher-ranked university than ours, and got tenure there, and I think there is fairly wide agreement at this point looking at that man's career that we blew it. . . .

There have been quite a few outstanding women candidates over the years who got turned down . . . [and] where looking at their career subsequently, you could say that we blew it.

Sarah reported that this insight crystalized for her the previous year when she became aware of discriminatory remarks made by colleagues during the process of voting on an underrepresented minority faculty candidate.

People in our department [have become] pretty savvy about these issues, and even when they are biased, they are not so stupid that they would come out and say something. . . . People don't make [openly racist or sexist] remarks like that here, and I think it's because they are smart enough to know that they shouldn't. . . . [They] have cleaned up their language, but I [also] think that the bias is very subtle, and I think for some people, actually, it's unconscious bias.[21]

Sarah's critique is consistent with Jessica's: departmental failures to hire and promote faculty from underrepresented groups, even those who have the right pedigree, credentials, and publications, are shaped by a cultural misperception that excludes certain groups from the definition of excellence.

The ways in which many faculty members maintain their belief in a meritocratic system of recognition and reward in STEM, in spite of under-representation and bias, shields them from critically evaluating hiring and promotion practices in their departments. It also affects how they treat women and racial/ethnic minority colleagues on a day-to-day basis.

When we asked Amy, a woman of color, about whether her department climate is welcoming toward underrepresented racial/ethnic minorities, she answered, "I have to say no. [But] on the surface, yes." Similarly, we asked about whether her department climate is welcoming toward women, she answered,

On the surface, yes, because the department hired over the last ten years or so significant numbers of female faculty members.

However, she said that although the department is willing to hire women as assistant professors, it has a poor track record of promoting them.

Once [the department] hires them, that's the end of story, and [it doesn't] care so much about how much they excel. Again, those little things like taking their [lab] space, taking this and that [away], the accumulation of that [treatment] essentially over the long run hurts certain populations and gives more advantages for others. And I think I have to say our division is certainly very happy that they got a lot of women, but I don't think they are promoting us to do well after we get here.

As discussed earlier in the chapter, new faculty at the assistant professor level need to apply for competitive research funding and develop an extensive research portfolio, in addition to teaching and service, prior to evaluation for tenure and promotion. This is a crucial "up or out" phase of their career. All assistant professors need support from established colleagues to make connections, be invited to collaborate on new projects, and receive feedback on grant proposals and research papers before they are submitted. The absence of each of these forms of mentoring would, in Amy's word, "accumulate" and create conditions under which building a career would be much more difficult.[22]

Amy said it took a long time for her to become aware that many women assistant professors were either ignored or treated with hostility, while men at their level were deliberately groomed for success. In response, many women left for jobs at other universities. This insight crystalized when Amy realized that in her multiyear faculty career, during which she had attended many departmental events honoring full professors who were retiring, there had never been an instance of a woman full professor retiring.

> When people retire from this division, we all have some sort of ceremony, and I haven't seen *one* for a female full professor retiring from this department. And partially perhaps it's because everybody left because of the way that they were treated.

Reflecting on this experience made it impossible for Amy to continue to believe that her department operated meritocratically.

Jessica, Antonio, Sarah, and Amy only gradually became disenchanted with their department's claim to operate meritocratically. They are a handful of critics at a university largely convinced that it judges scientists purely on the basis of scientific excellence. Their critiques are also consistent with our quantitative results that minoritized faculty are just as dedicated and productive as their colleagues.[23] Yet underrepresented groups, including women across racial/ethnic identities and Black and Latinx men, receive fewer rewards of respect and professional integration.

Tiptoeing on Eggshells

Some faculty also provided vivid reports of how their department poorly treats underrepresented faculty. These accounts help us see how devaluation and exclusion unfold in everyday faculty interactions within the very departments many professors defended as purely meritocratic.

Earlier, Zhangyong puzzled that his department remains so demographically dominated by white and Asian men because he believes that "we don't have anyone really biased against women or minorities." But Kristen, an early senior professor in Zhangyong's department, provides another view. She believes that their unit's persistent demographic imbalance alongside a formal commitment to diversity is awkward for some white and Asian colleagues, who often fail to communicate well with the small numbers of racial minority colleagues who are hired.

> People tiptoe around underrepresented minority faculty all the time. I think they feel like it's always like an elephant in the room. . . . It must feel extremely weird to be, like, in a really obvious underrepresented minority status. . . . In our [department], we have really great leaders who have really good points to raise about how to increase diversity, and so I think [the department] makes it clear that this is a priority

and something we value and care about, but I still think it's weird, it's too—because it's [5] percent, they just stand out too much, and I think it makes people feel uncomfortable.

By her first word, "people," Kristen means white and perhaps Asian faculty. The disconcerting "elephant" refers to the extremely low representation of Black and Latinx faculty even though her department formally values diversity. Her colleagues dislike being confronted with their ineffectiveness at increasing diversity in their units.

Antonio says that overall, the climate in his department is "not exceptionally bad"; in fact, his former university was worse. Yet he goes on to say,

Related to diversity of the faculty . . . people just don't know what the issues are. Like, you know, they are insecure about what they think. And, they walk on . . . eggshells, like you know, because like they—they don't what to say [something wrong] and—and often they have misconceptions.

As an underrepresented person of color, Antonio experiences his majority colleagues as "walking on eggshells" around him. This is echoed in Kristen's description of the majority faculty in her unit "tiptoeing around" their Black and Latinx colleagues.

The discomfort of some overrepresented professors may also stem from their feeling that the very presence of racial minority faculty brings up "political" matters of racial identity rather than scientific matters. Rather than interrogating their own discomfort and developing skills in self-reflective communication, majority faculty often either avoid or stumble through interactions with racially minoritized colleagues.

The unease of many white and Asian men produces negative outcomes for their Black and Latinx colleagues. Kristen explains that majority faculty's discomfort reduces the support and warmth they would otherwise extend, especially to early career scientists. Such collegiality is not an optional nicety. It is necessary for those at the assistant professor level to gain access to connections, collaboration, support, and information in order to thrive and then attain tenure and promotion.

Several faculty told us that the competition for extramural grants was becoming increasingly intense, and that there were insufficient funds to support every good proposal.[24] Recall Kristen's comment that, assuming the same high quality of the science and the scientist, a proposal's success depended on how many people provided comments on it. Kristen says that younger underrepresented professors she knows are not getting the "crowdsourcing" from senior faculty that every junior person needs in the competitive race for grant money.

Calvin, a tenured professor of color in the same unit as Kristen and Zhangyong, agrees. He says that even if "stellar" underrepresented early career faculty are hired at a top institution like this university, they will not get promoted with tenure unless senior members of the department mentor them. The department's willingness to do this, he states diplomatically, is still a "big challenge."

At this level, if no one has heard of you, then it is hard [for junior professors] to move forward in these top tier institutions. . . . So the [department's] challenge [for] the top women or people of color . . . they have a stellar CV, but the big challenge is that you need to develop a tenure relationship with them.

Calvin's statement is consistent with Amy's earlier report on her department's failure to actively develop and mentor women assistant professors, compared with the favorable mentoring that men assistant professors tend to receive.

The full professors—those with the most intellectual and social resources to share—are even more disproportionately likely to be men and to be white or Asian than the overall faculty body.[25] Although many of these senior professors may be well-meaning, their social chilliness around their racial minority and women colleagues interferes with developing collegial relationships. The unease (if not outright bias) some of these majority faculty express erodes their willingness to mentor younger faculty and share resources and collaboration opportunities. The interactional burden typically falls on underrepresented faculty as they try to soothe awkwardness and subtly counteract negative stereotypes while trying to access the same resources their majority peers enjoy.

The Minority-Meritocracy Trap

Earlier, we described faculty reports of the "pipeline issue" and the "pedigree issue," which faculty used in their attempt to explain the tiny numbers of racial minority STEM faculty on campus. Recall Perry's statement that there are "very, very few people who are actually qualified" who are racial minorities. This section considers how the belief in a tension between faculty diversity and scientific excellence unfolds. We describe what we call the *minority-meritocracy trap*, the catch-22 that minority STEM faculty face where they are often seen as "diversity hires" who advanced through STEM due in part to their minority status rather than their academic excellence.

"If They Are So Good, Why Aren't They at Stanford?" Beliefs That Underrepresented Colleagues Lack Scientific Excellence

Some professors claim that the few "actually qualified" underrepresented professors in the discipline are hard to recruit to the university, given their rarity. Amy, a professor of color, says,

And they're very highly sought after. And we can barely afford to hire them because we just can't compete with [the elite private universities] like Stanford.

Similarly, Heather, a white professor, maintains,

[Underrepresented faculty applicants] have so many options. . . . The strong women and the strong underrepresented minorities, they can write their ticket where they want to go. . . . [And] we can't win a battle with Princeton.

In light of the belief that only the wealthiest elite private universities can afford to woo the top minority candidates, some majority faculty assume that their Black or Latinx colleague down the hall is not one of the "very, very few" minorities "who are actually qualified," is not one of those "strong underrepresented minorities," but a charlatan. If they were truly excellent, the reasoning goes, they would have been recruited by a top private university with deeper pockets.

Belief That Underrepresented Colleagues Received Unfair Advantages

Further, some faculty told us that their underrepresented colleagues are getting undeserved extra "diversity" benefits unavailable to others.[26] Zhangyong says that the brutal competition for extramural grants was the greatest source of stress in his work (chap. 4). Further, he also believes that racial minorities have "a better chance to get funding compared to average people." Note that by "average people," he means the most common demographic—white and Asian faculty, the taken-for-granted typical people in STEM. Zhangyong elaborates:

Because there are a lot of special programs that promote diversity and encourage minorities and women. And they have these fundings. . . . I think they're actually funded really well. At least in [my department], I think the minorities, I think they have pretty good funding.

Jia-Xin, an assistant professor, says that she often hears views (like Zhangyong's) discounting her accomplishments winning NSF and DOE (Department of Energy) grants because she is a woman. Jia-Xin says,

Yeah. One thing I feel really offended sometimes is that there are a lot of male colleagues, and they really think that we get an NSF or DOE grant because we're a woman, because of Affirmative Action. And that's like truly an insult for us. because we go through the same peer review [as they do].

Jia-Xin said she refutes the argument that granting agencies favor women applicants because in her experience reviewing grant proposals, gender is never mentioned.

Yet Zhangyong's statement that women and underrepresented racial minority scientists get access to "special programs" echoes several other professors' concerns that underrepresented groups may receive unfair advantages disconnected from the quality of the research. For example, Melissa suggests that a focus on diversity reduces the excellence of the department.

I think the [department's] attitude is that we shouldn't ever sacrifice on research quality. . . . [But] if you try to recruit someone who's an underrepresented minority . . . some people will make the assumption that because [minorities are] being recruited, there's less [quality there] than if they were to do a broad search and find the best applicant.

Casey offers a stronger statement of his belief that some faculty from underrepresented groups are unfairly hired and promoted.

Top places should never promote someone who doesn't deserve it. Probably because of lawyers and liability, it's easier to promote someone who doesn't deserve it [than not to promote them] . . . especially if they're a minority. . . . We must require excellence. . . . Once you've started hiring individuals that aren't excellent, or promoting them, you've already . . . damaged the department.

Not Just "Diversity Hires"

In contrast, others argue that the view that underrepresented faculty on campus have less value is the real attack on meritocratic standards.

For example, Elizabeth, a white full professor, stated with frustration that the only underrepresented racial minority in her department is one newly hired scientist.

With exasperation mounting, Elizabeth says that professors in her department should simply assume that this new colleague was hired "based on meritocracy. . . . He works, he does his job, [and] he increases our assets because he gets a ton of money" in federal grants. Instead, Elizabeth reports, faculty claim that their new colleague got hired primarily because he is an underrepresented racial minority.

The numbers of underrepresented minorities and women are small in many units. If these professors are viewed as subpar, then they, in the imagination of other faculty, stand in for all academic scientists who share their demographic categories.[27]

We see this process unfold in Elizabeth's remarks. She believes generally that for a woman to be hired, "she has to be extraordinary, but a man just has to do good work." Nevertheless, Elizabeth also thinks that there have been a few cases in which "marginal women were given tenure that shouldn't have been." Because these particular women scientists were regarded as "marginal," their promotion, in Elizabeth's words, "degrades the accomplishments of all women."

Similarly, Melissa, a white woman, feels that her own reputation is vulnerable to being damaged if the department hires a woman who is not seen as measuring up.

I do feel like *my* research is high quality, and I want to be recognized for that, and it probably hurts women or underrepresented minorities to bring in people just because of their gender or ethnicity, who are going to be viewed as subpar in certain areas.

Calvin, an underrepresented professor, also feels that his own reputation is vulnerable to devaluation. In addition to his dedication to pushing forward his field of study, he works hard to manage the impression he gives as a person of color in a society that is still surprised when faculty of color are articulate, knowledgeable experts.[28] He also counters his "isolation" in his own department by building up networks nationally and internationally to thrive in a field that moves quickly and penalizes insularity.

Calvin seeks to make the most out of being the only underrepresented scientist in the room at conferences. When giving talks, he is "on his game" and "very mindful of being stellar . . . and creating a huge buzz." This buzz "makes you stand out, people want to work with you, then you get interactions and networks that are important, your scientific ideas move faster." He has become a superstar. Yet when asked whether he had ever been treated differently than majority faculty in his department, he answered, "I sure have." After a pause, he explained that he had felt isolated at several points during his career and that "it was a little bit lonely to break the ice."

These interviews offer accounts that are consistent with our survey findings presented in the previous chapter. Compared with men at the same job level, in the same department, and with the same scholarly productivity, women are less likely to feel that their research is respected in their department, and they are more likely to agree that they "have to work harder than others in their department and in their discipline to be perceived as a legitimate scholar." This pattern is particularly striking for Black and Latinx women.

The "unconscious bias" and "entrenched racial stereotypes" that Sarah, Elizabeth, and others name are found in many occupations and social groups. Over and above this bias, the schema of scientific excellence as a professional belief system in STEM amplifies the devaluation and disrespect of underrepresented scientists. These are emergent patterns that play out among colleagues committed to the ideal of research excellence.

Conclusion

The professors in our study are smart and analytical individuals. How do so many maintain the belief that STEM is meritocratic in light of the demographic underrepresentation of many groups among faculty on campus? The answer lies in taken-for-granted assumptions in the professional culture of STEM that explain away this underrepresentation and divert blame for its resolution from STEM faculty and institutions.

These faculty see the hiring and promotion procedures in their own departments as fair, and most report that scientific merit is objectively recognized and rewarded. When their faith in STEM meritocracy is threatened by statistical evidence to the contrary, they dismiss this evidence and hold fast to the belief that their departments and disciplines fairly recognize and reward scientific excellence.

These cultural beliefs ensnare many women and racial/ethnic minority faculty in a minority-meritocracy trap. First, to be hired, underrepresented groups must convince departmental evaluators that despite their demographic identity, they are above the hiring bar purely on the basis of their research. Second, when they are hired, underrepresented faculty are often denied full credit for their accomplishments and are not provided with the same collegiality and resources as white and Asian men. Third, if underrepresented professors who are viewed by some as subpar are hired or promoted, then the respect for others in that demographic group is vulnerable to damage by association.

However, speaking up about these dynamics is often seen as allowing political and social concerns to pollute scientific objectivity. The belief that STEM can and should be a depoliticized space thus explains away existing patterns of inequality and sidelines conversations about these issues in otherwise "pure" STEM spaces. The seemingly noble defense of the definition of excellence from concerns deemed too politicized exacerbates inequality, marginalizes underrepresented groups, and reproduces the dominant status of heterosexual white and Asian men.

SIX

The Moralization of Merit: Consequences for Scientists and Science

This book investigates a paradox. On the one hand, STEM professors typically believe that their fields are meritocracies that reward the best science, regardless of the identity of scientists. On the other hand, we have shown how STEM faculty from many groups—women, mothers, people of color, LGBTQ individuals—are not only underrepresented but are also often devalued and disrespected. We show that the problem of enduring inequalities is not driven primarily by a few bad apples with old-fashioned biases. Neither is it just a matter of a university's hiring and reward system sometimes falling short of its meritocratic ideals. Instead, we find that the problem also lies in scientists' very understandings of merit.

Previous chapters examined the revered schemas of work devotion and scientific excellence as separate entities. This chapter will explain how these schemas share tangled cultural roots and together reinforce a white, heteronormatively masculine, and *moralized conception of the scientific calling*. We show that many well-intentioned faculty defend what they understand as the purity of scientific excellence and devotion from perceived threats from identity politics, family responsibilities, and illegitimate claims to excellence. The harder they try to protect their profession's ideals, the more they reinforce beliefs and practices that marginalize and devalue many STEM professionals and their scholarship.

Although our investigation of these cherished schemas may be disconcerting, advancing the understanding of scientific culture can help STEM become more equitable and inclusive and enhance its capacity for innovation. We end this chapter by pointing to avenues for changing this culture for the better.

Schemas Entwined in the Moral Defense of Professional Purity

Our empirical results show that the schemas of work devotion and scientific excellence help define the scientific vocation as a meaningful life. These two schemas frame the profession as a calling devoted to the pursuit of new knowledge about the heavens and the earth, a quest that is simultaneously rational and inspired. Furthermore, the two schemas work together to construct a system of morality that many STEM professionals share. This system maintains a symbolic boundary[1] between purity and pollution, between those who are seen as true scientists and those who do not fully belong.

Although STEM is on the cutting edge of knowledge advancement and innovation, its cultural roots reach back centuries (chap. 2). Understandings of the purity of the scientific vocation are anchored in 2,400-year-old Platonic and Aristotelian beliefs about the rationality and superiority of white, free men of European origin.[2] In the sixteenth and seventeenth centuries, scientists were often understood as the faithful recorders of God's glory. This commitment was gradually replaced by more secular understandings of science in the eighteenth century Enlightenment. Yet a moral belief persists that academic scientists should pursue knowledge and truth for its own sake and protect this pursuit from influences that might corrupt it.[3]

Moreover, STEM's contemporary admiration of creative brilliance is rooted in old understandings of scientists as inspired geniuses—men who were personal recipients of divine knowledge handed down through traditions that trace back to Socrates, Aristotle, and Newton.[4] Such men were believed to follow their vocations selflessly, unmotivated by social status or monetary gain.[5] Beliefs about scientific brilliance have secularized, but STEM continues to valorize a sense of inspired and individualized creativity.

Further, the formalization of science into a profession during the Enlightenment entrenched the ideal that scientific progress is made possible through careful attention to the scientific method and vigorous evaluation by the scientific community. While this cultural development sought to neutralize social influence on the emergence of scientific truths (even though STEM work is always inherently cultural and social), it promoted the idea that scientific knowledge could be and should be sealed off from culture and politics.[6] These norms framed explicit considerations of scientists' identities and backgrounds as outside the pale of legitimacy in the evaluation of their research. Bringing in such considerations would threaten the foundations of objectivity.

These deeply rooted beliefs about the exclusion of personal perspectives from science still ring true for most STEM faculty today: most want objective, neutral STEM work without reference to the identities of individual scientists. But there's a catch. Historically—and today—that unmarked, unobtrusive identity of scientist can be embodied only by white, heterosexual men. Scientists who do not fit those characteristics—white women, women and men of color, openly LGBTQ professors—have never enjoyed the privilege of having their identities seem invisible.[7] Their very presence can be seen as a threat to cultural norms of objectivity, impersonality, and depoliticization.

Academic science today, like in the past, is understood to be sanctified and set apart from the messiness of politics, identities, caregiving, and other worldly preoccupations. Yet in contrast to previous eras, where white men had a near-monopoly on professorships, women and people of color, though still minoritized, have a clear presence in academic STEM. In our study, Latinx, Black, and Native American faculty and white women produce work at the same pace and of the same quality as their white and Asian men colleagues, on average,[8] even as they are confronted by a professional culture that flags their identities as potential violations of the purity of scientific excellence and devotion.

The professors we interviewed vigorously defend their commitment to scientific excellence and devotion against perceived threats, including the siren call of profit and the competing demands of childcare. They assert that they can clearly discern excellence in other scientists without bias or regard to demographics or politics. Some strive to protect their vision of excellence from what they see as the illegitimate diversity goals imposed by their university. This defense of professional purity is based in a set of moral convictions that are not easily swayed by scientific evidence contradicting those beliefs (chap. 5).[9]

Learning and Solidifying Moral Convictions: The Long Novitiate of the Scientific Calling

Those who seek a place in academic STEM must first go through a long, formative training period to demonstrate their worthiness and alignment with the cultural and moral commitments of the profession. This novitiate period of graduate school and postdoctoral appointments can last a decade or longer before a first faculty appointment. It is during this period that novices are socialized into the cultural norms of the profession and are expected to take up its values as their own.[10]

Due to the increasingly competitive job market for research-intensive faculty positions, many STEM academics take a series of postdoctoral positions that pay comparatively low salaries before being eligible for faculty positions.[11] For instance, John, a full professor, says,

We are a fantastic department. . . . We only hire people who have passed the PhD by several years. They have done penal servitude as postdocs, they have a publication record. We are very careful [about whom we hire as assistant professors].

By "penal servitude," John figuratively refers to how early career scientists (although privileged in many ways) face strenuous expectations of devotion and excellence under conditions of short-term, precarious employment, with the hope of eventually becoming tenured faculty with their own laboratories and research teams.

After entering their first faculty appointments, professors go through another probationary period of five to eight years at the rank of assistant professor without security of employment. At this stage, the pay improves but the pressure mounts. Assistant professors are required to intensely focus on an innovative research trajectory while also managing obligations to research teams, students, funders, departments, and disciplines, often within a fiercely competitive research funding and publishing environment. At the end of this period, they go through a year-long process of tenure evaluation. By this time, most are in their late thirties or early forties.[12] If their research output is judged sufficiently excellent by departmental colleagues and by experts in the broader discipline, they receive the privilege of promotion to associate professor and tenure with lifetime job security, which is designed to protect their academic freedom. However, if their work is not seen as above the bar, the probationer must leave the university.

Most faculty in our study believe these tenure requirements are reasonable and are based on research excellence alone rather than politics or demographics (chap. 5). Although the game is tough, most faculty believe that the rules are fair. Through this long novitiate, early career scientists must demonstrate their alignment with the cultural norms of their field. By the time they reach the professoriate, their faith in a meritocratic STEM has become an inextricable part of their understanding of their profession and their identities as professionals.

Following the Scientific Calling for Love, Not Money

Maintaining this intensive work focus over decades is presumed to require—and elicit—strong emotions, including love, passion, and desire.[13] The long novitiate selects for dedicated scientists who are devoted to charting their own course within the relative freedom of academic science. Recall Joseph, who in chapter 3 described his engagement with scientific discovery as a passion and an addiction.[14]

The scientists in our study have chosen to follow an academic path rather than a potentially more lucrative career in industry.[15] For instance, Peter recounts that he works nights and weekends, and that he does it for the sense of discovery, not money.

I like that it's explorative, that I get to do things that nobody has ever done. . . . I would say the devotion is more important to me than money. I'm glad I get paid, but I don't do it for that reason.

Many faculty described their jobs as something they would continue to do even if they were independently wealthy. Recall Michael's words that launched chapter 3: "I take work home with me all the time. I really love my work. I feel lucky to be able to do this job. If I were independently wealthy, I'd be perfectly happy to pay for the opportunity to have this job."

Gabi, a distinguished professor featured in chapter 5, is among the most senior faculty in his department. Describing his current situation, Gabi notes that he is "highly devoted" to his work and is now essentially "working for free," because his current salary is about the same size as his pension would be if he retired. Less senior faculty are keenly aware that they likely could fetch much higher salaries if they left academia for industry.[16] For instance, Charles, who started his career in industry, "took a 40 percent pay cut" when he transitioned into academia.

Academic STEM is hailed for the protection it is believed to offer from the potentially corrupting influence of profit-seeking.[17] For example, Alan explains that he prefers working in a domain buffered from the pressure of revenue generation.

[I and] most of my friends would do what they're doing even if they didn't get paid, because you really care about your subject. . . . Because I like the freedom to explore things that I want to explore. And I like universities. I like the idea of not necessarily [needing an] obvious use of research. . . . I like the mission of universities. I don't have a great drive to make other people money.

Alan's term "freedom" aligns with two additional core values of academic science: the freedom from outside influence conferred by the job security of being a tenured professor, and the freedom from conflicts of interest linked to financial gains associated with particular results that might corrupt disinterested, objective research.

The contributions of basic research tend to be on a different timeline than that of industry's applied research. To illustrate, Delfina says that her lab's focus is on "basic science, fundamental studies" at the molecular level. However, a distant, long-term application could be to "take nitrogen out of the atmosphere and turn it into fertilizer and feed the world." The applications of this research may not be realized for several generations. Similarly, Michael says his desire is

to make scientific contributions that will benefit society, broadly put. And because I'm a . . . neuroscientist, I hope that the things we discover will at some point contribute to clinical improvements that will help my children's children's children's children and all of our descendants have a better life. So that's what drives me.

In actuality, there are collaborations between academic science and industry.[18] Some of the professors in our study own patents or have founded start-up companies, which are sources of additional income.[19] The university administration frames the commercialization of faculty research as socially and financially beneficial. Previous research finds that professors who do industry-funded research argue for its legitimacy by maintaining that they bring their professional norms of disinterested objectivity into the collaboration.[20]

Patents and commercial activities are governed by complex university rules limiting conflict of interest, which are designed to contain the potential drain on faculty time and devotion and the potential corruption of their scientific judgment. Although these conflict of interest rules may not always fulfill their purpose, they function as cultural guardrails, preserving the norm that academic research should be uncontaminated by personal or corporate profit.

Singular Devotion

The world of elite academic scientists was not too long ago virtually all (white) men. In a 1953 study of sixty-four elite men scientists, one respondent quipped that the "archenemy of the successful scientist" was a wife who wanted her husband home for dinner most nights. Further, some of these scientists argued that women lacked the intellectual drive, "physical stamina, single-mindedness, and emotional detachment" required for producing excellent scientific research.[21]

Today, at our case university, 16 percent of STEM faculty are women, and two-thirds of these women are mothers. In contrast to faculty's tolerance for entrepreneurial and commercial activity (despite its potential to distract from basic research or introduce conflicts of interest), the culturally feminine work of involved motherhood is seen as a threat to the scientific calling.

Many fathers explained that although they participate in childcare to some extent, their time belonged to their scientific vocation first and foremost. For instance, Francisco memorably described how his wife and child tiptoe around his scientific concentration at home, knowing that if even he appears to be just sitting around, he might be thinking about science (chap. 3). Francisco's declaration that his wife and child have "learned" to be "very good" about not distracting him when he is working illustrates a moral claim for the sanctity of research time that is protected from family obligations.

In contrast, Joseph explains that he believes his wife—also a science professor—and other academic mothers he knows have lost the focus to keep up with the field and sustain a high quality of creative scientific thought. He reported that his wife struggled with feeling "guilty" about "neglecting our toddler" in day care (chap. 3). These words indicate a sense of moral culpability that Joseph believes most mothers struggle with. Feelings of "competing tensions for her time" suggest, in his view, that mothers' caregiving responsibilities do not primarily constitute a time management problem, solved perhaps by hiring a more efficient laboratory manager and a babysitter/cook/chauffer, but a moral dilemma between the work devotion expected of STEM faculty and the family devotion that women—even highly accomplished scientists—are expected to fulfill.[22]

The mothers we interviewed grappled with the competing moral claims of science and motherhood. Some agreed that childcare responsibilities pulled them away from staying on the "cutting edge" of their fields. Others defended themselves against this accusation by sacrificing sleep rather than neglecting their research or their children—even resuming work twenty-four hours after birthing a baby. Nonetheless, we found evidence of a stigma against mothers, who are often viewed as less committed to their careers than their colleagues are (chap. 3).[23]

This understanding among established faculty is consistent with research on STEM graduate students and postdocs, who are taught from their student days onward that motherhood is an abject and stigmatized condition that should be avoided, repudiated, or hidden.[24] These experiences of guilt, blame, stigma, and betrayal signal that motherhood is culturally framed as a moral violation of the schema of work devotion.[25]

Our results show the inaccuracy of the assumption that mothers are less committed to their careers. Mothers themselves are equally devoted to their STEM work as fathers and childless faculty are. Analysis of our Scholarly Production database demonstrates that mothers in our study have similar grant dollars on average and similar quantity and impact of publications as the men and childless women at their level and department (chap. 3).[26] Although there is variation in faculty productivity, this variation is not associated with gender, motherhood, or fatherhood status.[27] By defining openly involved mothers (not fathers or other groups) as too distracted to stay on top of their fields, faculty reinforce an old cultural story that women with children lack the singleness of heart to be true disciples in the scientific vocation.

To cope with assumptions that motherhood is practically and morally incompatible with the scientific calling, some mothers in our sample tried to "pass" as childless or "cover" as parents whose work practices were unaltered by the addition of children to their households. Recall Yolanda, whose career reputation "survived" the birth of two young children in part because she maintained her full focus on her research and forwent parental leave. And Jessica, a single mother of a child with special needs, used a secret "army" of paid caregivers to maintain the image of a single-minded scientist, "always available" for professional responsibilities (chap. 3). As a consequence of conforming to the work devotion mandate, parents deprive themselves of campus resources designed to help with family responsibilities. Unfortunately, their decisions reinforce the stigma associated with using these resources. By concealing their family lives, parents may miss out on informal connections that could develop into collegial and mentoring relationships.[28] More broadly, these processes reinforce the notion that the scientific vocation requires faculty to renounce openly time-intensive, close, connected care of children, elders, and others in the human community (chap. 3).

Defending Judgments of Excellence from Identity Politics and from Accusations of Bias

The schema of scientific excellence mandates that science should be evaluated objectively. Many professors insisted that they disregard race, gender, and sexual identity when evaluating colleagues (chap. 5). The declaration that academic STEM objectively appraises research while ignoring the personal identity of the scientists is a moral claim for the purity of the evaluation of scientific excellence, uncontaminated by identity politics.

As noted above, the catch-22 is that scientists are culturally assumed to be white heterosexual men. Identities that deviate from that description become visible and thus violate the expectations of depersonalized, disembodied excellence. Underrepresented faculty are less likely to be recognized and rewarded for living up to the expectations of scientific excellence, even though they are equally likely to do so (chaps. 4 and 5). They are often viewed as recipients of resources illegitimately linked to their identities rather than earned on the basis of their scientific work (chap. 5).[29] Many professors assume that underrepresented colleagues are less than stellar. Black, Latinx, and white women are sometimes dismissed as "diversity hires" who received an easier pass at hiring or promotion than their heterosexual white men colleagues.

Reinforcing these views, some professors we interviewed asserted that truly excellent racial minority scientists are exceedingly rare. Faculty attributed this rarity to upstream pipeline problems or an inability to convince racial minority candidates (and in some fields, women) to apply in the first place. Some professors laughed awkwardly when reporting that their units interviewed very few or zero Black and Latinx candidates. Following that, they were quick to emphasize that they would welcome more racially diverse colleagues, but the truly qualified candidates were snatched up by wealthier private universities that could offer more resources. Similarly, Benjamin said his unit had a warm and welcoming climate toward women—or would have, he clarified, if there were any women in it.

To help scientists talk about their taken-for-granted conviction that science is generally meritocratic, we asked them to help us make sense of a *Science* research article documenting the lower rates of NIH grants received by Black scientists compared to whites with similar productivity (chap. 5).[30] Even when confronted with this finding, published in the most hallowed of scientific journals, many faculty continued to insist that academic STEM was meritocratic. In the face of rigorous data, faculty often fell back on their own anecdotal experience as counterevidence to the study's results.

Recall that Ruben rejected the study's findings because they were at odds with his personal experience with an African American collaborator (chap. 1). Christopher rejected the results because he insisted that he and his fellow NIH reviewers never think about race or gender but only focus on the science (chap. 5). Benjamin, another NIH proposal reviewer, says that he knows all the scientists whose proposals he reviews, and he uses his personal knowledge to assess their training and abilities while ignoring their race and gender. He notes, "If you cannot write a proposal, you don't get the money," and states further that many Black scientists "are not getting the right training." He asserts that "the racial discrepancy is not intentional. There is no discrimination," and he seems naïve about the fact that implicit bias is a cognitive process that operates under the radar of intentionality and conscious awareness.[31] These declarations that all STEM faculty are evaluated without prejudice, even in the face of clear evidence to the contrary, is a cultural defense of the legitimacy of the yardstick of scientific excellence.

Some professors worried that members of some groups—Latinx and Black faculty and white women—were hired or promoted *because* they were members of underrepresented populations and, not, in Benjamin's words, "normal candidates" (white heterosexual men). Benjamin stated that universities would bring out "a lot of resources to try and attract" faculty candidates from underrepresented groups. Yet he asserted these resources "don't become available to the normal candidates. . . . And I think that this is completely warped and wrong."[32] Similarly, Casey warned that the fear of "liability" leads departments to promote the undeserving, "especially if they're a minority." Further, he fears that once the university allows this, "you've already . . . damaged the department" (chap. 5). Aware of these kinds of assumptions, some women and Black and Latinx men feel caught in a minority-meritocracy trap, worrying that their own scientific reputations could be injured by association if another underrepresented scholar is viewed as underperforming. Importantly, in contrast to the concerns of faculty like Casey and Benjamin, our SPI database analysis finds that the number and dollar level of grants and the number and impact of publications do not statistically differ by race or gender among the STEM faculty at this university (chap. 5).

Fundamentally, their fear is that underrepresented scientists are often undeserving, and efforts for their inclusion is like a toxin that harms the department's work and reputation. The very presence of underrepresented colleagues is thus seen as potentially violating the moral community of excellent scientists.

Like at all institutions, STEM faculty at this university vary in their level of productivity and grant success. Because our analyses find no systematic variation between white and Asian men and their colleagues, there is an equal proportion of white and Asian men and underrepresented faculty who perform above and below average. *Yet in our eighty-five interviews, not one person expressed concern about white and Asian men who were ruining their department's reputation through their underperformance.*

In sum, many STEM professors—from many demographic backgrounds—are convinced that STEM is generally meritocratic, even in the face of scientifically rigorous counterevidence. Their faith in meritocracy is not a rational or scientific belief but, for them, a moral conviction.

The Cost of Concealed Identities

Striving to preserve the boundaries of what he views as objective scientific evaluation, Christopher claimed that it would never cross his mind to be influenced by a scientist's demographics. Similarly, Mateo stated that he and his colleagues would not "even want to know" about the identities of faculty candidates as they assessed their work (chap. 5). The moral valorization of "not knowing" about a scientist's identity is particularly salient for the experiences of LGBTQ professors, whose status is often less visually identifiable than other demographic characteristics. Our quantitative findings demonstrate that LGBTQ faculty feel less included and respected then their non-LGBTQ peers and are more likely to cordon their personal lives off from departmental conversations and events.[33] Our interviews reveal that some "pass" as non-LGBTQ or "cover" or play down their status by remaining silent about their personal lives during hallway chitchat and after-work gatherings (chap. 4).

Several professors we interviewed believe that there are no LGBTQ colleagues in their departments at all. Yet descriptive statements such as "there *are no* openly LGBTQ faculty in my unit" sometimes become prescriptive, i.e., "there *should be no* openly LGBTQ faculty in my unit."

Recall Perry, who illustrates the view that the very presence of openly LGBTQ colleagues would illegitimately pull personal and politicized issues into professional settings. He disproved of openly identifying LGBTQ people "who are just out there in your face" because he doesn't want to "know this in a *professional* context. It's not an issue for me but *I don't need to be reminded of it every day* necessarily" (emphasis added). Perry presents the preference that LGBTQ faculty cover or pass as non-LGBTQ as a moral request to keep scientific contexts neutral.

This drive to maintain the purity of scientific judgment comes at great cost not only to minority scientists but also to broader academic departments and disciplines. The cases of professors who share multiple marginalized identities vividly illustrate this point.

For example, Sophia, an LGBTQ-identifying woman of color, describes herself as a "devoted" and "workaholic" scientist who joined our case university because of the opportunities it offered to work alongside scientists with similar specialties. She works long hours, publishes amply, and mentors many graduate students.

She says that she avoids talking about her woman partner to anyone at work other than a couple of colleagues she feels "very close to." When asked whether she would feel comfortable bringing her partner to department gatherings, Sophia responded that it feels "almost natural" to decline these invitations.

It's almost natural that she doesn't want to go, and I don't. You know? And I don't do very many social functions in the department. . . . So, it's like, it never occurred [to decide whether to bring her with me].

For Sophia, avoiding these events means missed opportunities for informal discussion and collaboration. At the same time, the department is impoverished by her absence. Faculty miss out on opportunities for collegial discussions with her, and students lose the chance to get to know her in a more informal setting.[34] She and some other LGBTQ professors believe that beneath the claim from colleagues that only the science matters, there lies the risk that their LGBTQ identity could be seen as politicizing and polluting. They isolate themselves to reduce the chance of rejection by their departmental colleagues and disciplinary communities.

Broadly, we find several common experiences across the diverse spectrum of underrepresented faculty, including LGBTQ professors, Black and Latinx faculty, women, and mothers. We see evidence that some white and Asian men professors view underrepresented faculty as inherently politicizing because they fear they could raise the specter of diversity at any time. As a result, majority-group professors sometimes find their underrepresented colleagues "awkward" to interact with—an awkwardness that typifies the othering so often experienced by women, mothers, LGBTQ faculty, and faculty of color.

Defending the Schema of Scientific Excellence from Diversity Goals

Some faculty are personally sympathetic to the goal of increasing the diversity of their departments, but they are constrained by the assumptions of their professional culture about what are legitimate actions to take. For example, Gabi and Zhangyong are looking for tools to implement small changes to the demography of their departments but are confused by why their efforts have failed. Their good intentions are hindered by the schema of scientific excellence, which defines the explicit consideration of demographics and unequal opportunities as a violation of universality. Bill would also like to see a demographic shift in his department but worries that the tools the university uses to increase faculty diversity "breed cynicism" among departmental members.

Other faculty are opposed to even the goal of increasing the diversity of their units, a goal they view as incompatible with scientific objectivity and the quest for excellence. One element of job application files on this campus (and others)[35] is a "contributions to diversity" statement, in which applicants to faculty positions discuss their present and future efforts to improve demographic diversity among students or faculty on campus. This requirement has plenty of critics. For example, Ronald, a white senior full professor, fears that this requirement discourages the brightest new PhDs from even applying. He places himself in the shoes of a young candidate for a faculty position:

And if I'm trying to choose between Stanford and [case university], and [case university] is asking me to write another four-page document on diversity, and I don't really know where they're coming from, and I don't know what they're going to hold me to. . . . I think it scares people away.

Ronald's statement implies that "people" who are truly excellent would be put off by this requirement, not proud to share their contributions.

Benjamin also fears that asking applicants to write about their current or planned contributions to diversity in their application materials would discourage the best candidates—who might have many employ-ment options—from applying. He sees this statement as an illegitimate part of the evaluation process in faculty recruitment. He believes it is "ridiculous" to expect "those guys" who have been trained to be meri-torious STEM academics, particularly those from other countries, to be well-versed in social inequality and the lack of diversity in US higher education.

Those guys are kids. They were trained to be a scientist in a major university. You [also] want them to be aware of diversity in education and how to create equality? It's just ridiculous . . .

Benjamin's comment illustrates his presumptions about who the quality candidates are that he does not want to put off—"guys" who would be burdened by this requirement rather than those who might welcome the recognition of their contributions.

Benjamin then describes how his department games the system by helping top candidates write their "contributions to diversity" statement.

You know what we do? We [sometimes] write it for them. [They might turn one in and ask,] "Is this the right way to do it?" No. We write it. Sometimes we tell them, if they're very good, go ahead and write it, we'll edit it for you. . . . And then you have to explain to the dean in writing why we just selected this [candidate], and you have to give them points for awareness when it comes to diversity, blah, blah, blah.

He defends this behavior as ethical because he believes it supports the broader professional mandate of a fair and objective evaluation of scien-tific excellence.

Benjamin thinks that the real travesty is what he sees as the pres-sure from the university to increase the number of underrepresented candidates in the applicant pool and among finalists. He says this pres-sure from the university has "broken" what had been a fair evaluation process. He continues:

[Can we] actually evaluate a file based on its merit? [No,] I just don't see an objective way of doing it. Not when you're pressured to try and increase the number of . . . [to] increase diversity.

He condemns this attention to the diversity of candidate pools as "com-pletely dishonest," a phrase that underscores his moral outrage over what he sees as an affront to scientific excellence.[36]

The paradox of academic science's commitment to fair and objective evaluation alongside the persistent devaluation and exclusion of many excellent, underrepresented colleagues is thus not due to a few bad apples who fail to apply meritocratic values. Instead, the paradox is rooted in a moralized professional culture beloved by its many true believers. This culture mobilizes STEM faculty to defend the purity of the calling to scientific excellence and devotion from perceived threats, such as profit, family caregiving, identity politics, false accusations of bias, and campus diversity goals.

Consequences for Academic Scientists and for STEM

We have documented how standard processes of evaluating merit come with an array of negative consequences for faculty who are women, racial/ethnic minorities, or LGBTQ individuals. The schemas of scientific excellence and work devotion, in other words, give unspoken advantages to white and Asian heterosexual men. These consequences have ripple effects for marginalized and minoritized students. The lack of diversity among faculty means that women, students of color, and LGBTQ-identifying students have fewer opportunities to work with mentors with whom they share identities. These students may internalize the message that STEM professionals do not generally look like them, which can discourage students from seeking careers along this path.[37] Moreover, the gendered, racialized, and heteronormative attribution of work devotion and excellence is likely as burdensome for graduate and undergraduate students as it is for the faculty we study.[38] The same shortcomings of faculty diversity efforts that ignore the racism, sexism, and heteronormativity embedded in the definitions of merit and excellence in STEM likely also hamstring efforts to recruit and retain a more diverse student body.[39]

Misconceiving Merit Is Bad for All STEM Faculty

Although the consequences of this misconception and mismeasurement of merit are especially negative for women, people of color, and LGBTQ persons in STEM, they can be harmful for all scientists.

First, living up to the work devotion schema requires tremendous sacrifices of personal time. Recall that Ruben works about fifteen hours a day, seven days a week, and still feels guilty about being the "bottleneck" holding up the progress of his students' and postdocs' projects.

He has little downtime and is glad that his two pets don't require much attention (chap. 1). Dan and Kristen (chap. 4 and 5, respectively) each describe feeling overworked and stressed that they are always falling behind as they attempt to live up to the demands of excellence.

As another example, Paul works long days, nights, and weekends. He literally shoots for the moon (with lasers) to test hypotheses of general relativity. He loves the exploration, yet he is exhausted with the constant rush to meet deadlines and requests:

The demands are so numerous that I'm incapable of satisfying everybody's demands to their full expectations. So I feel like my job is one of handing out disappointment, that I just can't do everything that everybody wants me to do. So that's the worst part.

Like others we interviewed, Paul thinks he is letting down pretty much everyone in his life.

Well, it can be students, it can be colleagues, it can be . . . collaborators. And that spills over into the personal life, because the . . . professional life is so busy that I fail to satisfy obligations elsewhere as well. So just all-around stress too.

Despite keeping up this "grueling" pace, Paul describes his research productivity as "a little on the low side." Like Ruben, Kristen, Dan, and so many others, he feels that he can never do enough.

Further, the schema of scientific excellence undermines faculty's sense of worthiness. By the standards of the scientific excellence schema, these STEM faculty are outstanding. Yet most faculty see themselves falling short of the ideal of someone "excellent" in their field: a creative, brilliant, assertive leader. For many, these definitions of excellence are too narrow. Faculty across all demographic groups, on average, view themselves as more fully embodying the relational qualities of collegiality and mentorship and feel more committed to diversity than the individualistic, assertive, depoliticized qualities praised in their profession (chap. 4).

For example, when we asked Michael, a white man, what he was most proud of in his career, he first gave the canonical answer, "scientific discoveries." Then while reflecting on this in real time during the interview, he mused,

Although the odd piece of this is . . . even if you ask most scientists what they're proud of, I'm guessing most of them will . . . talk about their discoveries.

[But really,] the thing that's going to be remembered, at least for a little while, are the people that we've trained. That's really our legacy. I mean, if you really put a gun to my head . . . and say, "C'mon, Michael, *name* it, really tell me [what is the most important]," the answer is: It's the people that we've trained, that I've trained. And that's been a good number of students and postdocs. I remain very attached to them and know where they are and what they're doing.

But I still aspire to making more scientific discoveries. And of course, in the process training more students and postdocs to help do that.

Student mentoring and collaboration can be part and parcel of a professor's main project of scientific discovery. For instance, Christopher describes his research as generative—not only in the construction of new molecules but also in bringing forth new ideas from himself and his students.

And also seeing the students bloom too. That's a big part. . . . Seeing the research ideas come to fruition is more collaborative.

The schema of scientific excellence celebrates individual brilliance, which is believed to be reflected in the quantity and impact of research articles. But the priorities in this schema constrain faculty's commitment to other important tasks of science. Performance reviews at research-intensive universities generally give far less attention to mentoring and fostering intra-department collaborations, and students and junior faculty suffer for that.[40] Mentoring and collaborating with the next generation is a vital responsibility of professionals, and scientists who do it well deserve more credit.

More pragmatically, to motivate STEM faculty to become aware of these misconceptions of merit, it is likely not enough to show them that these schemas are unfair for marginalized and minoritized groups. Chapter 5 illustrates the rhetorical contortions many professors performed to justify the ways that STEM is generally meritocratic, even in the face of scientifically rigorous counterevidence. Reevaluating the definitions of merit could benefit all faculty while countering many of the processes of bias we identify in this book.

Misconceiving Merit Is Bad for Science

Our results demonstrate that not only is misconceiving merit bad for scientists, but it is also bad for science. We uncovered four main negative consequences of misconceiving merit for STEM.

Consequence 1: The Assessment of STEM Merit Is Not as
Objective as It Seems

The processes discussed in this book are deeply rooted and difficult to
change. Most faculty believe that their departments and their professions generally operate neutrally, objectively, and meritocratically, in
accordance with the schemas of scientific excellence and work devotion. Yet these schemas are not neutral or objective yardsticks of merit.
Estimations of competence and assessments of what is most valued in a
profession are cultural constructs and have bias built into them. Every
time the schemas of excellence and devotion are deployed in STEM education and practice, they have the potential to reinscribe biases in hiring, promotion, salary, and funding decisions.

Further, our findings show that STEM professionals' defense of their
profession's yardstick for measuring excellence as objective reinforces
unfair practices in ways even beyond just the biased construction and
use of that yardstick (chap. 5). Faculty who vigorously defend the fairness of the schema of scientific excellence are, in practice, justifying
the patterns of disadvantage that the schema helps create. This defense
frames efforts to address these inequalities as irrelevant or even contaminating to the profession. Further, the professional culture of STEM
largely rejects serious engagement with the evidence that competent,
well-meaning scientists can make racist, sexist, and heteronormative decisions and—through inaction as well as action—support racist, sexist,
and heteronormative systems. These biases not only are harmful for faculty and students but also may restrict the development, funding, and
reception of innovative work.[41]

Consequence 2: The Way Merit Is Conceptualized Does Not Reflect the
Communal Way in Which Most Cutting-Edge STEM Work Is Done

The second consequence for STEM is that the way scientific merit is conceptualized may not reflect how STEM innovation actually takes place.
As we show in chapter 4, excellent scientists are seen as competitive risk-
takers whose sparks of individual genius lead to stellar publications and
flush grant funding. The academic review process assesses the work of
scientists as singular workers: faculty members must submit promotion
dossiers that trumpet their individual contributions. STEM faculty, moreover, are often cordoned off from colleagues in the spirit of competition
and disconnected from the broader populations their work impacts. This

is consistent with the admiration of scientists who are viewed as brilliant independent demigods and aggressive cowboys (chap. 2).

But that is not how STEM inquiry is typically accomplished today. As Kristen noted, most science is actually collaborative, completed in multi-investigator labs with groups of students, postdocs, and coinvestigators.[42] Grant proposals and publications are guided by others' comments and feedback, and STEM faculty share ideas at conferences, via email, and over coffee. Faculty whose work spans multiple disciplines collaborate even more. For instance, Mateo, a biology professor, offered a long list of faculty outside his department with whom he has worked:

Well, I, because of my interest, I tend to collaborate more with faculty in other divisions, computer science, materials, the medical school, biochemistry, people I sought—it's just purely my—you know, how my interests are kind of spread in areas that are too esoteric for [life sciences], like the area of architecture and neuroscience, I tend to work a lot more with people in the medical school and in engineering.

However, this kind of collaborative work is not always valued and is sometimes even resisted. As Ruben noted in chapter 1, his highly competitive departmental colleagues avoid collaborating with one another because of the perception that there isn't enough credit to go around. Junior faculty find it difficult to instigate such collaborations if more senior colleagues do not reach out first. He explained that this lack of intradepartmental collaboration can be counterproductive because it requires multiple separate grants to do similar work, pitting colleague against colleague.

Yet collaborative and interdisciplinary work is precisely where many we interviewed see STEM going in the future.[43] For example, Rich noted that collaborative work is increasingly important as his field becomes more complex.

It's not the old days of a PhD being narrow and deep. PhDs in my field are getting shallower but broader. You have to take on skill sets that are so broad that I think the people that are most successful and therefore are admired have shown how to work nicely across these massive disciplines, to integrate big-scale projects together and make them work.

He explains that academic STEM still doesn't "get the teamwork concept." "It's always what have *you* done recently, not what has your *team* done."

Rich states that fostering the skills necessary to be effective collaborators requires "a much more inclusively large collegial environment, rather than a competitive environment" and that "it makes work life more satisfying if you have a really good social interactive dynamic with colleagues." Unfortunately, he finds his own department competitive, individualistic, and hierarchical. Similar to Ruben, Rich finds it challenging to collaborate with departmental colleagues. Rich says, "Ninety-nine percent of the time, my joint proposals are outside the department." He regrets not feeling more connected to his own unit, and he places the blame on a reward system that prioritizes individual contributions.

I wish I could get my colleagues to . . . be more collaborative, or more proactive in being amenable. . . . I don't think anyone is going to turn you down if you say, "Hey, I'm willing to do 90 percent of the work and write the proposal." . . . But that's not what I call collaborative. "Let's sit down and really hash out how we can do something interesting and see how we can get the work done." That's rare in our department. And I think that goes back to the fact that *ultimately universities don't reward teamwork. They reward the individuals.*

He says these norms of evaluation impoverish the social and professional lives of almost everyone and hinder progress on big scale projects.

Kristen's and Rich's comments are consistent with the changes in STEM over the last several decades. By the early 1970s, almost two-thirds of Nobel prizes were given to teams of researchers rather than independent scholars.[44] STEM work is more collaborative and more complexly entwined with sociopolitical processes than ever.[45] Today, STEM research is increasingly conducted under the umbrella of "team science," where professionals work collaboratively in labs and share expensive equipment.[46] Even some of our respondents doing theoretical rather than experimental work describe research in their areas as increasingly collaborative. Yet because the work of lone geniuses is the cultural ideal, collaboration and maintenance of professional relationships are devalued as less serious, less valuable, less rewarded, and feminized (see chap. 4).[47]

At a more fundamental level, STEM knowledge is itself a product of collaborative social processes. Knowledge advances are collective creations: science claims are only seen as "truth" to the extent that they are collectively agreed upon by other members of the profession.[48] In other words, scientific truth-making is itself inherently social, relational, and collaborative. To deny this collective element not only misrepresents how STEM work is done but also underestimates the power of the collaborative relationships between scientists and the importance of equality in those relationships.

These patterns call for serious and sustained conversations in STEM fields about how scientific merit is measured. It is possible that merit could be measured differently—measured in ways that more closely align with how STEM work is actually conducted and STEM breakthroughs are actually made. If STEM professionals were to use as markers of success the characteristics that actually lead to the most cutting-edge, most visible, and most lauded work, then collegiality and collaboration—relational characteristics—would sit front and center. Instead of valorizing assertiveness and self-promoting competition, which we show in chapter 4 to not actually be associated with greater productivity, the schema of scientific excellence should emphasize collective, collaborative work, with significant investments in students and junior scholars. Put another way, if STEM uses impact, visibility, and innovativeness as markers of successful outcomes of the scientific enterprise, then the skills and characteristics that actually produce those outcomes should get proper credit as markers of excellence.

Consequence 3: Widely Used Indices Are Warped Indicators of Productivity

This section considers the problems of two common measures of "good" scientific work: publication indices and contributions to "mainstream" science. First, our study includes measures of published articles and grant dollars because these are widely regarded by STEM faculty as indices of productivity. However, these indices do not necessarily align with quality and impact of the work. For example, Mateo explains how people in his department rely on publication counts and journal rankings as shortcuts for making judgments about the excellence of their colleagues rather than holistically assessing the impact of their work.

Unfortunately, in attempts to be quantitative, numbers of papers or ranking of a journal have become kind of the factors that are looked at [in faculty hiring and promotion], particularly by administrators who don't know the fields. I believe there is too much emphasis on publishing in *Science*, for example, and not enough recognition of the *content* of the contribution of the paper. . . . You publish in *Science*, no one cares what the impact is really, or don't care to know what it is. . . . We're so busy all the time that we take shortcuts. . . . So you look at a CV, and you say you count impact [metrics] as opposed to really trying to understand the contribution within the field.

Sometimes you make a contribution that gets other people thinking but they don't quote you because they're maybe not doing what, you know, you're doing, or they may not want to quote you to tell where their idea came from. But I think we've fallen into many traps in science. . . . I do very basic science, and I do it with nontraditional approaches; then the value of what I do is less immediately obvious, but, you know, I'm convinced that I'm doing good things.

The standard measures of productivity revered by the cultural notions of scientific merit do not capture, and thus do not generally reward, these less "obvious" contributions to scientific inquiry.

These indices also do not capture other forms of labor that are important to scientific innovation, such as training younger scholars and communicating ideas to broader audiences. Recall Michael's reflection earlier in the chapter that his real legacy is not his scientific discoveries but rather all the students and postdocs he has taught to participate in discovery-making. Similarly, Mateo suggests that scientists' impact should also be judged by their ability to communicate that impact to students and to the broader public.

I think ability to communicate what you do at all levels including the general public, ability to train students to excel and become independent researcher, independent thinkers. . . . [You asked] what are the qualities that make a really [excellent] scientist. And I think that it's the ability to look at what you [are] doing and look in a wide context, as I said to communicate to all levels of people who have an interest or to create an interest, and to make a lasting contribution.

Academic reviews for promotion and salary increases should value the teaching of early career scientists and the communication to the public as highly as it valorizes article production.

The second problem is that academic STEM culture tends to marginalize scientists who may offer something different than mainstream views and experiences. The schemas of scientific excellence and work devotion devalue and marginalize groups of colleagues—including mothers, women, racial and ethnic minority professors, and LGBTQ professors—who seem to violate expectations for a depoliticized profession. Attempts to protect the sanctity of STEM against identity politics (such as Mateo's statement in chapter 5 that he "doesn't want to know" colleagues' LGBTQ status) can lead to the isolating or silencing of underrepresented scientists—and the contributions they make to STEM.

Recall Sophia, the LGBTQ-identifying professor of color above who felt it was "natural" for her and her partner to stay away from departmental events. When we asked Sophia what characterizes excellence in her field, her response was illuminating.

It's a really hard question because half of me is trained as a scientist or just thinks there is objective measures of excellence. But half of me is a woman scientist and is very critical of thinking of scientific excellence as something that is objective. . . . In [my field], your value is how much you inspire others, or how much they cite you, or how much they listen to you. So it's particularly hard because it's this weird balancing of like deep, really fundamental work but then [also how much they cite you]. . . . It's a catch-22. . . . So you just realize that the measurement of excellence is very subjective. . . . I think it's a question of, like, people's background and their general outlook on life, like a combination of all of those. Right? So I feel *like people who are more from the elite institutions and come from that kind of elite pedagogy tend to be less critical of the ways that [the] scientific community works as any other community of human beings . . . and how there sort of is subjective privileging that gets to be done at all times.* (emphasis added)

If scientific creativity and assessments of excellence are at least partly defined by, in Sophia's words, "people's background and their general outlook on life," then efforts to preserve depoliticized, homogenous work spaces deprives science of the full range of critical and innovative perspectives that are needed to solve pressing societal problems.

Recall reports from faculty respondents that when senior men do provide mentorship, they disproportionately give this time and attention to majority-race men. These practices have been amply documented in previous research.[49] Yet marginalized scientists are among those most likely to add value to the scientific enterprise. Previous research using a near complete population of PhD dissertations in the United States found that underrepresented students "innovate at higher rates than majority students, but their novel contributions are discounted and less likely to earn them academic positions."[50] Decades of research has found that diverse teams are more groundbreaking, productive, and fact-based than more homogenous teams.[51] Similarly, interdisciplinary teams produce more innovative ideas than single-discipline ones.[52] These studies robustly document that more rigorous and more pioneering results come out of collaborations among groups of people with diverse perspectives, backgrounds, and experience. Processes that exclude or devalue these voices thus stunt scientific innovation.

Consequence 4: STEM Innovation Is Undermined by Overwork

In accordance with expectations for work devotion, many academic scientists seem to never stop working. Dan attributes his feelings of stress to what he sees as impossible demands of producing a high volume of research articles that must also be pathbreaking.

So I feel that I spend lots and lots of time trying to make my work very solid and bul-letproof. . . . And because I do that . . . one of my papers would be three of somebody else's papers. And so I battle the fact that I have decided that I was going to go for quality but then sacrifice the quantity. [But] the quantity is important as well. And so . . . that's a stressor, and . . . I really overanalyze and overthink every little thing, every single word that I write, every sentence to make sure that it's correct, it's precise, it's well-written, that nobody can criticize—any part of it.

Like many others we interviewed, Dan works under conditions of chronic worry, stress, and exhaustion—conditions that can actually undermine clearheaded and creative thinking.[53] Even without Dan's specific concerns, constant busyness and the sacrifice of personal time may not be a recipe for the most innovative and significant scientific advances. Consider the comments of John, a highly respected mathematician.

I have never thought of myself as very methodical or optimally efficient. . . . Many of my tasks are perfunctory, and those get resolved with a measure of procrastination and often a bit of a last-minute panic. . . .

But no, when something interests me deeply—and many things do—I wake up with those things on my mind, and I solve them in waking dreams, or I . . . I get a lot of my best writing done in the morning. And my clearest thinking . . . that I do at the kitchen table.

John describes himself as inefficient in getting through his perfunctory tasks. But he opens up his mornings—and his dreams—to his most creative thinking.

Recent research in psychology and neuroscience has shown that creativity is sparked in time that is not crammed with tasks. Scientific discovery is more likely to flourish if there is time for active rest, time to let the mind wander, and time for wakeful dreaming. The celebration of grinding, workaholic individualists who do not take the time to relax, reflect, or care for the next generation does not foster the creativity or commitment needed to conceptualize or provide scientific solutions for threats facing our planet today.[54]

Thus, time away from work, in the form of rest and time off, actually enhances creative thinking and efficiency, which is contrary to the presumptions of the work devotion schema.[55] Research on working professional mothers has found that their experiences raising children can make them more productive and more resilient workers.[56] This might be part of what drives mothers' overproductivity compared to their faculty peers (see chap. 3). In addition, research on faculty from other universities has found that mothers who take parental leaves are actually more likely to maintain their research productivity than new parents who do not take leaves after the birth or adoption of children.[57] Counterintuitively, then, taming the stigma of not working might foster, not stifle, the creativity that is foundational to scientific and technical innovation. The work devotion schema promises single-minded, meaningful, creative work as a pathway to a life well lived. This promise can only be fulfilled when time away from work is also protected and when devotion to important personal, family, and community commitments is also honored.

Avenues for Positive Change

STEM professionals enjoy prestige and privilege, good salaries, and (for faculty with tenure) job security. They have the trust of the public and opportunities to educate the next generation of scientists. With these privileges come obligations to think critically about their work and how it can best serve the needs of society. Our research suggests that meeting these obligations requires STEM professionals to take a critical look at how scientific merit is conceptualized, measured, and conferred. Faculty tenure is designed to protect academic freedom; we encourage academic scientists to use that freedom to question some of the precepts of their scientific culture.

As noted in the introductory chapter, most research on inequality in STEM has attended to how implicit biases and prejudicial behaviors harm marginalized and minoritized faculty. The solutions typically recommended to address these issues focus on instituting policies and practices that promote more equitable behaviors and providing resources to support individuals from groups historically disadvantaged within the academy.[58] Scholars have recently recommend systemic approaches to change that combine interventions at the institutional and departmental policy levels with increased resources for individual support. Though these approaches are important, they leave unchallenged the hegemonic beliefs we have chronicled in this book.

To address the biases and beliefs imbedded in the cultural definitions of scientific merit, we have to rethink science itself. We see at least four avenues for change.

First, in our study, professors across demographic groups personally value the qualities of collegiality, mentorship, and diversity promotion with more sincerity than what they see being valued most highly in their STEM disciplines. The daylight between scientists' own values and what they see as valorized in STEM creates an opportunity to think critically about the dogma of excellence in the profession.

Second, an important subset of faculty questioned whether their departments and their profession really operate meritocratically. These faculty are aware of social structural factors like networks and ideologies that restrict the advancement of racial and ethnic minority women and men as well as white women. In related research, we found that professors who have an understanding of these barriers are also more likely to recognize poor climates for underrepresented colleagues.[59] This suggests that faculty from various demographic backgrounds—disadvantaged and advantaged alike—could serve as supportive allies and enlist their colleagues in work toward social structural perspectives that supports a fuller set of characteristics that foster excellent science. When STEM professionals recognize that conceptions of scientific merit are social constructs susceptible to being warped by bias, they are better armed to implement hiring, recognition, and reward structures with greater transparency and accountability that could mitigate that bias.[60]

Third, as an example of bias recognition and change, our previous research found that many faculty without children at home are nonetheless aware of and troubled by stigma in their department toward caregivers.[61] In part inspired by our research, faculty-administrative partnerships have gone on to implement more equitable, generous, and less stigmatized family caregiving policies.[62]

Further, the COVID-19 pandemic, which occurred after our study was completed, may have long-term consequences for the careers of STEM professionals with children, especially women.[63] Yet the cultural expectation for devoted, intensive work in STEM has survived the pandemic undeterred. The short- and medium-term postpandemic period is a critical time to reckon with schemas that contribute to the misrecognition of the scientific excellence of mothers in STEM.

Fourth, we have also seen promising results at our study site and elsewhere of peer-to-peer education about the causes of unequal outcomes for certain colleagues. Previous studies have found that diversity training is generally ineffective in the medium- to long-term.[64] Yet context matters. When faculty recruitment committee training workshops are presented by peers who are star scientists in their disciplines in addition to being knowledgeable about diversity and equity in academia, and when workshops present evidence of bias in departments similar to their own, participants are more likely to embrace more equitable and inclusive practices in faculty hiring.[65]

We encourage academic scientists to think more deeply about the limitations of the schemas of scientific excellence and devotion as markers of merit. What if conceptions of scientific excellence fully valued faculty's commitments to collaboration and social connections with colleagues and students? Acknowledged the reality that STEM work is always inherently cultural and social? Embraced diversity as an amplifier of innovation and not a threat to it?[66] What if advancement reviews systematically tracked and rewarded these efforts? If STEM professors had time to engage in a more varied set of life experiences (playing with the kids, improvisational theater, intramural soccer), would they do so with less anxiety about research bottlenecks and actually produce more creative science?[67]

Alternative approaches to notions of scientific excellence have already been developed in spaces beyond dominant Western scientific traditions. Feminist, postcolonial, and indigenous approaches to science exalt characteristics like perspective-taking, collaboration, credit-sharing, and humility in the process of knowledge creation as critical to idea development and problem solving.[68] Such approaches contrast sharply with the culturally masculine, individualistic, and self-promoting dimensions of scientific excellence and work devotion found in our case university. Dominant Western approaches to science have much to learn from such perspectives.

These shifts in how scientific merit is measured and defined will require critical reflection and a break from deeply held assumptions that have been foundational to science since its earliest days as a profession. Doing so will require decentering and destabilizing the very cultural structures that have privileged the same groups in STEM for centuries. It is a tall order but a vital one.

Scientific and technological innovations are needed now more than ever to help address the gravest concerns we face as humans. From climate change to cyber warfare to superviruses, we need as many bright, creative, well-mentored individuals engaged in diverse and closely connected teams working on solutions as possible. Outmoded, biased, and constraining notions of who can be excellent scientists and what excellent science looks like are not just bad for individual STEM professionals or bad for science. They are bad for us all.

Acknowledgments

A book is a community endeavor, and both authors thank the many scholars, students, and friends who contributed their time and talent. We thank Jeanne Ferrante, a founding member of our team, whose involvement was instrumental in launching the project and garnering funding. We acknowledge the vital support of the National Science Foundation (grant number 1107074). We thank the remarkable group that assisted with data collection and coding, including Laura Pecenco, Zach Leffers, Sidra Montgomery, and Jordan Packer; we especially call out Erica Bender and Laura Rogers for their amazing assistance. Our advisory boards and community liaisons provided valuable feedback on our multimethod research design and findings; we thank Maria Charles, Shelley Correll, Amy Wharton, Moshe Hoffman, Bob Bitmead, Lisa Levin, Bob Continenti, Marnie Brookolo, Shaun Travers, and Edwina Welch. We are grateful for all of the other scholars who offered valuable advice in the early phases of the project or commented on versions of chapter drafts, including Akos Rona-Tas, Sigtona Halrynjo, Liza Reisel, Mari Teigen, Erin Kelly, Dana Britton, Kate Antonovics, Kim Barrett, Mandy Bratton, Ruben Garcia, Kathleen Gerson, Christine Hunefeldt, Martha Lampland, David Schkade, Cathy Nagler, and anonymous reviewers for the press. We thank Isabella Furth and Stacy Williams for expert editorial assistance. We are grateful for the sustained support and enthusiasm of Elizabeth Branch Dyson, executive editor at the University of Chicago Press. We acknowledge all the STEM professors who gave their time and trust by participating in surveys and interviews. Without their openness and generosity, this book could not have been written. Finally, we are grateful for one another. This book was a product of hundreds of in-person, virtual, and email conversations—all of them thoughtful and generous. Our respondents talked about the joy and inspiration that can come from collaborative work; we know firsthand what they mean.

Mary Blair-Loy

My scholarship depends upon the generative engagement of so many. I thank my friends for their support and encouragement on this project and so much else, especially Shari Young, Amy Binder, Ruth Bush, Ann Mische, Ellen McLarney, Miranda Worthen, Gershon Shafir, and April Sutton. I am incredibly grateful for the love and support of my family, including Louis Blair-Loy; Martin LaPlaca and Reuben Isenberg; Anne, Michael, Carla, and David Romero; Rebecca Coolidge and John, Madeline, and Josephine Blair; and Peter Blair, Ana Almeida, and Luana Pacheco. I am continually awe-inspired and humbled by my parents, to whom I dedicate this book: Joan Frances MacDonald Blair—teacher and artist, and the Rev. Dr. Alexander Blair—engineer, mathematician, and theologian.

Erin A. Cech

I am grateful to colleagues and friends who were enthusiastic about this work from its very beginnings, especially Alexandra Vinson, William Rothwell, Lindsey Trimble O'Connor, Greta Krippner, Sandy Levitsky, Karin Martin, Sergio Chávez, Müge Göçek, and Elizabeth Long. I am deeply thankful to my partner, Heidi Sherick, who was an unwavering cheerleader, sounding board, and source of reassurance that this book could and should be written. I dedicate this book to my parents. My mother, Meg, a special education teacher, taught me that how people see, and how they are seen by others, has tremendous power. My father, Mike, has been unflinchingly supportive of my STEM inequality research, even when it means I am critical of his own field of engineering. I cherish their lessons of curiosity, compassion, and humility.

Appendix

This appendix summarizes the theoretical and empirical innovations our study makes to sociological, STEM inequality, and science and technology studies research. It then provides supplemental details about our case site, describes our methodology, and reviews our analytical approach.

I. Theoretical and Empirical Innovations of Our Study

Studying cultural schemas is complicated, and so is attempting to uncover the cultural processes embedded within the taken-for-granted, deeply venerated belief systems of prestigious professions. Our investigation of the contours and consequences of the two schemas that shape definitions of scientific merit required an approach that is multimethod and intersectional.

Our case is the STEM faculty of a research-intensive university. As we describe in detail later in this appendix, our bounded, medium-sized sample and unusual access allowed us to collect comprehensive data on the entire population as well as learn deeply about the lives of individual professors. Our multiple data sets include personnel data from the case university, our Scholarly Production Indices (SPI) database with information we gathered through bibliometric websites and funding databases, our own survey, and in-depth interviews with eighty-five professors. After focusing intently on our case, we widened our gaze and found evidence to show that the patterns we discover appear across academic STEM more broadly. Section II describes our case site, and section III details the data sets and methods we employed.

In this book, we investigate how STEM professional culture creates disadvantages for many marginalized and minoritized groups in STEM spaces while also helping to maintain the power of white and Asian heterosexual men. We study the cultural processes that shape advantages and disadvantages along the intersecting dimensions of gender, family status, race, and sexual identity.[1] Whenever possible, we assessed intersectional patterns in our analyses such as the specific forms of disadvantage encountered by women of color, which we discuss in chapters 4 and 5.[2] We also found patterns of similarity across different groups of faculty, including the broad embrace of hegemonic cultural understandings of merit. We encourage scholars of inequality in STEM to similarly move beyond single axes of ascriptive difference to consider ways that cultural processes in STEM uphold multiple forms of disadvantage simultaneously across many demographic groups.

Uniting the Strengths of Multiple Subfields

Our focus on the cultural (mis)conceptions of merit in STEM unites the strengths of the sociological subfields of inequalities, professions, and culture with science and technology studies (STS) scholarship. Sociologists of inequality have long studied the experiences of historically underrepresented groups in STEM, particularly women. Many STEM occupations remain dominated by white and heterosexual men, even as other professions have become more diverse.[3] Much past social science research has examined society-wide cognitive biases and stereotypes;[4] other work has examined interpersonal actions that create chilly working environments for underrepresented groups.[5] These studies of broad societal patterns are important but often miss tacit processes residing in professional cultures that allow inequalities to persist. In other words, this prior work has tended to black box—or dismiss the importance of the inner workings of—academic STEM culture.[6]

We also take inspiration from STS literature, which has demonstrated how scientific processes that seem disembodied and objective are in fact never devoid of politics and culture.[7] Scholars have illustrated that social institutions of gender, race, and sexuality have always been imprinted onto the work of scientists and engineers even while they claim a "view from nowhere" of objective knowledge.[8] Borrowing insights

from STS scholars, we focus on how STEM faculty themselves understand and evaluate what they consider objective qualities of merit, and
we show that these understandings are inherently cultural and political. However, the work of STS scholars rarely centers concerns about
social inequality. Our work combines inequality literature's goal of
understanding sociodemographic disadvantage with the core STS insight that the yardsticks used to evaluate STEM excellence are culturally
constructed.

Further, we join this with several insights from the sociology of professions. While much research on academic STEM considers how departments as educational spaces inequitably train students,[9] we focus
instead on academic STEM units as spaces of white-collar employment.
From the professions literature, we know that professions are bounded
communities of those who are deemed experts by their peers, with spe-
cialized knowledge in their jurisdictional areas.[10] Professions have their
own historically rooted and semiautonomous belief systems about the
work that is done within their jurisdiction—what demonstrates merit,
and what achievements are counted and most valued. Professions are
given wide latitude by government, business, and other institutions to
define their own criteria of merit and excellence.

STEM faculty at research-intensive institutions like the one we study
are on the cutting edge of their profession. As discussed in chapter 2,
they spent a decade or more in higher educational training and have
been socialized into the expertise, orientations, and habits that allow
them to win competitive positions in the academy. Most earned PhDs
in top-rated programs, where they were steeped in beliefs about merit.[11]
Most were hired into postdoctoral positions, and then five- to nine-year
probationary positions as assistant professors. During that time, they
develop an independent research trajectory and produce publications
and nurture a national or international reputation that allows them to
win tenure and job security. They are in charge of mentoring the next
generation of professionals in their classrooms and labs. Some of the
students they train will take their professional cultural beliefs with them
to other universities; other students will graduate and take up positions
in for-profit industry, government, and other employment sectors.[12] The
professors we study socialize students into preexisting cultural beliefs
and practices of their discipline and, in doing so, help perpetuate those
beliefs and practices. Thus, academic STEM, and the faculty we study,
are key sites of the production, enactment, and perpetuation of STEM
professional culture.

Analyzing Schemas within Professional Culture:
A New Approach to STEM Inequality Research

This book studies STEM *professional culture* as a set of intersubjective meaning systems bounded by the historical understandings and emergent relationships within the STEM professions, which in turn are situated within societal culture. We employ STEM professional culture as a floodlight into the black box of merit in STEM to understand the ways that such definitions of merit can perpetuate inequality.

We offer a major conceptual innovation by theorizing key cultural schemas at the heart of these cultural definitions of merit. The term *cultural schema* underscores that these elements of merit are historically rooted, widely shared, taken-for-granted understandings that shape what their adherents know as reality.[13] In addition to identifying two schemas in the definition of scientific merit, our book advances understandings of how these schemas work.

The term *schema* is used in social psychology to denote the cognitive categories that help individuals to process and sort information.[14] We agree that schemas create cognitive maps, "a network of associations that organizes perception."[15] The cognitive maps are nested within broader cultural meaning systems.[16] Schemas provide cognitive shortcuts that allow people to more quickly link new information with previously understood concepts.[17] They define particular experiences and characteristics as belonging together.

Importantly, we show that schemas serve not only as cognitive categories but also as moral and emotional categories. They not only help people sort information; they also help them forge identities, express feelings, and create meaning. Cultural schemas designate a career worth having and a life worth living.[18]

Previous research has typically focused on schemas embedded in the broader societal culture.[19] This book demonstrates that professional cultures are also important sources of schemas (chap. 2). Professional socialization involves absorbing the profession's mental maps that structure the cognitive understandings and moral commitments presumed of a responsible professional.[20]

This work thus serves as a template for investigating the definition of merit and excellence in other professional occupations. Scholars of inequality within other professions should similarly attend to how the justificatory narratives within the cultures of the professions they study help uphold an unequal status quo. Careful attention to these cultural beliefs can help open up the black box of merit in other professions.

II. Description and Justification of Case Site

As we describe in chapter 1, our data are drawn from STEM faculty at a top-ranked research university in the United States. Our research site is not representative of all STEM faculty, but it is similar in several respects to other highly ranked institutions. Our site offers the advantages of detailed data on faculty embedded in multiple departments in a single institution, removing cross-institution heterogeneity in policy and climate. We describe these data sources in more detail in section III.

Ragin explains that sociological research can be described as either "variable-oriented" or "case-oriented."[21] Whereas variable-oriented research treats individual and social-structural properties as predictive indicators of a particular outcome, case-oriented research studies a particular case of theoretical interest. Case-oriented research identifies a small, nonrandom sample and investigates it deeply in order to fully understand the contextual complexity of the case. While not meant to be generalizable, the benefit of case-oriented research is its ability to illuminate social and cultural processes that may otherwise be overlooked. Case-oriented research "sheds new light on social phenomena and . . . adds specificity and complexity to our understanding" of social reality.[22] Many high-impact studies of social inequality focus on a single-organization case with rich data.[23]

We chose to study STEM faculty at this particular university for several reasons. First, as described in the next section, we procured unique access to multiple sources of high-quality data. Second, our study uses the strategy of studying an exemplar case—a highly ranked public research university—to understand mechanisms of disadvantage.[24] Our case highlights the social and cultural processes that are theoretically meaningful to inequality in this profession. The faculty we study have access to significant resources, including scientific prestige and a value system that venerates meritocracy and excellence. Professors pride themselves on their ability to fairly and objectively analyze the quality of colleagues' work. Academics, administrators, and the public view the university as a sacred space that fosters basic science largely buffered from markets and politics.[25] Moreover, our site, like other highly rated US public universities, lauds not only its academic excellence but also its transparency and fairness. Faculty governance is strong, and faculty salaries are published annually.[26] The university is committed to recruiting and fairly rewarding the best and brightest faculty, alongside its commitment to educating the most talented of the public's children without regard to their gender or race. In the recent past, the university has also taken concrete steps to assess and then address gender gaps in salary among ladder-ranked faculty.[27]

In addition to being an elite public university, the culture of the university we study is shaped by the prominence and prestige of its STEM departments. The university asserts its institutional identity by emphasizing scientific innovation.

Although our case university is exemplary, it is not idiosyncratic. We do not claim generalizability, but we note similarities to other institutional contexts. Our university is comparable to other highly ranked research institutions in size, student-faculty ratio, and number of full-time faculty.[28] STEM faculty at our case institution were trained and professionally socialized at top research universities in the country, suggesting some degree of professional isomorphism in these taken-for-granted understandings of merit. Specifically, 81 percent of our survey sample received their PhDs from a university that was ranked in the top fifty nationally and/or globally.[29]

Like other similarly research-intensive institutions,[30] nondominant groups in our sample face disadvantages. As with the academic STEM contexts examined in other research, women, underrepresented racial/ethnic minority, and LGBTQ individuals who are faculty at this university are more likely than heterosexual white and Asian men to report chilly climates in their departments. Compared to national faculty populations, our study population has similar proportions of white, Asian, and underrepresented racial/ethnic minority (URM) faculty. Specifically, STEM faculty at our case university are 73.8 percent white, 20.4 percent Asian, and 5.8 percent URM, and STEM faculty nationally are 71.5 percent white, 20.7 percent Asian, and 7.7 percent URM.[31] Women are somewhat less well represented in our study population than in national data of all STEM faculty. Our population is 84 percent men and 16 percent women, and the national STEM faculty workforce is 72.5 percent men and 27.5 percent women.[32] However, these national data include both universities and four-year colleges, and there are proportionally fewer women STEM faculty at Research I universities than at other four-year institutions of higher education.[33] In addition, full professors, among which women are most underrepresented, make up 67 percent of our total sample. The proportion of LGBTQ-identifying faculty in our sample is slightly below national estimates of LGBTQ persons with advanced degrees at 3.4 percent.[34]

Many of our findings are consistent with information from other studies of academic scientists at highly research-active universities. These include the intense competition for professional accomplishment,[35] which is often difficult to reconcile with responsibilities of family life.[36] The experiences of marginalization, stereotyping, and double standards reported by disadvantaged group members in our population mirror the chilly climates and unequal outcomes documented in research on STEM faculty at other universities.[37]

Unlike previous studies, we systematically analyze how unequal and unfair outcomes persist alongside sincere commitments to objectivity and excellence. In doing so, this research sheds light on the contradictions and limitations of human agency.[38]

Our intensive focus on one university helped us identify a set of schemas prominent in the cultural definitions of merit in STEM. We then looked more widely and discovered that these schemas are pervasive across academic STEM more generally. To assess the salience of the work devotion and scientific excellence schemas beyond our sample, we conducted supplemental analysis of the 2018 STEM Inclusion Study survey (principal investigator: Erin Cech).[39] This survey encompassed data from 7,647 PhD-level STEM professionals employed at four-year universities that included indicators for the central measures of work dedication and scientific excellence we use in our quantitative survey of STEM faculty. We find very similar patterns of work dedication and scientific excellence beliefs in the STEM Inclusion Study data as we find within our own faculty survey data. Specifically, the STEM Inclusion Study data show no significant difference in work dedication by gender and race/ethnicity (even though the survey sample is many times larger). Yet echoing both our quantitative and qualitative data, the STEM Inclusion Study data show that women and underrepresented racial/ethnic minority respondents are significantly more likely to report marginalization and professional devaluation than white men peers.[40]

In addition, we find in the STEM Inclusion Study data the same pattern of valuation on the four strands of the schema of scientific excellence we document in chapter 4: creativity and assertive leadership were most highly valued in the STEM Inclusion Study data (4.20 and 3.82, respectively, on the same 1 to 5 scale). Relational skills were valued less (mean = 3.59 on a 1 to 5 scale). Diversity promotion was the least valued characteristic (mean = 3.23), and as with our faculty data, more people disagreed than agreed that diversity promotion was characteristic of a successful member of their STEM discipline.

The STEM Inclusion Study data include respondents from a much wider range of four-year institutions than the research-focused institution that we study in this book. And yet the cultural schemas we identified in our case site are clearly reflected among this much broader population of academic scientists. This suggests that our results, and the focal schemas that they center around, are far from idiosyncratic. As this supplemental analysis indicates, work devotion and scientific excellence schemas are alive and well among academic STEM professionals in departments across the United States.

III. Data Sources

This book takes advantage of our ability to triangulate the quantitative and qualitative data sources we have collected among our population. We use quantitative data measures to chart the overarching structures of advantage and disadvantage among STEM faculty at the university. We then add qualitative data, which illuminates the subjective understandings that make sense of, and perhaps perpetuate, inequality.[41] While quantitative measures strengthen our understanding of the systematic effects of individual and social-structural variables on career outcomes, qualitative data are necessary to unpack the "subjective experiences and cultural sense-making" that undergird social structures of disadvantage.[42] These methods complement each other and provide a more complete picture of the social world.[43]

We combine university personnel data on the more than five hundred STEM tenured or tenure-track faculty members in this university with our own detailed survey data on over half of these faculty and in-depth qualitative interviews with eighty-five of them. In addition, we amplify this information with a database containing external, standardized measures of productivity and visibility. We secured IRB approval for each phase of this research.

As a white, cisgender, heterosexual woman trained in sociology and religious studies and a mother of a child of color (Blair-Loy), and as a white, cisgender, childless queer-identifying woman trained in sociology and engineering (Cech), we recognize that our positionality may have made certain patterns more salient than they may have been to other authors, and may have obscured from our view patterns that would have been clear to scholars of color conducting this research. Throughout the data collection, analysis, and writing phases of this project, we challenged ourselves and each other to be reflexive about the opportunities and limitations our perspectives offered.

Academic Personnel Data

The university personnel office at our case site provided us with confidential data on the rank, department, salary, and demographics for our entire population of 506 STEM faculty. Specifically, we obtained personnel data for each population member on the following measures: self-identified gender, self-identified race/ethnicity (Asian, Black, Latinx, Native American, white), salary, hire date as a ladder-ranked faculty, highest degree, year of highest degree, year since highest degree, number of years it took to reach assistant professor rank, number of years it took to reach associate rank (if applicable), number of years it took to reach full rank (if applicable), university division, department, title (rank), step, and whether they obtained recent formal retention packages (and the year retention package was sought). This academic personnel dataset served as our reference population and the basis of our survey recruitment and productivity and visibility data collection.

Survey Data

In the spring of 2012, all members of the population of STEM faculty at this university were invited to participate in a confidential online survey.[44] The survey was programmed and hosted by Cornell's Survey Research Institute. Of the total faculty in our study population, 266 (53 percent) participated in the survey. This response rate is quite high for a busy population of faculty, is equal to or higher than surveys of STEM faculty at other institutions (e.g., UCLA, Cornell), and is higher than nationally representative surveys such as the National Survey of the Changing Workforce.[45] Survey items covered several topics, including demographics, educational and career background, family status, work-life and work-family issues, professional integration, department and disciplinary climate, networks, and "schemas of inequality" or cultural accounts of broader disciplinary disparities.[46]

Following standard analytic procedures, multivariate analyses use multiple imputation to handle missing data due to skipped questions.[47] Compared to the full population, the survey sample overrepresents women (sample: 27 percent women; population: 16 percent women); no significant differences in the representation of racial/ethnic groups emerged between the population and survey sample. The sample also underrepresents full professors compared to the population (sample: 59 percent full professors; population: 67 percent full professors). Although we cannot confirm this with our data, we expect that the full professor men who did participate in the survey would have been more inclined to be reflexively concerned about diversity and inclusion issues and that, conversely, full professor men who are most resistant to diversity and inclusion issues would have been most likely to opt out of the survey.

Scholarly Production Indices (SPI) Database

To complement our survey and personnel data with standardized measures of scholarly productivity and visibility, we constructed a database with two set of externally generated data on our faculty population: a list of grants awarded to each faculty and bibliographic information on respondents' publication and citation records.

Grants Data

The grants dataset was created using online records from the university's office of grants. The university tracks all federal and foundation-based grants awarded to faculty. The following variables were created for each grant respondent received: dollar amount of the grant, the time duration, and whether they were the principal investigator (PI) or Co-PI. We also created measures for total grant dollars and total number of grants awarded to each faculty as well as average grant dollars per year.[48]

Bibliographic Data

Data on respondent publication and citation records were collected using a web-scraping program written for this purpose. The web-scraping program collected information on scholarly output and visibility for each faculty member from the online bibliographic database SCOPUS. Some previous productivity studies have used individual curricula vitae (CVs) as their information source, whereas others have utilized the Web of Science (another online database).[49] Because it would be almost impossible to gather up-to-date CVs for everyone in our sample, we decided to find the best bibliographic database available that would provide standardized measures of publications and visibility.[50]

To conduct the web-scraping, we found the SCOPUS identification number for each faculty member in our population. We then designed a web-scraping program to gather the following information for each SCOPUS identification number: articles published, number of citations (with and without self-citations), H-index (with and without self-citations), and the average SJR journal prestige metric (the average journal impact factor rating for the journals in which the faculty member publishes).[51] We gathered this publication and visibility information for the entirety of respondents' career and for the five years prior to the study.[52] We also constructed a number of secondary measures from these indicators, such as the log average number of articles published per year since faculty earned their PhD. These publication and visibility measures are commonly used in research on faculty productivity.[53]

Because STEM faculty often say that the number and impact of scientific articles are the most objective and valued metrics of productivity, we also augmented the SPI with publication rates, measures of visibility (citation counts and impact measures), and grant dollars for each professor in our study.

Objective Indicators of Productivity?

Previous research documents that underrepresented groups generally have to produce more and higher quality work for the publications and funding they do receive. For example, research on academic scientists shows that white men are more likely to get grant proposals funded compared with women and to men of color with similar qualifications,[54] and that men tend to receive more credit than women do for collaborative work.[55] Further, research finds that men are more likely to cite their own work in their research articles, and this pattern is particularly prevalent in STEM fields. Self-citations directly and indirectly increase an article's total number of citations, with potentially large and cumulative effects in the sciences.[56] Citation indices and impact factors seem to be objective indices of merit, but the numbers for many men are inflated. By controlling for these indices of productivity in our analyses, we likely underestimate the professional devaluation faced by underrepresented researchers.

In-depth Interviews

In addition to these quantitative data sources, we also conducted confidential, in-depth, semistructured interviews with eighty-five faculty. Our goal was to better understand the "subjective experiences and cultural sense-making" that reinforce or potentially challenge social inequality,[57] and we oversampled faculty from underrepresented groups, whose experiences may be substantively significant but fail to reach statistical significance in quantitative models.

Interview recruitment proceeded along two avenues. First, survey participants were asked whether they would be willing to be contacted to participate in an interview. Among those who agreed, we invited all women faculty and racial/ethnic minority faculty to participate in an interview, and we invited a randomly selected subset of white and Asian men to participate in an interview. Second, we implemented a cluster sampling strategy in order to increase the number of women of color and LGBTQ individuals in our interview sample.[58] We asked members of the project's advisory board and directors of campus centers that provide support and advocacy for diverse constituencies (LGBTQ, women, and underrepresented racial/ethnic groups) to reach out to LGBTQ faculty and women faculty of color directly to invite them to participate in an interview.

The interview sample includes thirty-four white women, thirty-one white men, and twenty women and men of color. Of these, six professors identify as lesbian, gay, or bisexual.[59] Interviews were conducted by the authors or by trained research assistants. The interviews covered the following themes: faculty career history; family and personal life (including partner/spouse's employment, career aspirations for self and partner, and work-life issues); personal beliefs and understandings of department and disciplinary standards of excellence, ideal qualities of a profession member, and publication norms; department and disciplinary climate; networks; respondents' beliefs about inequality in STEM; and questions about the degree to which members of underrepresented or devalued groups (including LGBTQ faculty, underrepresented minorities, and parents) feel comfortable and accepted in their departments.

It can be challenging for interviewers to elicit details from respondents about their taken-for-granted beliefs.[60] To give us leverage on interview respondents' beliefs about the fairness of their profession, as we discuss in chapter 5, our interview guide contained two short, factual scenarios designed to prompt professors to articulate their views more fully. In the first, we asked faculty to help us understand why, among STEM faculty at this university, less than 15 percent of faculty are women (of any race), and barely over 5 percent are Latinx, Black, and/or Native American.

The second scenario briefly summarized a finding in the flagship scientific journal *Science*, coauthored by a director of the NIH, that found

African American applicants for NIH grants were less likely to be funded than white applicants with the same productivity (see study description in chap. 5). This approach provided all respondents with the same specific, scientifically validated reference points from which to respond.

Interviews were recorded and, except in instances where the interviews contained particularly sensitive information, were professionally transcribed. The interview transcripts were coded and analyzed in NVIVO, as we reciprocally and iteratively combined inductive evidence into more abstract themes.

IV. Scale Operationalization

Operationalization of Quantitative Variables Used in Chapter 3

The quantitative analyses in chapter 3 draw on a range of items from our personnel, survey, and SPI databases.

Dedication Scale: Our four-item dedication scale (1 = low, 5 = high, alpha = .647) is the mean response to four Likert scale items (ranging from Strongly Disagree = 1 to Strongly Agree = 5) as follows: "I am willing to put in a great deal of extra effort into my research beyond that normally expected in my department" taps respondents' cognitive acceptance of the legitimacy of research demands. "I find that my values and the values of many of my colleagues in the department are very similar" shows a sense of moral identification with departmental norms. "I really care about the fate of my department" explores the emotional investment respondents have in their departments and, by extension, their discipline. "My colleagues and students really inspire the very best in me" taps the dimension of inspiration and transcendence of personal limitations. Ninety-one percent of respondents somewhat or strongly agreed with at least two items of the dedication scale; 73 percent agree with at least three items, and 42 percent agreed with all four.[61]

Flexibility Stigma: We measured flexibility stigma by respondents' agreement (coded 1 = Strongly Disagree to 5 = Strongly Agree) on three sets of beliefs in their departments: "Female faculty who have young or school-aged children are considered to be less committed to their careers than colleagues who are not mothers" (mean = 2.1); "Male faculty who have young or school-aged children are considered to be less committed to their careers" (mean = 1.5); and for those who use formal or informal arrangements for work/life balance, this usage "often has negative consequences for their careers" (mean = 2.5). We combined these three measures into a flexibility stigma scale (alpha = .661; mean value = 2.13). Mean values and standard errors are reported in Cech and Blair-Loy (2014, 96, table 1).[62]

Persistence and Satisfaction Measures: To measure the effects of flexibility stigma, we use two persistence measures: the likelihood that respondents consider leaving the university for industry (1 = Strongly Disagree to 5 = Strongly Agree) and their agreement that they are likely to remain at the university for the remainder of their career (1 = Strongly Disagree to 5 = Strongly Agree). Our satisfaction measure asks, "Overall, how satisfied or dissatisfied are you with your experience at [institution]?" (coded 1 = Very Dissatisfied to 5 = Very Satisfied). Mean values and standard errors are reported in Cech and Blair-Loy (2014, 96, table 1).

Salary: Our salary measure is the natural log of the salary reported for each faculty by the office of academic personnel at the university we study.

Departmental and Job Measures: We also draw on the following departmental and job-related variables: respondent department (listed as generalized titles, e.g., "Engineering Department 3" to protect confidentiality), respondent step (or their place in the faculty hierarchy at the case site, ranging from 0 to 33), the total number of hours per week respondents report working, the number of hours per week respondents spend on research, and whether they held a Teaching Professor position.

Demographic Measures: Our quantitative analyses control for respondent self-identified gender (woman = 1),[63] underrepresented racial/ethnic minority status (yes = 1), LGBTQ status (yes = 1), whether they are married or partnered (yes = 1), and whether they are a parent of at least one child (yes = 1). Certain models (especially in chap. 4) also separate whites and Asians for the purpose of understanding more nuanced racial/ethnic and intersectional race and gender differences. Gender and race/ethnicity are self-identified measures from personnel data. The rest of the demographic measures were ascertained in the survey. To protect the confidentiality of our respondents, we did not collect data on citizenship status (although some individuals volunteered that information in interviews). Our measures of race/ethnicity include US citizens and international faculty who identify with each racial/ethnic group. For example, the term *Asian* includes Asian Americans and Asians, and *Latinx* includes US citizens and international Latinx scholars with citizenship in Central America, South America, Europe, and beyond. Supplemental analyses for figure 3.2 and figures A.3 and A.4 use intersectional race-by-gender interaction terms (e.g., URM × woman, Asian × woman, and white × woman) in separate models.

For parenthood status, we aggregate children of various age groups into a single indicator for two reasons. First, we expect that the consequences of having children on one's salary and productivity may accumulate over the course of one's career, rather than be isolated to the particular set of years when respondents' children are young or school-age. Second, because ours is a medium-N sample, disaggregating parenthood status would mean that the cell sizes in each interaction term would be quite small. Models in table 3.4 include an interaction term for motherhood, which was computed as woman × parent.

Productivity and Grants: The productivity measure we use in chapter 3 is the natural log of the average articles per year that each respondent has published since earning their PhD. Specifically, we took the number of total articles that respondents have published in their career and divided that by the number of years since PhD. As noted above, this publication information came from SCOPUS. Grant activity is measured as the grant dollars that each respondent has received divided by the number of years since PhD.

Operationalization of Quantitative Variables Used in Chapters 4 and 5

Assertiveness Scale—typical successful person: Respondents were asked the extent to which they agree or disagree that the following set of qualities are characteristic of a "typically successful person" in their discipline (1 = Strongly Disagree to 5 = Strongly Agree): "competitive," "promotes own accomplishments," "strong leader," "risk taker." Questions were summed and divided by four to create a scale (alpha= .619).

Assertiveness Scale—self-conceptions: Respondents were asked the extent to which they agree or disagree that the following set of qualities characterize them personally (1 = Strongly Disagree to 5 = Strongly Agree): "competitive," "promotes own accomplishments," "strong leader," "risk taker." Questions were summed and divided by four to create a scale (alpha = .627).

Relational Scale—typical successful person: Respondents were asked the extent to which they agree or disagree that the following set of qualities are characteristic of a "typically successful person" in their discipline (1 = Strongly Disagree to 5 = Strongly Agree): "good mentor," "good at interpersonal relationships," "empathetic." Questions were summed and divided by three to create a scale (alpha = .672).

Relational Scale—self-conceptions: Respondents were asked the extent to which they agree or disagree that the following set of qualities characterize them personally (1 = Strongly Disagree to 5 = Strongly Agree): "good mentor," "good at interpersonal relationships," "empathetic." Questions were summed and divided by three to create a scale (alpha = .660).

Diversity Promotion Measure—typical successful person: Respondents were asked the extent to which they agree or disagree that the following is characteristic of a "typically successful person" in their discipline (1 = Strongly Disagree to 5 = Strongly Agree): "cares about promoting diversity."

Diversity Promotion Measure—self-conceptions: Respondents were asked the extent to which they agree or disagree that the following quality characterizes them personally (1 = Strongly Disagree to 5 = Strongly Agree): "care about promoting diversity."

The list of tables and figures in the book's front matter includes all these portrayals of our results. Table A.1 and four figures (A.1–4), which provide supplemental detail on the measures in chapter 4, appear at the end of this appendix.

Funding and Land Acknowledgment

This research was supported by an ADVANCE-Paid grant from the National Science Foundation, PI Mary Blair-Loy (Award #110707). Any opinions, findings, conclusions and recommendations expressed in this material are those of the authors and do not necessarily reflect the views of the National Science Foundation.

We acknowledge that the academic institutions where we worked while conducting this research, like almost all institutions in the United States, exist on grounds obtained through colonialist practices that have for thousands of years been part of the traditional lands of the Akokisa, Chippewa, Kumeyaay, Ottawa, and Potawatomi peoples. We honor these lands and are grateful to have lived and worked there.

Appendix Tables and Figures

Table A.1 OLS Regression Models Predicting Self-Conception Measures with Gender, Race/ Ethnicity, Department, and Career Stage

	Assertive Self-Conception		Relational Self-Conception		Diversity-Promoting Self-Conception	
	Coeff.	Std. Error	Coeff.	Std. Error	Coeff.	Std. Error
Woman	.001	.100	.284**	.101	.321**	.119
Underrepresented racial/ethnic minority	−.065	.163	.074	.151	.212	.178
Asian/Asian American	.071	.110	.101	.108	.161	.129
LGBTQ indicator	.321	.262	.141	.287	.261	.332
Academic step	−.001	.005	.002	.193	.008	.005
Teaching Professor	−.205	.198	.498*	.193	.428†	.228
Chemistry	.197	.154	.187	.155	.020	.182
Computer science	.050	.160	−.096	.157	−.056	.189
Math	−.292	.184	−.109	.193	.167	.223
Physics	.114	.187	−.001	.174	.001	.227
Biology specialty 1	.047	.182	.218	.182	.096	.221
Biology specialty 2	.202	.189	.227	.191	−.001	.224
Biology specialty 3	.263	.284	−.035	.285	−.179	.338
Engineering specialty 1	−.090	.213	.161	.244	.235	.292
Engineering specialty 2	−.005	.183	.082	.168	−.006	.208
Engineering specialty 3	.153	.180	−.067	.222	−.035	.198
Engineering specialty 4	.148	.213	.003	.213	.031	.253
Engineering specialty 5	.116	.303	−.096	.158	.125	.361
Engineering specialty 6	.013	.238	.288	.304	.053	.252
Constant	3.639***	.142	3.706***	.139	3.804***	.167

Note: *** $p < .001$; ** $p < .01$ * $p < .05$; † $p < .10$. A multidisciplinary STEM department is the reference category for department; white is the reference category for race/ethnicity (respondents could select multiple racial/ethnic categories). In supplemental models run with Gender × Race interaction terms, we did not find intersectional gender-by-race patterns in these self-conception measures.

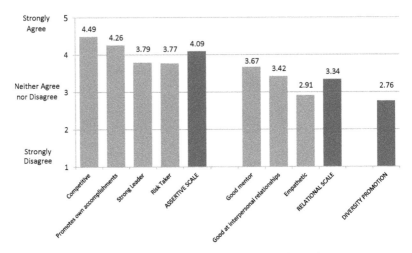

A.1 *Mean Values on Perceived Characteristics of Successful STEM Professional*
Bars represent averages across the sample of STEM faculty on the individual characteristics that make up each strand of the scientific excellence schema. Respondents were asked the extent to which they agree or disagree that each characteristic was "typical of a successful person in my discipline" (1 = Strongly Disagree to 5 = Strongly Agree). Values on the assertive and relational scales are averages of their component characteristics.

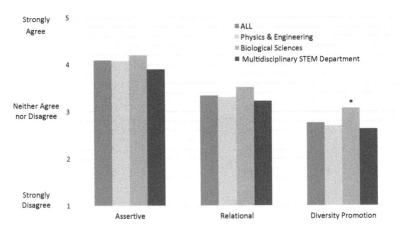

A.2 *Averages on Each Strand of Scientific Excellence Schema, by Broad Disciplinary Field*
Bars represent averages on each of the strands of the scientific excellence schema by broad disciplinary category. See figure A.1 for means on the characteristics that make up the assertive and relational scales. Respondents were asked the extent to which they agree or disagree that each characteristic was "typical of a successful person in my discipline" (1 = Strongly Disagree to 5 = Strongly Agree).

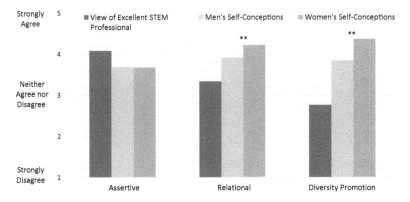

A.3 *Schema of Scientific Excellence Strands versus Self-Conceptions, by Gender*
The leftmost bar in each set represents the average agreement among STEM faculty that the typical successful person in their discipline exemplifies that trait. The other bars represent respondents' agreement that each characteristic is part of their self-conceptions (i.e., respondents were asked, "To what extent do you agree that each of these characteristics are typical of you personally?"), displayed separately by gender. Specifically, the middle bars represent the extent to which those characteristics are part of men's self-conceptions on average, and the rightmost bars represent the extent to which those characteristics are part of women's self-conceptions on average. Women have significantly higher relational and diversity promotion self-conceptions than men, net of controls (see table A.1). Supplemental OLS regression models with race × gender interactions (URM × women, Asian × women, white × women) suggest that these gender differences do not vary intersectionally by race/ethnicity.

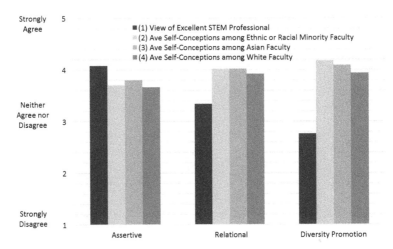

A.4 *Schema of Scientific Excellence Strands versus Self-Conceptions, by Race/Ethnicity*
The leftmost bar in each set represents the average agreement among STEM faculty that the
typical successful person in their discipline exemplifies that trait. The other bars represent
respondents' agreement that each characteristic is part of their self-conceptions (i.e.,
respondent were asked, "To what extent do you agree that each of these characteristics are
typical of you personally?"), displayed separately by racial/ethnic group. Specifically, the second bar represents extent to which underrepresented racial/ethnic minority (URM) faculty
see those characteristics as part of their self-conceptions on average, the third bar represents
the extent to which Asian respondents see those as part of their self-conceptions, and the
fourth bar represents the extent to which white respondents see those characteristics as part
of their self-conceptions on average. There are no statistically significant differences by race/
ethnicity in self-conceptions, net of controls; see table A.1.

Notes

1. In a study of non-STEM academics from the humanities and social sciences, Lamont (2009) also finds a common belief among faculty that the best academic research rises to the top and is recognizable to experts in the field.
2. Throughout this book, we use "STEM" and "science" interchangeably to refer to science, engineering, and mathematics professions, excluding social science professions. In the United States, "science" is often used as shorthand that is inclusive of engineering and mathematics disciplines (e.g., the National Science Foundation encapsulates all STEM disciplines).
3. For research on biases affecting faculty and faculty candidates, see Knobloch-Westerwick, Glynn, and Huge (2013), Madera et al. (2019), and the review by O'Meara, Culpepper, and Templeton (2020). For studies on biases affecting students, see Milkman, Akinola, and Chugh (2012) and Moss-Racusin et al. (2012). For a broad synthetic review and set of recommended practices on faculty recruitment, development, and promotion, see Stewart and Valian (2018) and Laursen and Austin (2020). Further, see studies by the National Science Foundation (2019) and by the National Academies (National Academy of Sciences 2007; National Academy of Sciences 2011) that document disadvantages for women, racial and ethnic minorities, and other groups in STEM fields.
4. National Science Foundation (2018, 3).
5. Stephan (2012). As we discuss in chapter 6, some faculty do engage in commercial work such as starting a company, patenting, or consulting for other organizations. This can

create potential conflicts of interests and shifting normative boundaries that universities and individual faculty must navigate (Johnson 2017; Lam 2010; Mars, Bresonis, and Szelényi 2014; Vallas and Kleinman 2008).

6. Of the $96.5 billion spent on basic research in 2018, government agencies provided $43 billion, and universities, many of which are public institutions, paid $13 billion (Congressional Research Service 2020, table 1). See also Mervis (2017).

7. To protect the confidentiality of our respondents, we do not name the university. In addition, all persons' names are pseudonyms, and we occasionally obscure or alter particular details (e.g., changing a professor's specific research specialty) to ensure we protect respondent confidentiality.

8. Lamont (2009).

9. For example, faculty pay scales are widely publicized, and the salaries of each faculty member and administrator are published annually. Academic files of candidates considered for hiring are viewed by all members of the hiring department, plus a university-wide faculty committee, plus administrators. Similarly, academic files of candidates up for promotion are viewed by all members of the department at the candidate's rank or above, and major promotion decisions are also reviewed by the university-wide committee. A policy of checks and balances across different university units limits the degree to which individuals can amass special perquisites or retention incentives.

10. DiMaggio (1997); Corrice (2009).

11. Blair-Loy (2003).

12. This book moves beyond previous research on cultural schemas in several ways. Previous research has not fully identified the social boundedness of schemas (Blair-Loy and Williams 2017). For example, the first study of the schema of work devotion (Blair-Loy 2003) did not clearly identify whether this schema exists at the analytical levels of national cultures, in the managerial and professional workforce, or within particular organizations and professions. Our book focuses on the schemas of work devotion and scientific excellence within the bounded professional spaces of academic STEM. See chapter 2.

13. Blair-Loy (2003, 2010).

14. Sociologist Max Weber described the "scientific vocation" as a calling, referring specifically to men in the social sciences disciplines (Weber 1958). As we show, this notion of a calling is highly salient among these twenty-first-century STEM faculty.

15. Work devotion is related to but conceptually distinct from Cech's (2021) notion of the "passion principle." The passion principle is a cultural schema that elevates finding fulfillment and self-expression as the most important factor in choosing a career path. When doing work one is passionate about, one also gets emotional inspiration from the work. Work devotion, in contrast, is the expectation that one's work ought to elicit such

dedication and, importantly, that nothing else in one's life should compete with work.

16. When presenting our qualitative interview data, we use pseudonyms that convey respondents' gender identity. We refer to white faculty as white. Given the small numbers of some other racial/ethnic groups on campus and in STEM, including Black and Latinx men and women and Asian women, we use the aggregate "faculty of color" category rather than the specific racial/ethnic identities. Because of the need to protect the confidentiality of respondents, particularly for LGBTQ faculty and faculty of color, we only reference quoted respondents' race/ethnicity and LGBTQ status when these categories are relevant for the contexts under discussion.

17. Abbott (1988); Cech (2013a).

18. Branch (2016); Zippel (2017).

19. National Center for Science and Engineering Statistics (2021). For example, the proportion of women who earned engineering majors has only increased by 1 percentage point since 2002 (National Center for Science and Engineering Statistics 2019b, table 5-1). The employment of women in physical sciences and engineering has increased by 4 percentage points and 2 percentage points, respectively, since 2008, but the proportion of women employed in computer science and mathematics has declined by 3 percentage points (National Center for Science and Engineering Statistics 2019b, table 5-1).

20. Branch (2016); Zippel (2017); Laursen and Austin (2020).

21. Sexual harassment against women is widespread in academic STEM. The most common type of sexual harassment is gender harassment, which includes actions that communicate disrespect and hostility toward women in the workplace. Severe gender harassment, like other types of sexual harassment (unwanted verbal or physical sexual advances and sexual coercion) have damaging consequences, including harm to the health and well-being of targeted scientists, their careers, and the scientific community. A culture that tolerates gender harassment is also more likely to propagate other forms of sexual harassment (National Academies of Sciences, Engineering, and Medicine 2018). Gender harassment and other forms of sexual harassment against women and gender nonconforming men are, at their core, abuses of power and are especially common in masculinity-contest workplaces (Berdahl, Cooper, Glick, Livingston, and Williams 2018).

22. Cech and Waidzunas (2021).

23. We did not collect data on citizenship status (although some individuals volunteered that information in interviews). Our measures of racial/ethnic identity include both US citizens and international faculty who identify with those racial/ethnic categories. For example, the term *Asian* includes Asian Americans and Asians. Latinx includes US citizens and international Latinx scholars with citizenship in Central America, South America, Europe, and beyond. Because Asians are not proportionally underrepresented,

we include them with white faculty in the racial majority category that is compared with minoritized Black, Latinx, and Native American faculty. However, other research on racial differences in the professional workforce generally has demonstrated that Asian (including Asian American) faculty are more likely than white peers to face marginalization, stereotypes, and exclusion from leadership roles (Sy et al. 2010). Further research is needed to examine subtle ways that Asian STEM faculty may be racialized and disadvantaged by the work devotion and scientific excellence schemas in ways that differ from their white peers. Moreover, Asian women and white women are underrepresented compared to the national population of adults.

24. National Science Foundation (2013). Exacerbating the problems of underrepresentation and devaluation of many groups, the swell of STEM PhDs and postdoctoral positions over the last two decades has been met with stagnated tenure-line faculty positions. In engineering disciplines specifically, Larson, Ghaffarzadegan, and Xue (2014, 1) calculate that "a professor in the US graduates 7.8 new PhDs during his/her whole career on average, and only one of these graduates can replace the professor's position. This implies that in a steady state, only 12.8% of PhD graduates can attain academic positions in the USA."

25. National Center for Science and Engineering Statistics (2019b, table 9-34). While the proportion of Latinx students in STEM has increased by about 5 percentage points since 2006, the representation of Black and Native American students has declined: Black students earned 8.4 percent of bachelor's degrees in STEM in 2006, but only 8.2 percent in 2016. Native American students were 0.7 percent of STEM BS degrees in 2006 but just 0.4 percent in 2016 (National Center for Science and Engineering Statistics 2019b, table 5-3). As with gender, there has been little increase in the proportion of the representation of racial/ethnic minorities employed in STEM (National Center for Science and Engineering Statistics 2019b, table 9-34).

26. National Center for Science and Engineering Statistics (2019b, table 9-25). Ong et al. (2011) argue that the "underrepresentation of women of color in STEM fields represents an unconscionable underutilization of our nation's human capital and raises concerns of equity in the U.S. educational and employment systems."

27. National Academy of Sciences (2011); Eaton et al. (2019); Stolzenberg et al. (2019); Posselt (2020); Sue and Spanierman (2020).

28. National Center for Science and Engineering Statistics (2021).

29. Castro and Collins (2021).

30. Williams et al. (2016).

31. Marx, Engels, and Arthur (1974); Gramsci (1992); Connell and Messerschmidt (2005); Seron et al. (2018).

32. Gerson and Damaske (2020); Posselt (2020).

33. The authors of this study include celebrated economist Donna Ginther as the first author and Raynard Kington, who had served as deputy director

and acting director of the NIH, as the senior author. The authors examined the submissions of all 81,188 new project NIH R01 grant applications submitted between FY2000 and FY2006 (Ginther et al. 2011). Generally, only about 20 percent of R01 applications receive funding (Lauer 2019).

34. A follow-up study (Ginther et al. 2018), conducted after our data were collected, added additional variables from each faculty proposer's biographical sketch, including all past educational institutions, the NIH funding rank of the employer, previous grants in addition to NIH R01 grants, and additional bibliometric information on publications. Including these variables narrowed the Black-white disparity to 6.9 percent, but it remained statistically significant. This new analysis also revealed that on average, white scientists worked at institutions with much higher NIH funding rates than African American scientists (Ginther et al. 2018). Other research finds gender bias in grant proposal reviews and funding decisions (Kolev, Fuentes-Medel, and Murray 2019), with reverberating negative effects on women's careers.

35. As another part of his claim that the results were flawed, Ruben stated that the study of the funding decisions on the entire set of actual grant proposals used the wrong method of data collection. He stated that the study authors should have instead run a randomized control experiment. Specifically, Ruben said the authors should have randomly placed some scientists in a "treatment" group and in the grant application pool, and other scientists in a "control" group, although it is not clear what "treatment" some applicants would get that the controls would not get. In other words, Ruben offered up methodological suggestions for research far outside his own specialty to counter the flaws he presumed to be in the methods of the study whose results he did not agree with.

36. Wharton and Estevez (2014) recognize similar practices at their institution and find that department chairs view the struggles of parents as a personal issue, ignoring broader cultural and institutional processes.

37. Chapter 3 presents the evidence for these patterns among academic scientists. For a study of work devotion among science professionals more broadly, see Blair-Loy and Cech (2017).

38. Similarly, Kmec (2013) finds that mothers in STEM, regardless of their productivity and time spent at work, feel that they need to work harder to be seen as legitimate scholars.

39. In chapter 3, regression models predicting pay control for log of scholarly articles per year, advancement level, department, gender, race, and family status. Specifically, our models predicting pay (using productivity indicators and other controls) show that fathers were paid about $3,800 more than mothers in annual salary the year of the study. More broadly, pay penalties for mothers in the general population of workers are well documented (Budig and England 2001; Correll, Benard, and Paik 2007; Budig and Hodges 2010).

40. We discuss these findings in chapter 3 and in Cech and Blair-Loy (2014).
41. We discuss this fully in chapters 2, 4, and 5. The qualities most strongly identified with disciplinary conceptions of excellence are creative brilliance and assertive traits. Previous research on broader social norms shows that white heterosexual men are assumed to naturally embody the positively valued brilliance and assertive traits (McIlwee and Robinson 1992; Pierce 1996; Cuddy, Fiske, and Glick 2004; Tilcsik 2011; Cech 2013a; Rudman and Mescher 2013; Vandello et al. 2013). Respondents report that their disciplines give a somewhat lower valuation to another grouping of characteristics (empathy, mentoring, and being skilled at interpersonal relationships), which are culturally associated with feminine qualities (Gorman 2005; Gorman and Kmec 2009). Finally, those who have commitments viewed as violating the objectivity and neutrality of STEM (e.g., social justice and diversity commitments) or identities deemed as too political (e.g., LGBTQ identity) may be seen as inconsistent with excellence in STEM (Cech and Waidzunas 2011; Cech 2013a, 2014).
42. Leahey (2006); Maliniak, Powers, and Walter (2013); King et al. (2017); Sarsons (2017).
43. In chapter 4, regression models control for log average of articles published, advancement step, department, gender, underrepresented minority (URM), LGBTQ, and family status. URM faculty are generally considered those who identify as Hispanic or Latinx and/or identify as Black/African American, Native American/American Indian/Alaskan Native, or Native Hawaiian/Other Pacific Islander. To protect confidentiality, we combine these groups into one URM category due to very small sample sizes of some of these groups.
44. Williams and Dempsey (2014).
45. Fox and Stephan (2001); Kemelgor and Etzkowitz (2001); Ong et al. (2011); Sheltzer and Smith (2014); McGlynn (2017).
46. Stephan (2012).
47. Cech and Waidzunas (2011); Cech (2014).
48. Gewin (2020).
49. See chapter 6.
50. Pang (2016).
51. Moen, Kelly, and Hill (2011).
52. National Academy of Sciences (2007).
53. Fox and Stephan (2001); Kemelgor and Etzkowitz (2001); Sheltzer and Smith (2014).
54. Domestic Policy Council (2006); Kuenzi (2008); Page (2008); Perez (2019); Hofstra et al. (2020).
55. Ragin (1987).
56. See Lamont and White (2005, 157). Many high-impact studies of social inequality focus on a single-organization case with rich data. For example, see the books by Hochschild (1997), Kunda (2006), Armstrong and Ham-

ilton (2013), and Kelly and Moen (2020). See also the articles by Blair-Loy and Wharton (2002), Castilla (2008), and Cech and Waidzunas (2011).

57. We constructed the scholarly productivity and impact measures from the SCOPUS bibliographic database. We used university records on funding to add measures of grant dollars earned as PI and Co-PI. See the appendix for details.

58. The appendix includes a discussion of ways that bias is often encompassed in these seemingly objective indicators of productivity. Our models that include productivity measures likely underestimate the productivity of marginalized and minoritized faulty who have the same rates of publications and grants as their white male colleagues. For example, studies find that white men are more likely to get grant proposals funded compared to women and to men of color with similar qualifications (Ginther et al. 2011; Ginther et al. 2018; Kolev, Fuentes-Medel, and Murray 2019), and that men get more credit than women do for collaborative research (Sarsons 2017). Further, research finds that men are more likely to cite their own work; self-citations directly and indirectly increase an article's total number of citations, a metric for "impact," with potentially large and cumulative effects in the sciences (Leahey 2006; King et al. 2017; Maliniak, Powers, and Walter 2013; West et al. 2013; King et al. 2017).

59. Chapters 3 and 4 presents our measures of the degree to which professors see themselves as having the traits valorized by the work devotion and scientific excellence schemas.

60. US News and World Report (2014).

61. Processes of isomorphism mean that the structure and operation of research universities are strikingly similar. This structural similarity helps produce cultural continuity as well (DiMaggio and Powell 1983).

62. US News and World Report (2016a, 2016b).

63. This supplemental analysis used 2018 STEM Inclusion Study data (principal investigator: Cech). See appendix for details.

64. MIT (1999); UCLA (2003); Cornell University (2006).

65. Cech, Blair-Loy, and Rogers (2017).

66. National Science Foundation (2012). See the appendix for more information.

67. As stated earlier, underrepresented minority (URM) faculty are generally considered those who identify as Hispanic or Latinx and/or identify as Black/African American, Native American/American Indian/Alaskan Native, or Native Hawaiian/Other Pacific Islander. We combine these groups into one URM category due to small sample sizes. Because Asian/Asian Americans are not underrepresented in our sample or in STEM more broadly (National Science Foundation 2013), we do not include this group within the URM category. See the appendix for comparison of proportions of women, URM, and LGBTQ faculty in our sample to national data.

68. Throughout our analysis and writing, we carefully considered intersectional processes by gender, race/ethnicity, and LGBTQ status. We found a number of instances in which patterns of inequality differ across sociodemographic and intersectional categories. We also found evidence of similarity across categories in beliefs in the cultural schemas of merit, consistent with calls by Elizabeth Cole (2009) that intersectional research should attend not only to differences but also to convergences of patterns.

69. National origin is a common point raised in policy discussions surrounding racial/ethnic inequality (Stephan 2012). Although first language was occasionally raised as a factor by our respondents, country of origin was not a salient status when respondents described the cultural values that anchored the two schemas we study. There was no differentiation between the work devotion of US-born versus non–US-born mothers, for example. Race/ethnicity, regardless of the country of origin, was much more salient than nationality in how respondents understood and applied the schema of scientific excellence. Hence, we do not center nationality in our investigation or in our discussion of results.

70. Chapter 5 explains that the dominant pipeline narrative faculty use to account for the small proportions of underrepresented STEM faculty at the university contrasts with how the actual numbers of underrepresented scientists with recent PhDs far exceed the numbers of underrepresented scientists in assistant professor positions in the United States. For instance, while over 10,300 Black, Latinx, and Indigenous US citizens and permanent residents graduated in the United States with PhDs in STEM fields over the last five years (about 2,100 per year), there are only around 3,600 Black, Latinx, and Indigenous Assistant STEM professors employed in US four-years colleges and universities (Authors' calculation from National Science Foundation data; National Center for Science and Engineering Statistics 2019b).

CHAPTER 2

1. Cole and Cole (1973); Long and Fox (1995); Cech and Blair-Loy (2010). Note that we are not attending to the prevalence of the meritocratic ideology more broadly, as other scholars have done among other populations (Young 1958; Kluegel and Smith 1986; Hochschild 1995; DiTomaso 2012; McCall 2013). Rather, we are interested in cultural understanding of merit as a characteristic of professionals and the extent to which that merit is believed to be fairly or unfairly rewarded within the context of STEM.

2. Bloor (1976); Knorr-Cetina (1999).

3. Shapin (2008).

4. Stephan (2012).

5. As explained in more detail in the Appendix, this university is an elite research-focused university that is ranked as a "Highest Research Activity" university in the Carnegie Classification of Institutions of Higher Educa-

tion. At institutions like our case university, faculty evaluation aligns most closely with the norms of meritorious research productivity within STEM disciplines. The definitions of merit among faculty at other institutions may be somewhat distinct from what we describe here. This may be particularly the case in more teaching-oriented institutions. However, we argue that the schemas of merit we describe are embedded within the broader professional culture of academic STEM. Even when faculty at other institutions are assessed along somewhat different criteria (e.g., teaching excellence), they likely recognize these schemas from the socialization they received at their own PhD-granting institutions. In the appendix, we describe supplemental analyses with STEM Inclusion Study data of over 7,000 PhD-level STEM professionals employed in universities. We find very similar patterns in how these professionals view excellence in STEM.

6. Stephan (2012).
7. Lamont (2009).
8. Specific qualitative and quantitative analyses showing professors' attitudes about the fairness of promotion and hiring at their university are presented in chapter 5. The broader argument about a pervasive belief that science is a meritocracy is supported by evidence throughout the book.
9. Xu (2008); Charles (2011); Cech, Pecenco, and Blair-Loy (2013).
10. Leslie, McClure, and Oaxaca (1998); National Academy of Sciences (2011); Stephan (2012); Cech, Metz, and Smith (2019); Flaherty (2021).
11. Eisenhart et al. (1998); Valian (1998); National Academy of Sciences (2000); Xie and Shauman (2003); Smith-Doerr (2004); National Academy of Sciences (2007); Blair-Loy and Cech (2017); Shafran (2017); National Academies of Science, Engineering, and Medicine (2018). These patterns have also been documented for women in other professions and occupations (Correll 2001; Gorman 2005; Ridgeway 2009; Turco 2010; Williams, Blair-Loy, and Berdahl 2013).
12. Bilimoria and Stewart (2009); Cech and Waidzunas (2011, 2021).
13. MIT (1999); National Academy of Sciences (2007); Burrelli (2008); National Science Foundation (2008); Ecklund, Lincoln, and Tansey (2012); Kelly and Grant (2012); Cech, Pecenco, and Blair-Loy (2013); King et al. (2017).
14. Reflecting STEM faculty nation-wide, women and certain racial/ethnic groups are underrepresented in our population (National Science Foundation 2012). See the appendix for detailed information comparing our study sample with national statistics on gender, racial/ethnic, and LGBTQ representation.
15. Cech, Blair-Loy, and Rogers (2017).
16. Cech and Blair-Loy (2010); Cech, Metz, and Smith (2019); Cech and Waidzunas (2021).
17. Kuhn (1962); Fleck (1979); Hughes (2004); Shapin (2008).
18. By "Western" we mean beliefs and practices of the global sociocultural west, which generally includes Europe, North America, and Australia.

19. Harding (1991, 1998); Cajete (2000).
20. Harding (1998); Cajete (2000).
21. Harding (1998).
22. Duhem (1996).
23. Hughes (2004).
24. Jordan (1994).
25. Harding (1991).
26. In their book, Ecklund and Lincoln (2016) discusses the notion of the "ideal scientist" and examine the extent to which biology and physics faculty feel constrained in managing expectations of parenting alongside their career. However, their conception of "ideal scientist" focuses specifically on the intensive time investments embedded within that ideal. While we see this intensive time norm as part of the ideal scientist conception generally and part of work devotion among STEM faculty specifically, our book examines the cultural meaning structures that exist around this intensive time norm and how it interfaces with conceptions of merit—including scientific excellence and devotion to a scientific vocation—*within* STEM.
27. Stephan (2012).
28. Shapin (2008, 32–33).
29. Kuhn (1962); Fleck (1979); Hughes (2004). An example of this is a lab group coming together to debate whether feedback from lab equipment is "real" or "just noise" (Latour and Woolgar 1986; Knorr-Cetina 1999).
30. Kuhn (1962); Fleck (1979). Scientific truth, in other words, is not a characteristic of the knowledge being claimed but the outcome of a social process: scientific claims are only seen as "true" to the extent that they are collectively understood as such by other members of the profession (Kuhn 1962).
31. Shapin and Schaffer (1985).
32. These beliefs broadly reinforce hegemonic masculinity, a set of normative practices and beliefs that embody "the currently most honored way of being a man" and that ideologically legitimate the "subordination of women to men" (Connell and Messerschmidt 2005, 832).
33. Des Jardins (2010).
34. Des Jardins (2010, 120).
35. Powerful counterexamples of the exceptional mathematical abilities of women can be found across the history of science and engineering. Women were, for example, on the forefront of computer science and were among the first computer coders (Des Jardins 2010). Popular accounts of women's mathematical genius, such as in the 2016 film *Hidden Figures* and the 2021 PBS documentary *Picture a Scientist*, attempt to undermine these gendered (and racialized) stereotypes of STEM excellence.
36. Harding (1986); Des Jardins (2010).
37. Nye (1997, 158).
38. Nye (1997); Hughes (2004).
39. Traweek (1988); Des Jardins (2010).

40. Schiebinger (1999).
41. Sinclair (2004). This engagement could have been as hired help in labs, or in the case of some scientific work in the eighteenth and nineteenth century United States, as the forced labor of enslaved or indentured persons.
42. For example, new drugs were tested on predominantly African American and indigenous communities, frequently without their knowledge (Schiebinger 1999; Cajete 2000).
43. Herzig (2004); Sinclair (2004); Cech, Metz, and Smith (2019). The apparent contradictions between the "nerd identity" of science and engineering and subcultural identities in Black and Latinx communities can also make it difficult for Latinx and African American men to succeed in STEM without accusations of "acting white" (Eglash 2002; Beasley 2011).
44. Eglash (2002).
45. Cech (2014, 2015).
46. Zippel (2017); Settles et al. (2020).
47. Schiebinger (1999); Des Jardins (2010).
48. These societal-level beliefs, often called "status biases," are implicit and often precognitive assumptions that women, LGBTQ individuals, and people of color as less competent, less reliable, and less worthy professionals than heterosexual white men (Cuddy, Fiske, and Glick 2008; Ridgeway 2009, 2011; Stewart and Valian 2018).
49. Corrice (2009).
50. Correll, Benard, and Paik (2007); Ridgeway (2009, 2011); Tilcsik (2011).
51. Scholars have documented how organizational practices may amplify biases through processes such as opportunity hoarding (Tilly 1999) and job title differentiation (Tomaskovic-Devey 1993) or how organizational approaches to reduce bias through diversity and inclusion efforts often fail to do so (Dobbin 2009; Dobbin and Kalev 2016). Still others have looked more intently at power relationships within organizations, the demography of intra-organizational work units (Blair-Loy and Wharton 2002) and organizational-level cultural narratives and symbols (Kunda 2006; Morrill 2008). Further, neoinstitutional scholars consider how organizational myths of rationality help sustain the legitimacy of organizations within organizational field (Meyer and Rowan 1977) and the cultural construction of seemingly rational processes such as organizational control (Fligstein 1990) and equity and grievance procedures (Edelman 1990; Sutton et al. 1994; Edelman, Uggen, and Erlanger 1999). Scholars concerned with intra-organizational cultural processes have examined how normative expectations about ideal workers and ideal work embedded within organizational culture can devalue workers with family responsibilities (Acker 1990; Wharton, Chivers, and Blair-Loy 2008).
52. Cech et al. (2011); Blair-Loy, Pecenco, and Cech (2013).
53. Abbott (1988); Blair-Loy, Pecenco, and Cech (2013). Although professional cultures are distinct from organizational cultures, institutional

isomorphism likely means that organizations dominated by particular professions may have organizational cultures that are powerfully shaped by professional cultures. Organizational cultures lack the coherence of professional cultures. They are also not insulated and perpetuated through institutional-level processes of closure and socialization as professional cultures are.

54. Kunda (2006).
55. Bourdieu (1984); Abbott (1988); Grusky and Sorensen (1998); Weeden and Grusky (2005).
56. Due to changes in regulation, globalization, and the subordination of professional autonomy to bureaucratic processes, professions have less power of self-regulation than they had half a century ago (Leicht 2016; Liu 2020; Gorman and Sandefur 2011). Professionals, in turn, are increasingly employed in multinational corporate organizations that put limits on their enactment of professional authority and autonomy (Freidson 2001). However, structural and cultural processes like closure and socialization (described later) still foster shared norms and practices among professionals who work across industries about the profession's epistemologies and norms of excellence (Abbott 1988; Schleef 2006; Gorman and Sandefur 2011).
57. Freidson (2001); Stephan (2012); Jacobs (2014).
58. Abbott (1981); Sandefur (2001).
59. These professional cultures are often unfamiliar—even inexplicable—to the uninitiated. In their classic ethnography of medical school students, Howard Becker and colleagues (1961) provide a window into the meanings within medicine's professional culture. Here, Becker and colleagues describe the ways that the cultural meanings nurtured in medical school often differ from meanings of laypersons outside of medicine.

> Many occupations deal routinely with things that are shocking, horrifying, or revolting to laypeople. Their members develop a technical vocabulary and point of view based on that routine acquaintance with the horrible and reflecting the specific occupational interest they have in it. . . . The medical student sees many things laymen customarily think of as "traumatic"; in particular, death and disabling or disfiguring disease. The medical profession has a language and a point of view toward these things which provide a technical and impersonal way of experiencing them . . . [they learn to see] death not so much as a human tragedy as a problem in the use of medical responsibility. . . . This does not mean that the student becomes cynical and unfeeling; it simply means that he [sic] has the reactions appropriate to one in his situation. . . . (Becker et al. 1961, 272–73).

In the process of learning techniques of healing, medical students also adopt the meanings around death and disfigurement that are part of their profession. These meanings are recognizable and reasonable to most within medicine, yet they may seem puzzling or even cynical to those outside its professional culture.

60. Abbott (1981); Haas and Shaffir (1991).
61. These processes are also why specific aspects of a professional culture can be found across different geographic regions and work contexts.
62. Abbott (1988).
63. Freidson (1971); Larson (1977); Grusky and Sorensen (1998).
64. Abbott (1988, 3); Trice (1993); Tilly (1999).
65. Stephan (2012); Posselt (2020). See also Jacobs (2014) for discussions of interdisciplinarity in academia generally.
66. Zippel (2017); Posselt (2020). As we explain in chapter 6, the schema of scientific excellence challenges the prestige of interdisciplinary team science in ways that undermine its potential as a more inclusive alternative model of STEM work.
67. Rhoten and Pfirman (2007); Pfirman and Begg (2012).
68. Abbott (2001).
69. For instance, the professional engineers' licensure is supposed to protect "the public by enforcing standards that *restrict practice to qualified individuals* who have met specific qualifications in education, work experience, and exams" (http://ncees.org/engineering/pe/; emphasis added).
70. Abbott (1988); Freidson (2001).
71. Abbott (1988); Weeden (2002); Waidzunas (2015).
72. Blair-Loy et al. (2017).
73. Becker et al. (1961); Dryburgh (1999); Schleef (2006). This process of socialization inculcates neophytes into a "web of values, norms, rules, beliefs, and taken-for-granted assumptions" of the profession, which helps them develop the "habits of mind" of a committed member (Barley and Tolbert 1997, 93).
74. Cech (2015).
75. Wilensky and Jack (1967); Haas and Shaffir (1991).
76. Some intraprofession research (e.g., Weeden 2002; Weeden and Grusky 2005) has begun to acknowledge professional cultures as an important social force that binds professions and entrenches mechanisms of inequality reproduction within them. Although this research takes professional cultures seriously as cohesive forces that support structural sources of inequality, this scholarship largely black boxes the content of professional cultures (their myths, norms, practices, scripts, habits, etc.).
77. Blair-Loy (2003, 5).
78. The conception of schema we use here diverges from the way psychologists have traditionally used the term to describe individualized constructs like gender identity (Bem 1983). In contrast, we emphasize that schemas are cognitive, moral, and emotional constructs that emerge out of structural and cultural processes (Blair-Loy 2003).
79. Following Sewell (1992, 27), we understand social structure as made of "mutually sustaining cultural schemas and sets of resources that empower and constrain social action." Schemas can be transposed to novel social

settings where they are used to make sense of new sets of social interactions. Several studies have developed Sewell's notion of schemas within empirical contexts (Blair-Loy 2003; Beisel and Kay 2004; Williams, Blair-Loy, and Berdahl 2013; Enriquez and Saguy 2016).

80. Blair-Loy (2003, 2010).
81. Blair-Loy (2003); Blair-Loy and Williams (2016).
82. For example, Turco's (2010) study of leveraged buyout firms found that women faced "intense questioning of their work commitment" if they were seen as potentially getting married or getting pregnant. "Even when they went to great lengths to prove their commitment to work, having children had negative consequences for women's careers. Several described incidents in which women were fired or involuntarily transferred to non-deal roles after announcing they were pregnant. One woman said, 'I call each of my kids my "million dollar babies" because of how much each of them has cost me.' Despite never taking maternity leave, her year-end bonus was substantially docked each year she gave birth" (Turco 2010, 902).
83. Blair-Loy and Williams (2016).
84. Blair-Loy (2003).
85. Blair-Loy and Williams (2016).
86. Our previous work found evidence of the work devotion schema among senior women in science and technology industries across different firms in the same broad geographic region (Blair-Loy and Cech 2017).
87. For example, the characteristics that culturally define excellence in elementary school teaching are not the same as those that define excellence in physics (Traweek 1988; Williams 2014).
88. Abbott (1981). For example, Becker and colleagues describe how medical students value neurosurgeons not necessarily because they wield such great medical responsibility but because of their "detective-like" characteristics:

> Neurosurgery is seen by some as possessing a great deal of medical responsibility because brain surgery is so difficult and the chances great of making a fatal mistake. . . . students think it is interesting and challenging, remarking on the detective-like character of the diagnostic processes used. The other major feature of the student stereotype is its emphasis on the necessity for certain personal qualities if one wants to be a neurosurgeon: an interest in science, mental capacity, and so on. (Becker et al. 1961, 414)

89. Although an important empirical question, it is outside the scope of this book to contrast the features of the professional cultures within each discipline of STEM.
90. Shapin (2008).
91. Hughes (2004).
92. Harding (1998).
93. Haraway (1988); Harding (1991); Waidzunas (2015).

94. Merton (1973); Latour (1987); Huutoniemi (2012); Lincoln et al. (2012); Cech (2014).
95. Merton (1973); Shapin (2008); Fox, Fonseca, and Bao (2011).
96. Hunter and Leahey (2010).
97. Kuhn (1962); Ezrahi (1971); Cech and Waidzunas (2016).
98. Knorr-Cetina (1999); Huutoniemi (2012).
99. Long and Fox (1995); Valian (1998); Ridgeway and Correll (2004); National Academy of Sciences (2007); Ridgeway (2009); Leslie et al. (2015); Stewart and Valian (2018).
100. Biernat (2003); Quillian (2006).
101. Cech and Waidzunas (2011).
102. Ridgeway (2009); Hoffman, Gneezy, and List (2011).
103. These schemas do not exhaust the values that make up the conception of STEM merit. Other dimensions, such as meanings around educational pedigree, are likely also part the cultural conception of merit in STEM. We encourage other scholars to investigate the connection between these aspects of the cultural definition of scientific merit and the reproduction of inequality.
104. Wharton, Chivers, and Blair-Loy (2008); Halrynjo and Lyng (2009).
105. Perlow (2001).
106. Ecklund and Lincoln's study (2016) of biology and physics professors in elite departments in the United States found that expectations for long work hours is part of the understanding of what it means to be an ideal scientist in academic STEM.
107. The pace of work in STEM industry is also shaped by management concerns about corporate profitability. A study of US informational technology professionals in a large company discusses intensive work as overload caused by management decisions to increase shareholder profit by downsizing and by shifting jobs to cheaper contractors in the United States and offshore (Kelly and Moen 2020).
108. Perlow (2001).
109. Blair-Loy et al. (2017).
110. Fox and Stephan (2001); Ecklund and Lincoln (2016).
111. Fox, Fonseca, and Bao (2011).
112. Merton (1973).
113. Weber (1946).
114. Weber (1958, 122).
115. Shapin (2008, 35).
116. Merton (1973).
117. Shapin (2008, 36–37, 124–26).
118. We discuss the commercialization of academic science further in chapter 6.
119. Our survey data include quantitative proxies for the elements of work devotion: dedication to, identification with, emotional investment in, and inspiration derived from work. See the appendix for details.

120. Des Jardins (2010, 120–21).
121. Roe (1953, as discussed in Des Jardins (2010, 124–25).
122. Blair-Loy (2003).
123. Even a scientist as illustrious as Marie Curie was accused of being neglectful of her children as she focused on her research. Men scientists, in contrast, "could be revered for their single-minded devotion to their work. . . . Regardless of how much children actually interfered with [women's work in science], male colleagues perpetuated the idea that home life and science were two distinctly different and incompatible realms" (Des Jardins 2010, 121, 125).
124. Williams, Blair-Loy, and Berdahl (2013).
125. Shapin (2008, 32–33).
126. As we explain in chapter 1 and the appendix, while Asian men differ in some ways from white men in work experiences generally, they are similarly overrepresented compared to their proportion in the US population and are similarly stereotyped as competent in STEM pursuits, compared to white women and Latinx, Black, and Native American men and women.
127. Leslie et al. (2015).
128. Schippers (2007).
129. We care about the content of this schema of scientific excellence—the characteristics that make it up—to the extent that those characteristics are not assumed to be equally distributed across demographic categories.
130. Rudman (1998); Williams and Dempsey (2014).
131. Misra et al. (2017).
132. Furthermore, measures of productivity are themselves biased, as systematic biases favor white men in citations (King et al. 2017), evaluation (Sarsons 2017), and funding (Ginther et al. 2011; Ginther et al. 2018; Kolev, Fuentes-Medel, and Murray 2019). See the discussion in the appendix.
133. Broverman et al. (1972); Abbott (1988); Gorman and Kmec (2009); Blair-Loy, Pecenco, and Cech (2013). Schemas of excellence are more specific to STEM than a more general notion of competence that is often associated with hegemonic masculinity, where men are stereotyped as more broadly "competent" than women (Broverman et al. 1972). These schemas are also distinct from what Gorman and Kmec (2009) call "role-incumbent schemas"—the narrower image employers have in mind of the "ideal fit" for a particular position. Schemas of scientific excellence likely help shape these role-incumbent schemas, but the continuity and transferability of the former lend them resonance throughout the profession.
134. For example, earlier research suggests that racial/ethnic minority women and men and white women are more likely than white men to experience bias, isolation, and intolerance (Bobo 2000; Fox 2001; Trower and Chait 2002; Quillian 2006; Trower 2008; Rhoton 2011; Ecklund, Lincoln, and

Tansey 2012; Morimoto and Zajicek 2012). Beyond STEM, previous research on the US labor market finds that individuals who are more successful (i.e., white men) are more likely to assert meritocratic explanations of inequality (Ellemers 2001).

1. Throughout this chapter and the empirical chapters that follow, we consistently reference interview respondents' gender but redact their race/ethnicity and LGBTQ status unless we are specifically discussing the variation of beliefs or consequences along those axes. This helps protect the confidentiality of our respondents.

2. The means and 95 per cent confidence intervals for hours worked among each ladder rank are as follows: Assistant professors: 61.17 hours per week (56.86–65.48 hours); Associate professors: 55.28 hours per week (51.04–59.52 hours); Full professors: 58.17 hours per week (56.35–59.98 hours). The correlation between hours and work dedication is 0.168* ($p = .013$). Survey and interview data were collected before the COVID-19 pandemic. We discuss later in this chapter the ways that the circumstances described here may have been exacerbated in the context of pandemic-related work and life disruptions.

3. Ecklund and Lincoln (2016) interviewed academic biologists and physicists across several top universities and found that mothers and fathers struggled with juggling professional and family obligations.

4. Similarly, Kmec (2013) finds that STEM mothers feel like they need to work harder than their counterparts, regardless of their actual hours worked.

5. Blair-Loy (2003); Wharton, Chivers, and Blair-Loy (2008); Blair-Loy and Williams (2016).

6. Williams, Blair-Loy, and Berdahl (2013).

7. Halrynjo and Lyng (2009); Blair-Loy and Cech (2017). In addition, supplemental analysis of data from STEM professionals across industry and academia from the STEM Inclusion Study found that the average on the work dedication scale across STEM professionals was 3.95 (on a 1 = strongly disagree to 5 = strongly agree scale), which was right in line with the average from our case study sample (average = 3.99). See the appendix for further discussion of our supplemental analysis of STEM Inclusion Study data.

8. See chapter 2 for a detailed discussion of science as a vocation.

9. For example, in an earlier qualitative study of executive women in finance, only half of the women continued to enthusiastically endorse work devotion, whereas the other half endured the demands of work devotion with ambivalence or resentment (Blair-Loy 2003).

10. One measure of work devotion is the dedication scale. We adapted this from our earlier study of women professionals in STEM industry and allied

fields, in which we developed a four-item dedication scale to measure the degree to which the cognitive, emotional, and normative expectations of intensive work were embraced. In that earlier study, nearly 90 percent of respondents somewhat or strongly agreed with at least two statements; 53 percent agreed with all four (Blair-Loy and Cech 2017).

11. Blair-Loy (2003).

12. In the survey of STEM faculty analyzed here, we found similar levels of agreement on these work devotion measures in our earlier study of professionals in STEM industries and allied fields (Blair-Loy and Cech 2017). Specifically, 91 percent of faculty respondents somewhat or strongly agree with at least two items of the dedication scale, 73 percent agree with at least three items, and 42 percent agree with all four. Comparisons of means across gender (women and men) and race (URM and non-URM) show similarly high levels of dedication. Furthermore, as we note in the appendix, our supplemental analysis of 7,647 PhD-level STEM professionals working in four-year universities from the STEM Inclusion Study data found no statistical differences in work dedication by gender or race/ethnicity.

13. The values in figure 3.2 control for variation by department, academic rank, and other career measures.

14. In supplemental analyses (not shown), parents of children aged six or younger are, on average, even more likely to personally embrace work devotion expectations than their colleagues. In an OLS regression model, we found that parents of children under age six had marginally higher levels of dedication ($B = .214$, $p < .067$), controlling for gender, race, LGBTQ status, weekly work hours, step, teaching faculty indicator, salary, and department. The other demographic measures were not statistically significant. As faculty step is highly correlated with age, we do not include a separate indicator for respondent age.

15. The similarity across STEM faculty is an example of the type of convergence across intersecting identity categories that Cole (2009) and others highlight as central for the perpetuation of multidimensional inequality.

16. See Cech (2021) for theoretical and empirical examination of the desire for, and broader consequences of, being passionate about the substantive tasks of one's career field.

17. Net of department, rank, and demographic measures in OLS regression models, organizational dedication is related to higher salaries (log salary $B = .078$, $p < .05$), greater average number of articles published per year ($B = .153$, $p < .05$), more job satisfaction ($B = .591$, $p < .001$) and lower intentions of leaving academia for industry ($B = -.394$, $p < .001$). In our survey data, only 6 percent said they would be somewhat or very likely to leave academia for industry, and another 8 percent were unsure. A full 60 percent said it was "very unlikely" that they would leave academia for industry.

18. In OLS regression models (not shown), organizational dedication is negatively related to personal experiences of marginalization (experiences of

marginalization scale $B = -.503$, $p < .001$) and positively related to perceptions that their department members view them as highly productive compared to the departmental average ($B = 1.172$, $p < .01$).

19. Hermanowicz (1998).
20. Cech and Blair-Loy (2014).
21. O'Meara and Campbell (2011); Ecklund and Lincoln (2016).
22. For discussions of violations of ideal worker norms, see Whalley (1986); Traweek (1988); National Academy of Engineering (2004); Fox, Fonseca, and Bao (2011); Cech (2013); Kmec, Huffman, and Penner (2014); and Kmec, O'Connor, and Schieman (2014). For ideal worker norms being based in the work devotion schema, see Blair-Loy (2003); Blair-Loy and Wharton (2004); Wharton, Chivers, and Blair-Loy (2008); Williams and Boushey (2010); and Cech and Blair-Loy (2014).
23. Specifically, across the entire STEM workforce in academia, industry, and government, 43 percent of new mothers and about a quarter of new fathers leave their full-time STEM jobs after having children (Cech and Blair-Loy 2019). In academia, early career women who have or want children often feel pressure to "decide" to leave academia (Goulden, Frasch, and Mason 2009; Mason, Wolfinger, and Goulden 2013; Ecklund and Lincoln 2016). These gendered parental pressures are in part why women are less likely than men to obtain faculty positions at research-oriented universities (Shauman 2017).
24. Williams, Blair-Loy, and Berdahl (2013).
25. Cech and Blair-Loy (2014).
26. Existing literature (e.g., Lundquist, Misra, and O'Meara 2012; Misra, Lundquist, and Templer 2012) have illustrated that faculty who do take leaves are better able to retain research productivity than those who do not. This highlights the irrationality of the stigma toward parents who take leaves after having or adopting children.
27. In OLS regression models (not shown), mothers of children under age sixteen spend significantly more time on average than fathers of children under age sixteen on childcare on the weekdays ($B = 1.485$, $p < .01$) and on the weekends ($B = 2.059$, $p < .001$), net of controls for demographics, department, and step.
28. Hays (1996); Blair-Loy (2003); Collins (2019).
29. According to self-reported hours worked from our survey data, net of demographics, department, and step within rank, although mothers and fathers do not work significantly different hours, parents of children under sixteen (mothers and fathers) work about fifty-five hours a week, or about six hours per week fewer than childless faculty. These work hours are roughly comparable to national trends (Rudman and Mescher 2013). Research on faculty across disciplines finds that compared with men, women spend a smaller percentage of their work time on research (Jacobs and Winslow 2004; Misra, Lundquist, and Templer 2012; Stone and Hernandez

2013). However, we find that there are no statistically significant gender differences in the amount of time spent on research among these elite STEM faculty. This could be due to selection and/or retention effects of only the most work devoted faculty into these positions. In addition, we find that mothers of young children are actually more work devoted than their colleagues (see note above), which may drive them to match or exceed the research time of their colleagues despite additional care responsibilities.

30. Because STEM faculty generally believe that the number and impact of scientific articles and grantsmanship are the most objective metrics of productivity, we constructed the SPI database. Of course, while publication and citation counts and grant dollars may seem like objective measures, previous research has shown that underrepresented groups generally have to produce more and higher quality work for the same publications and funding, and the citation counts for men are often directly and indirectly inflated by self-citations. Therefore, these indices may underestimate the scholarly contribution of many underrepresented groups. See the discussion of productivity indices and relevant literature in chapter 1 and the appendix. We discuss the methodology of our SPI database and the technical details of our analysis in the appendix.

31. In the models reported in table 3.3, figure 3.4, and the appendix, the motherhood and fatherhood measures are dichotomous measures (0 = not a parent, 1 = a parent of one or more children) that indicate whether respondents have children of any age. Supplemental analyses using two-category parenthood measures—one for parents of children under sixteen, and one for parents of children sixteen and older—found that mothers of children of both age categories were significantly more productive in terms of average publications per year than their colleagues (mothers of children under sixteen: $B = .489$, $p < .05$; mothers of children sixteen and older: $B = .648$, $p < .05$).

32. Andersen et al. (2020); Flaherty (2020); Kitchener (2020); Kreeger et al. (2020).

33. Of the eighty-five interviews, forty are with women and forty-five are with men. Sixty-two interviewees are parents. See the appendix.

34. The family devotion schema provides an alternative definition of a worthwhile life, particularly for white middle- and upper-class women (Blair-Loy 2003). Family devotion defines full-time motherhood and wifehood as a worthwhile calling. This schema promises a morally, emotionally, and financially rewarding life for women who dedicate their lives to caring for breadwinning husbands and vulnerable and sacred children (Blair-Loy 2003). The family devotion schema is rooted in the separate spheres ideology and arrangements of the eighteenth- to nineteenth-century industrial revolution (Cott 1977; Hays 1996; Davies and Frink 2014). Retreating from (or being pushed out of) work and into the private sphere to care for family

has historically characterized the lives of white middle- and upper-middle-class women more than the lives of women of color (Dow 2019; Blair-Loy 2003; Amott and Matthaei 1996). In addition, single mothers are less likely to hold themselves accountable to intensive family devotion and more likely to emphasize the importance of delegation (Christopher 2012). The cultural expectations and material resources for women to navigate work and family responsibilities also vary across different national contexts (Blair-Loy and Wharton 2002; Wharton and Blair-Loy 2006; Halrynjo and Lyng 2009; Collins 2019).

35. Ecklund and Lincoln (2016) found similar patterns in their study of academic physicists and biologists.

36. Garey (1995); Jacobs and Gerson (2004); Williams, Blair-Loy, and Berdahl (2013); Ecklund and Lincoln (2016).

37. Blair-Loy (2003); Williams, Blair-Loy, and Berdahl (2013).

38. Glavin, Schieman, and Reid (2011); Stephan (2012).

39. See Reid (2015) for a discussion of the process of "passing and revealing" that consultants use in response to the stigmatized identity of motherhood.

40. We include respondents in the mother or father categories if they have children of any age because we expect that salary differentials accumulate over the course of one's time as a caregiver, not just shortly after the birth or adoption of a child. Supplemental analyses using the two-category parenthood measures described above to predict salary found that the interaction terms for motherhood were both in the same direction; the measure for mothers of children under sixteen was marginally statistically significant and negative ($B = -.086$; $p < .055$), and the measure for mothers of children sixteen and older was negative but nonsignificant.

41. Pay penalties for mothers in the general population of workers are well documented (Williams 2010; Williams, Blair-Loy, and Berdahl 2013). A laboratory experiment asking evaluators to assign starting salaries to professionals with identical qualifications found a pay penalty of about six thousand dollars for mothers (Berdahl and Moon 2013).

42. Many individual faculty are not aware of broader trends related to gender and parenthood in faculty salaries. But even faculty in administrative leadership in our sample with more awareness of broader trends generally view personnel actions and salaries as largely fair and meritocratic. An alternative rationale that is given for the lower salaries of women and mothers is that faculty salaries are subject to "the market," and that men are more likely to strategically seek other job offers for the purpose of raising their salaries at their home institution. However, according to our Academic Personnel data, net of department, demographics, and step, there are no gender or parenthood status differences in the likelihood of seeking a formal retention package. We do not have consistent data on informal retention offers.

43. Table 3.5 is adapted from Cech and Blair-Loy (2014, table 3). See also Jacobs and Winslow (2004).

44. Figure 3.6 is adapted from Cech and Blair-Loy (2014, fig. 1).
45. In contrast to the stigmatization of leave for family reasons, departments and colleagues generally willingly accommodate absences or reduced research efforts when faculty start a company (Lam 2010; Mars, Bresonis, and Szelényi 2014) or take a multiyear position as a program officer at the National Science Foundation, even though such efforts may be far more disruptive to research productivity than childcare responsibilities. This underscores that flexibility stigma is not triggered by accommodations per se but by real or perceived need for accommodations for caregiving specifically. Views that childcare is more disruptive and thus more stigmatized for academic scientists than commercial activity reinforces gender inequality in the form of devaluation of mothers' work commitment. Additionally, gender inequalities persist in the realm of commercial research conducted by academics. On average, women secure patents for their work less frequently than men in general, particularly in hierarchical organizational contexts like academia (Whittington and Smith-Doer 2008), and women's patents tend to be under-counted and under-valued compared to men's (Whittington and Smith-Doer 2005; Melo-Martin 2013).
46. Cech and Waidzunas (2011).
47. Cech and O'Connor (2017).

CHAPTER 4

1. Self-conceptions are the beliefs or theories that people have about themselves as individuals (Cech 2013b). People hold many self-conceptions; we focus only on those that are connected to the strands of the schema of scientific excellence we examine here.
2. We measure research impact with the H-index, which represents the number of publications a scholar has with at least that number of citations. For example, someone with an H-index of 20 has twenty publications with at least twenty citations each.
3. Our interviews asked an open-ended question: "What kinds of qualities do you think characterize excellence in your field?" If needed, we followed up with clarifying questions about whether others in the respondent's discipline would agree with their statements. Seventy-five of the eighty-five interviewees (88 percent) explicitly discussed creative brilliance in research as a marker of excellence in their fields.
4. Specifically, in our interview sample, thirteen out of twenty-seven men who were full professors (48 percent) but only six of twenty women who were full professors (30 percent) talked about and identified with their own creative brilliance. Due to the small number of URM and LGBTQ professors, we do not report their views by rank.
5. Factor analysis of the survey data indicates that these assertiveness qualities are intertwined. Assertive leadership is also orthogonal to the other strands

of the scientific excellence schema discussed below. See the appendix and figure A.1 for details.

6. These four traits of the assertiveness strand, and the assertive scale measure, are displayed as the first five bars of figure A.1.

7. See figures A.2, A.3, and A.4. Supplemental regression models did not find that the importance to respondents of these assertive characteristics in their view of excellent scientists varied by gender, race/ethnicity, LGBTQ status, career stage, or department.

8. In the survey, we use the same set of traits to ask respondents about the characteristics of an excellent member of their discipline as we use to ask them about their self-conceptions. See the appendix for details.

9. See figure A.3 for self-conceptions by gender and figure A.4 for self-conceptions by race/ethnicity. Table A.1 presents OLS regression models predicting each of these self-conceptions by demographic characteristics, department, and other career stage controls. In supplemental models with gender × race interaction terms, we do not find intersectional gender-by-race patterns on these self-conception measures.

10. The second set of bars in Figure A.1 provides the means for these three qualities. Being a good mentor and being skilled at interpersonal relationships hover slightly above the "neutral" point, but faculty are more likely to disagree than to agree that being empathetic is a marker of scientific excellence.

11. See table A.1.

12. See figure A.3 for self-conceptions of relational qualities by gender and figure A.4 for self-conceptions of relational qualities by race/ethnicity. See table A.1 for regression models predicting each self-conception with the full set of demographic and department measures and controls.

13. Specifically, we replicated the models in table A.1 with added interaction terms for woman × URM and woman × Asian. These interaction terms did not approach statistical significance, meaning that the gender patterns did not vary substantially by race/ethnicity. The subsample of LGBTQ respondents was not large enough to reliably conduct similar intersectional analyses.

14. As figure A.1 indicates, the mean on this measure is just below "neither agree nor disagree." See figure A.2 for averages by disciplinary groups. Net of gender, race/ethnicity, and other controls, biological science faculty are significantly more likely than faculty in other disciplines to value diversity promotion in their understanding of scientific excellence. Regression coefficient for biosciences: $B = .515$, $p = .024$.

15. Chapter 5 discusses depoliticization in detail. For more information, see Cech and Waidzunas (2011), Cech (2014), and Cech and Sherick (2015).

16. Women are slightly more likely than men to emphasize the importance of diversity to them personally, net of controls. See Appendix figure A.3 and table A.1.

17. As discussed in the appendix, the STEM Inclusion Study data include over seven thousand PhD-level STEM professionals in four-year universities across the country. On the same 1 to 5 scale used in figure A.1, the means on each of the scientific excellence strands were as follows: creativity: 4.20; assertive leadership: 3.82; relational skills: 3.59; diversity promotion: 3.23. See Cech and Waidzunas (2021) for detailed description and methodology of the STEM Inclusion Study survey.

18. Kristen's experiences are consistent with studies of women in men-dominated professions. Women often have to do extra emotional work to appear to fit naturally into professional networks, which are culturally and numerically dominated by men. See Blair-Loy (2001), Turco (2010), and Williams and Dempsey (2014).

19. Those with assertive self-conceptions are rewarded more highly at the case university, controlling for scholarly productivity (measured here by log average of articles published per year) and other factors (advancement step, department, gender, URM, LGBTQ status, and family status).

20. Figure 4.2 presents predicted values that control for variation by demographics, department, academic rank, and other factors; see the note below figure 4.2 for details.

21. Specifically, a survey item asked respondents the extent to which they agree that "In my department, my research is respected" (1 = strongly disagree to 5 = strongly agree). URM faculty were marginally less likely than their white and Asian colleagues to report that their research is respected ($B = -.148$, $p = .077$). See also the results in note 23.

22. Net of controls, women were more likely than men to report that they have to "work harder than their colleagues in their department to be perceived as a legitimate scholar" (coefficient for women $B = 1.01$, $p < .001$).

23. For example, women were more likely than men, net of controls for demographics, department, rank, and productivity, to agree that "my work is respected in my department" (coefficient for women $B = .729$, $p < .001$).

24. See results of OLS regression models reported in notes 28 and 30. In our data, as in STEM, white and Asian men are numerically dominant. We examined effects of white men and Asian men separately and we found that both groups similarly enjoy the advantages of being assumed to fit the expectation of assertive and brilliant scientists. In the broader society, there are differences between how white and Asian men are viewed. Asian men are more likely to be seen as feminized. These stereotypes are rooted in histories of racial oppression. Asian immigrant men in the 1800s were barred from most work except manual labor such as farming, mining, and construction, and they were also prohibited from citizenship and from bringing their families to the United States. When they were banned from even manual labor jobs, many Chinese men opened small businesses offering domestic services. This association between Asian men and domestic work began a feminized stereotype of Asian men in the United States

that lingers today (Espiritu 1997; Chen 1999; Lee 1999; Galinsky, Hall, and Cuddy 2013). However, Asian men are also stereotyped as "naturally" talented at math and science (Eglash 2002), which helps buffer them from the questions about their potential for STEM brilliance that other faculty of color often endure. As such, we do not find intersectional patterns between Asian and white men (as we do between Asian and white women).

25. See Williams and Dempsey (2014) and Cuddy, Fiske, and Glick (2008).

26. Collins (2000); Zambrana et al. (2017); Misra, Curington, and Green (2020).

27. (Williams and Dempsey 2014). For more on gender stereotypes at work, see the reviews by Foschi (2000) and Ellemers (2018).

28. Compared to white women, and to Latinx and Black women with less assertive self-conceptions, Latinx and Black women with assertive self-conceptions are penalized: they are less likely to report that their research is respected in their departments (URM × Assertive interaction term in women-only model: $B = -1.61$, $p = .043$) and more likely to report that they have to work harder than their colleagues in their discipline to be perceived as a legitimate scholar, net of discipline, rank, and productivity (URM × Assertive interaction term in women-only model: $B = 4.51$, $p = .001$). Finally, assertive Black and Latinx women are more likely than white women and Black and Latinx women who are less assertive to report that they have to work harder than others in their department to be perceived as a legitimate scholar (URM × Assertive interaction term in women-only model: $B = 3.79$, $p = .012$). Exacerbated penalties for assertive Black women are consistent with research showing that Black women are more likely than white women to be seen as unfeminine, tough, pushy, and angry (Rosette and Livingston 2012; Rosette et al. 2016; Motro et al. 2019, 2021). Latinx women are also more likely than white women to encounter backlash as overly emotional or "fiery" when acting assertively (Williams and Dempsey 2014; Williams, Phillips, and Hall 2014).

29. Racialized gender stereotypes of Asian women as hyperfeminized, passive, and docile are connected to historical contexts, including the nineteenth-century trafficking of Asian women, brought to the United States against their will and forced to work as sex workers (Tajima-Peña 1989; Espiritu 1997; Pyke and Johnson 2003). Asian women in the workplace are often viewed as competent and hardworking, but they face stereotypes of being passive and demure that undermine others' assessments of their assertiveness (Berdahl and Min 2012; Williams, Phillips, and Hall 2014; Rosette et al. 2016).

30. Specifically, compared with white women, and with Asian women without assertive self-conceptions, Asian women who have assertive self-conceptions are more likely to report their research is respected in their discipline (Asian × Assertive interaction term in women-only model: $B = 2.69$, $p = .044$) and more likely to report that their research is respected in their department (Asian × Assertive interaction term in women-only

model: $B = 2.29$, $p = .071$). These patterns also hold when Asian women are compared to Black and Latinx women.

31. For example, see social psychology research on warmth versus competence (Cuddy, Fiske, and Glick 2008), double standards and shifting standards (Foschi 1989, 1996, 2000; Foschi, Lai, and Sigerson 1994; Biernat and Fuegen 2001), backlash (Williams and Dempsey 2014), and how this can play out in STEM specifically (Cech 2007; Shafran 2017). As seen in chapter 3, these disadvantages are aggravated further for women by the work devotion schema (Blair-Loy 2003; Benard and Correll 2010; Turco 2010).

32. See Hochschild (1983) and Williams and Dempsey (2014).

33. Women with the most relational self-conceptions are marginally less likely than men colleagues and women with less relational self-conceptions to say that their research is respected in their department (woman × Relational interaction term: $B = -2.03$, $p = .057$), net of controls for discipline, rank, and productivity. Relational women are also less likely to say that they feel they "fit in" with others in their discipline (woman × Relational interaction term: $B = -1.96$, $p = .029$). In supplemental models with race-by-gender interaction terms, and aligned with the penalization of assertive Black and Latinx women noted earlier, Black and Latinx women with relational self-conceptions are more likely to experience departmental respect than Black and Latinx women with less relational self-conceptions and than white women (URM × Relational self-conception interaction term in women-only model: $B = 2.00$, $p = .049$).

34. Some incidences of disrespect and devaluation in our data may constitute gender harassment, a form of sexual harassment. Gender harassment is harmful to the well-being of targeted scientists, their research, and the scientific community as a whole. Powerful tools for preventing harassment include creating a diverse, inclusive and respectful working environment, maintained by transparency of strong university policies and accountability for those who violate them (National Academies of Sciences, Engineering, and Medicine 2018).

35. Black and Latinx women with strong diversity commitments are less likely than other Black and Latinx women and than white women to say their research is respected in their departments (URM × Diversity commitments interaction term in women-only models: $B = -3.50$, $p = .012$).

36. In women-only models, Asian women with strong diversity commitments reported less respect for their research in their discipline than white women and other Asian women with less diversity commitments, net of controls (Asian × Diversity promotion self-conception interaction term in women-only model: $B = -.906$, $p = .071$).

37. See Herek (1998) and Cech and Rothwell (2020).

38. Cech and Waidzunas (2021).

39. Specifically, net of discipline, rank, productivity, and demographics, LGBTQ faculty are significantly more likely than their non-LGBTQ colleagues to

report that they have to work harder in their discipline to be perceived as a legitimate scholar ($B = 1.32$, $p = .017$) and are less likely to say that they fit in with others in their department ($B = -1.12$, $p = .020$).

40. Controlling for demographics, discipline, and rank, LGBTQ faculty more likely than non-LGBTQ peers to agree that they tend to separate their personal and professional lives ($B = 2.31$, $p = .045$).

41. We concur with intersectionality scholars (e.g., Cole 2009) who argue that it is just as important to highlight ways beliefs and practices converge across intersecting sociodemographic categories as it is to detail intersectional differences. Such convergences reveal powerful cultural perspectives that may be perpetuated and endorsed by both those who are privileged and disadvantaged by them (Collins 2000).

42. National Science Foundation (2012); Larson, Ghaffarzadegan, and Xue (2014).

43. Berdahl and Min (2012); Rosette and Livingston (2012); Williams and Dempsey (2014); Williams, Phillips, and Hall (2014); Motro et al. (2019, 2021).

CHAPTER 5

1. Tenure review is a yearlong intensive assessment of faculty's research, teaching, and service to the department and the discipline during the assistant professor period. In addition to the evaluation by department members and senior administration within the tenure candidate's university, anonymized evaluations from experts in the field outside the university are also sought. For faculty who are successfully promoted, tenure brings the privilege of security of employment (assuming faculty abide by professional norms and regulations). Although faculty continue to be reviewed every two to three years for consideration of further promotions and raises, the basic job security of tenure is designed to protect the academic freedom of faculty to pursue and publish their academic research, even if their research is high-risk or the results are controversial.

2. Tenure assessment questions were asked of all faculty who were on the tenure track or had received tenure at the case university ($N = 163$). Specific wording of items: "Please indicate your level of agreement with the following statements regarding the tenure process in your department at [case university] [Strongly Agree to Strongly Disagree]"; "Tenure decisions in my department are based primarily on excellence in research and teaching, rather than on politics, relationships or demographics"; "Requirements for tenure are/were reasonable"; and "I understand/understood the criteria for achieving tenure/promotion."

3. Faculty at this university perceived greater clarity in the tenure process than is typical at US institutions broadly. The COACHE survey of faculty across academic institutions in the United States found that faculty rated the clarity and reasonableness of tenure expectations at their institutions between "neither clear nor unclear" and "fairly clear" (between 3 and 4

on average on a 5-point scale). There was also gender differences in these results: Women report slightly lower clarity and reasonableness compared to men. There are no systematic racial/ethnic differences in clarity and reasonableness ratings by race/ethnicity in the COACHE data (Collaborative on Academic Careers in Higher Education 2008; Lisnic, Zajicek, and Kerr 2019). The clarity and fairness that faculty in our study perceive may be due to the case university's policies regarding transparency of tenure expectations and open communication about the tenure process.

4. Posselt (2020) found similar explanations in her interviews with STEM faculty in other universities. Previous research has critiqued the "pipeline" narrative as an inaccurate account of the dearth of underrepresented groups in STEM academic departments (Xie and Shauman 2003; Branch 2016; Posselt 2020).

5. For instance, while over 10,300 Black, Latinx, and Native American US citizens and permanent residents graduated in the United States with PhDs in STEM fields over the last five years (about 2,100 per year), there are only around 3,600 Black, Latinx, and Native American Assistant STEM professors employed in US four-year colleges and universities. Authors' calculation from National Science Foundation data (National Center for Science and Engineering Statistics 2019b)

6. The names of the colleagues he mentions are pseudonyms.

7. Compared to its peer institutions, our case university is about average in its underrepresentation of women and URM faculty. However, there is striking underutilization of diversity in the pool of academically oriented PhDs compared to hired faculty. For instance, the average availability of women PhDs in the academic labor market from which our case university hires averaged about 25 percent between 1987 and 2006 (the time when the majority of faculty currently employed at the university were hired). However, in 2008, only 14 percent of faculty in STEM were women. See also note 5.

8. As we stated in chapter 1, the university follows designations used by the National Science Foundation and others that among STEM faculty, underrepresented minority (URM) faculty are those who identify as Hispanic or Latinx and/or identify as Black/African American, Native American/American Indian/Alaskan Native, or Native Hawaiian/Other Pacific Islander. On our study campus, underrepresented faculty are primarily Black (including African American) and Latinx. Because Asian/Asian Americans, including South Asians, are not underrepresented in our sample or in STEM more broadly (National Science Foundation 2013) they are generally excluded from the URM category.

9. See Ginther et al. (2011).

10. A follow-up study (Ginther et al. 2018), conducted after our data were collected, added more variables from the grant applicant's biographical sketch (including the NIH funding rank of their employer) to the models

predicting a positive funding decision. Even with these new variables, the Black-white disparity remained at 6.9 percent, a statistically significant gap. Generally, only about 20 percent of R01 applications receive funding (Lauer 2019), so a 7 or 10 percent lower likelihood of getting funded based on race is highly impactful.

11. In contrast to Christopher's assertions, research shows that applicant names do matter. For example, Kang et al. (2016) conducted an audit study of how undergraduates with names associated with Black or Asian identities are less likely to be hired, net of qualifications. This negative effect is reduced when these students "whitewash" their names to hide or deemphasize their racial connotations (Kang et al. 2016). Similarly, in an audit study, Gaddis (2015) found that prospective employers were less likely to respond to applications ostensibly from recent college graduates with names associated with Black identity compared to identically qualified applications with conventionally white names, even when the Black candidate is from a prestigious university. Other research shows that evaluators of CVs (Steinpreis, Anders, and Ritzke 1999) and other scholarly materials (Knobloch-Westerwick, Glynn, and Huge 2013) rate materials with a woman's name lower than identical materials with a man's name.

12. The degree to which extramural research grants matter depends on specialty; they are less impactful for faculty such as theoretical physicists, who don't do expensive empirical research. See Lamont (2009) on how faculty evaluation panels in non-STEM fields are similarly invested in meritocratic criteria when evaluating grant proposals.

13. See Cech and Waidzunas (2011), Cech (2014), and Cech and Sherick (2015). We also discuss depoliticization in chapters 2, 4, and 6.

14. Of course, as we discuss in chapter 2, the operation of STEM is always imbued with social, cultural, and political concerns. Depoliticization reflects a belief about how STEM can and should operate, not an empirical assessment of its operation.

15. Rivera's (2017) study of recruitment committees in academic departments found that some faculty used Google and social media to learn about top candidates' personal lives, with the justification that they were looking for clues about the likelihood that the candidate was movable and would accept the department's offer.

16. Chapter 4 reports that net of discipline, rank, productivity, and demographics, LGBTQ respondents are significantly more likely than their non-LGBTQ colleagues to report that they have to work harder in their discipline to be perceived as a legitimate scholar ($B = 1.32$, $p = .017$) and are less likely to say that they fit in with others in their department ($B = -1.12$, $p = .020$). LGBTQ faculty are more likely to separate personal and professional lives than their similar colleagues ($B = 2.31$, $p = .045$).

17. These trends are echoed in recent research on the experiences of LGBTQ professionals in STEM more broadly (Cech and Waidzunas 2021).

18. Heteronormative beliefs are beliefs that there are only two binary sexes and that only sexual attraction between people of those two sexes is "normal" and "natural." Cisnormative beliefs deride transgender or gender nonbinary identities and privilege cisgender individuals, or those who identify with their assigned sex at birth (Schilt and Westbrook 2009; Collier and Daniel 2017).

19. Cech and Rothwell (2020).

20. Johnson et al. (1995).

21. Although possibly less common than more subtle biases with "cleaned up" language, other research has found that openly sexist language and sexual harassment are still common in academic STEM. See National Academies of Science, Engineering, and Medicine (2018).

22. Fox and Stephan (2001); Kemelgor and Etzkowitz (2001); Ong et al. (2011); Sheltzer and Smith (2014).

23. As presented in chapter 4, we found that among the STEM faculty at our campus, there are no statistically significant differences in academic productivity, impact, and grant dollars won by gender or race.

24. See chapter 4 as well as Lauer (2019).

25. The proportion of faculty from underrepresented groups among full professors is less than half the proportion among assistant and associate professors.

26. Warikoo (2016) finds similar beliefs among undergraduates at elite universities.

27. See Moss Kanter (1977) and Turco (2010).

28. Biernat and Manis (1994).

CHAPTER 6

1. Lamont (1992).

2. Des Jardins (2010).

3. Weber (1958); Shapin (2008). Shapin (2008, 334) also points out an anti-Semitic strain in twentieth-century US scientific culture.

4. Shapin (2008).

5. The notion of pure scientific research being unmotivated by profit and income is rooted in sixteenth- to eighteenth-century ideas of scientists as selfless, uncompromised by moneyed interests, and focused on their calling (Shapin 2008, 2010).

6. Weber (1958); Shapin (2008); Des Jardins (2010). During this era, scientific culture adopted the upper-class European norm that dissent is to be formally directed toward scientific ideas, not toward the scientists personally (Shapin and Schaffer 1985). See chapter 2.

7. Faulkner (2000).

8. As assessed by measures of publication rates, visibility, impact ratings, and grant awards; see chapter 4.

9. The moral defense of the STEM profession's view of merit is part of the process of closure. As chapter 2 explains, closure draws boundaries between insiders and outsiders and excludes those who seem misaligned with the profession's cultural values.

10. See the discussion of professional socialization in chapter 2.

11. National Science Foundation (2012); American Institutes for Research (2014); Larson, Ghaffarzadegan, and Xue (2014).

12. "The average for tenure receipt in the sciences was 26 in 1985, and extended out past age 39 by 2003" (Goulden, Frasch, and Mason 2009).

13. O'Neill and Rothbard (2017) analyze firefighting as another mission-driven occupation, but one with a culture characterized by love, affection, and compassion.

14. Stephan (2012). This exaltation of personally meaningful work is linked to the "work devotion schema" (Blair-Loy 2003) and is an example of the "passion principle," a cultural schema that elevates passion-seeking as the most preferred, morally valued consideration for career decision-making in the white-collar labor force (Cech 2021). It aligns with deep-seated notions of individualism and self-actualization in the US, and encourages participants in the white-collar labor force to search out work that is self-expressive and fulfilling over work that would simply offer a higher salary (Cech 2021).

15. Hanks and Kniffin (2014); National Center for Science and Engineering Statistics (2019a).

16. Stephan (2012).

17. Stephan (2012).

18. See Owen-Smith and Powell (2001). Professors may generally be more critical than their university administrations are of industry-academic science collaborations (Vallas and Kleinman 2008).

19. Eleven of our eighty-five interview respondents have or had some involvement with commercialization of their research.

20. Lam (2010); Johnson (2017).

21. See Roe (1953). Also cited in Des Jardins (2010, 124).

22. In a large sample of employed parents, Glavin, Schieman, and Reid (2011) find that women and men both find incursions of work tasks, emails, and phone calls into time at home to be stressful, but women uniquely feel guilty about these incursions.

23. See chapter 3 as well as Cech and Blair-Loy (2014).

24. Drawing on Pascoe (2005), Thébaud and Taylor (2021) argue that the cultural construction of motherhood as a specter "discourages and disadvantages young women on the basis of their status as potential, rather than actual, mothers" and helps explain the attrition of many women with PhDs out of academic careers.

25. Hays (1996); Glavin, Schieman, and Reid (2011); Blair-Loy and Cech (2017). This cultural expectation is directed most intensively at white women who are not single mothers (Christopher 2012; Dow 2019). See chapter 3.

26. We constructed our Scholarly Production (SPI) database for the entire population of STEM faculty at the university with information we gathered through bibliometric websites and funding databases with information on grants received and the number and impact of publications. See the appendix for more information.

27. The one exception to this broad finding is that mothers actually published more articles per year over their careers than fathers and childless faculty in our study (see table 3.3).

28. Cech and Blair-Loy (2014).

29. Similarly, Warikoo (2016) finds that minoritized undergraduates at elite universities are commonly regarded as beneficiaries of special programs earmarked for racial/ethnic minorities.

30. Ginther et al. (2011).

31. Corrice (2009).

32. Benjamin may be referring to university outreach efforts to increase the numbers of underrepresented faculty candidates in applicant pools or shortlists and/or efforts to become aware of underrepresented scientists who may be encouraged to become future candidates. These recruitment practices are recommended by social scientists studying diversity for several reasons: first, departments hoping to address a lack of diversity in their departments cannot hire candidates who do not apply. Second, social science studies show that employers have cognitive limitations that lead them to devalue the skill and talent of underrepresented candidates, especially when there are very few of them in the pool. See Stewart and Valian (2018, 171–75) for a discussion of this literature.

33. Our survey results show that LGBTQ faculty are significantly less likely to feel they "fit in" with others in their department and significantly more likely than non-LGBTQ professors to feel that they have to work harder in their discipline to be perceived as legitimate scholars and to separate their personal and professional lives. These differences remain net of productivity, department, step, and other demographic characteristics (chap. 4).

34. Because LGBTQ identities cannot necessarily be read off the body, faculty often have to reveal their status to students for this to be known. As such, if faculty who would wish to be out to colleagues and students keep their LGBTQ status concealed, students lose out on the ability to know and potentially be mentored by someone who shares their sexual or gender minority status (Cech and Rothwell 2018).

35. Posselt (2020).

36. As we show in chapter 5, not all faculty share Ronald and Benjamin's perspective. Several faculty championed the importance of diversification efforts for better science. Additionally, editorials from prominent STEM leaders (Gallimore 2019) and leading scholars on faculty diversity (Stewart and Valian 2018; Wingfield 2020) explicitly argue that diversity enhances innovation. Research we cite in this chapter supports these claims. Yet

perspectives like Ronald's and Benjamin's were common and a logical extension of hegemonic beliefs about purity.

37. Hyde and Mertz (2009); Cech and Waidzunas (2011); Handley et al. (2015); Canning et al. (2019). Puritty et al. (2017) write, "URM students do not only need support and allies, we must be able to see ourselves in our role models and mentors."

38. Posselt (2020).

39. Puritty et al. (2017); Price (2010).

40. Women and racially minoritized students tend to receive less mentoring support from senior faculty (Fox and Stephan 2001; Kemelgor and Etzkowitz 2001; Sheltzer and Smith 2014; Puritty et al. 2017).

41. Page (2008); Perez (2019).

42. Stephan (2012); Misra et al. (2017); Zippel (2017).

43. See also Misra et al. (2017). Jacobs (2014) argues that interdisciplinarity actually does not mean the breakdown of traditional academic disciplines, and Abbott (2001) argues that interdisciplinarity might actually strengthen, rather than undermine, disciplinary boundaries.

44. Des Jardins (2010).

45. Milojević, Radicchi, and Walsh (2018).

46. Stephan (2012); National Research Council (2015).

47. Faulkner (2000); Des Jardins (2010).

48. Kuhn (1962); Latour and Woolgar (1986); Knorr-Cetina (1999).

49. Fox and Stephan (2001); Kemelgor and Etzkowitz (2001); Sheltzer and Smith (2014).

50. Hofstra et al. (2020, 9284).

51. See Domestic Policy Council (2006); Sommers (2006); Kuenzi (2008); Page (2008); Diaz-Garcia, Gonzalez-Moreno, and Saez-Martinez (2013); Nathan and Lee (2013); Levine et al. (2014); Page (2017); Perez (2019).

52. Salazar and Lant (2018).

53. Siegel (2015, 2018); Kelly and Moen (2020).

54. Newport (2016); Pang (2016).

55. See Sonnentag (2003); Fritz and Sonnentag (2006); Pang (2016).

56. Krapf, Ursprung, and Zimmermann (2017).

57. For example, Lundquist, Misra, and O'Meara (2012); Misra, Lundquist, and Templer (2012).

58. For example, Stewart and Valian (2018); Laursen and Austin (2020); Posselt (2020).

59. Cech, Blair-Loy, and Rogers (2017).

60. Reskin (2003); Stainback, Tomaskovic-Devey, and Skaggs (2010); Correll (2017).

61. Cech and Blair-Loy (2014).

62. As one example, the former family accommodation policy had provided paid family leave only for women giving birth. The university broadened paid family leave to include bonding leave for all parents of any gender when a child under eighteen joins the family. This policy reform provides

practical support and legitimacy to a more diverse and inclusive array of family caregivers. The new policy is also designed to lessen the stigma of taking family leave by associating paid leave not only with younger pregnant women but also with fathers, adoptive parents who are often older and more senior, and LGBTQ parents.

63. National Academies of Sciences, Engineering, and Medicine (2021).
64. Kalev, Dobbin, and Kelly (2006).
65. Stewart and LaVaque-Manty (2008); Fine et al. (2014); Blair-Loy et al. (2017); Stewart and Valian (2018); O'Meara, Culpepper, and Templeton (2020); Blair-Loy et al. (2022).
66. Page (2008); Perez (2019).
67. Talbot (2021).
68. See TallBear (2014); Cajete (2000, 2005); Harding (1998).

APPENDIX

1. Misra, Curington, and Green (2020).
2. Following McCall's (2005) typology, our comparisons across different axes of inequality constitute an intercategorical intersectional analysis, and our highlighting of the challenges of faculty with particular devalued identities (e.g., women of color, mothers, LGBTQ persons) adds elements of an intracategorical approach.
3. See Blair-Loy, Pecenco, and Cech (2013).
4. For example, a common problem across the labor force is the double standards that often require women and underrepresented minority groups to provide more evidence of competence than white men to be seen as equally proficient (Williams and Dempsey 2014). As another example, gender-based favoritism or homophily helps explain why men-dominated groups of decision-makers are more likely to favor other men over women in hiring and promotion; this process has been studied in law firms (Ely 1994; Gorman 2005), finance (Roth 2004), large corporations (Stainback, Kleiner, and Skaggs 2016), and other areas.
5. See Cech, Blair-Loy, and Rogers (2017).
6. See Latour (1987).
7. Our move to open up the black box of cultural definitions of merit in academic STEM draws on STS literature that has demonstrated the social construction of scientific and technological knowledge (Haraway 1988; Harding 1991; Waidzunas 2015); merit, valuation, and evaluation (Merton 1973; Latour 1987; Huutoniemi 2012; Lincoln et al. 2012; Cech 2014); devotion (Merton 1973; Shapin 2008; Fox, Fonseca, and Bao 2011); scholarly productivity (Hunter and Leahey 2010); organization (Kuhn 1962; Ezrahi 1971; Cech and Waidzunas 2016); and epistemologies (Knorr-Cetina 1999; Shapin 2008; Huutoniemi 2012; Settles et al. 2020).
8. Harding (1986, 1998); Haraway (1988).

9. Cech et al. (2011); Seymour and Hunter (2019).
10. Abbott (1988); Gorman and Sandefur (2011).
11. Posselt (2020).
12. Roach and Sauermann (2017).
13. Blair-Loy (2003).
14. Hunzaker and Valentino (2019).
15. Bem (1983, 603).
16. Norton (2019).
17. For many cognitive psychologists, schemas are the "representations of knowledge and the information-processing mechanisms" that provide short-cuts to simplify cognition (DiMaggio 1997, 269; see also Zerubavel 1997).
18. Blair-Loy (2003).
19. Some arguments reduce culture to cognitive schemas and the taken-for-granted routines of action they motivate. For example, as part of the cognitive turn in sociology, neo-institutional research has argued that culture could be reduced to these cognitive schemas among actors (DiMaggio and Powell 1991; Friedland and Alford 1991). We take a more multifaceted approach to culture, one that sees cultural schemas not only as cognitive but also as moral and emotional (Blair-Loy 2003).
20. Seron et al. (2018).
21. Ragin (1987).
22. Lamont and White (2005, 157).
23. For example, see books by Hochschild (1997), Kunda (2006), and Armstrong and Hamilton (2013) and articles by Blair-Loy and Wharton (2002), Castilla (2008), Cech and Waidzunas (2011), and Kelly and Moen (2020).
24. See Blair-Loy (1999).
25. Stephan (2012).
26. The salaries of each faculty member and administrator are published annually on a public website, and policies of checks and balances severely limit the degree to which individual professors can acquire special perquisites or retention incentives.
27. Specifically, university administration commissioned a salary study that found women faculty were significantly underpaid compared to men in their same department and at the same rank. The university took action to address these salary inequities, raising the salaries of many women faculty to counteract these salary gaps. As such, aggregate salary differentials that often occur at other universities (and were present at our case site) may be much smaller in our data than they would otherwise have been without that administrative action. This is likely also why we do not see significant negative effects of the gender coefficient in our salary models (although we do see significant negative effects of the motherhood coefficient).
28. US News and World Report (2014).
29. US News and World Report (2016a, 2016b).
30. MIT (1999); UCLA (2003); Cornell University (2006).

31. National Science Foundation (2013).
32. National Science Foundation (2013).
33. Ginther and Kahn (2012).
34. Gates and Newport (2012).
35. Hermanowicz (1998, 2009).
36. Ecklund and Lincoln (2016).
37. Xie and Shauman (2003); Smith-Doerr (2004); National Academy of Sciences (2007); Stewart and Valian (2018); Posselt (2020).
38. Sewell Jr. (1992).
39. See Cech and Waidzunas (2021) for detailed description of the STEM Inclusion Study data collection and survey methodology. The STEM Inclusion Study was funded by the National Science Foundation (grant numbers 1665117 and 1535385).
40. See Cech and Waidzunas (2021, table S2).
41. Blair-Loy (1999).
42. Lamont and White (2005).
43. Gerson and Damaske (2020).
44. Our data were collected several years before this book's publication, but we do not expect that the foundational schemas we analyze have shifted greatly in the intervening years. As we note earlier, these schemas are salient in data collected in a much broader population of academic STEM workers in 2018. Schemas like work devotion and the scientific excellence schema are slow to change because they are deeply ensconced in the professional culture of STEM; see chapter 2.
45. www.familiesandwork.org.
46. Cech, Blair-Loy and Rogers (2018).
47. Allison (2002).
48. The grants office at our case site had data on grant awards that are currently active or have end dates after 2001.
49. Ginther et al. (2011).
50. To assess the quality of data produced by SCOPUS, we compared the listings of academic works across three sources: Academic Personnel CVs (graciously given to us by three STEM faculty members at our university), Web of Science, and SCOPUS. We found that Web of Science had significantly more discrepancies when looking for individuals with more common last names than did SCOPUS. During our comparison, we found that the data provided from SCOPUS matched identically to the CVs provided by the participants. Not only does SCOPUS give us the data on each publication, but the database also provides us with all of the aggregate productivity measures necessary for analysis.
51. See http://www.journalmetrics.com/sjr.php for more information on the SJR journal prestige metric.
52. For number of citations and H-index values, SCOPUS had data only since 1995. When using these measures in our analysis, our models control for respondents' step to help correct for the truncation of these variables.

53. Long, Allison, and McGinnis (1993); Wenneras and Wold (1997); Xie and Shauman (1998); McBrier (2003); Judge, Kammeyer-Mueller, and Bretz (2004); Hirsch (2005, 2007); Lee and Bozeman (2005); Leahey (2007); Ginther et al. (2011).
54. Ginther et al. (2011, 2018); Kolev, Fuentes-Medel, and Murray (2019).
55. Sarsons (2017).
56. Leahey (2006); Maliniak, Powers, and Walter (2013); West et al. (2013); King et al. (2017).
57. Lamont and White (2005).
58. Cluster sampling is a useful recruitment strategy for identifying potential underrepresented interview participants, as researchers have the opportunity to speak with individuals who otherwise would have declined to participate in research with a complete stranger (Lamont and White 2005).
59. None of the interview respondents identified as outside the gender binary.
60. Gerson and Damaske (2020).
61. A confirmatory factor analysis (CFA) suggests that these measures are a part of the same subjective experience of organizational dedication: coefficient estimates are all significant at the $p < .001$ level ($\chi^2 = 7.516$, $df = 2$, CFI = .960, RMSEA = .074), and the standardized coefficient estimates are as follows: "extra effort," .36; "same values," .60; "care about the fate," .62; and "inspire the best," .74.
62. The skewness and kurtosis values for the flexibility stigma variable are within assumptions for approximate normality: skewness = 0.31; kurtosis = 2.28.
63. None of our survey respondents identified as outside the gender binary.

References

Abbott, Andrew. 1981. "Status and Status Strain in the Professions." *American Journal of Sociology* 81:819–35.

———. 1988. *The Systems of Professions: An Essay on the Division of Expert Labor.* Chicago: University of Chicago Press.

———. 2001. *Chaos of Disciplines.* Chicago: University of Chicago Press.

Acker, Joan. 1990. "Hierarchies, Jobs, Bodies: A Theory of Gendered Organizations." *Gender and Society* 4 (2): 139–58.

Allison, Paul D. 2002. *Missing Data: Quantitative Applications in the Social Sciences.* Thousand Oaks, CA: Sage.

American Institutes for Research (AIR). 2014. *The Nonacademic Careers of STEM PhD Holders.* Washington, DC: STEM at American Institutes for Research.

Amott, Teresa L., and Julie A. Matthaei. 1996. *Race, Gender and Work: A Multicultural Economic History of Women in the United States.* Boston: South End.

Andersen, Jens Peter, Mathias Wullum Nielsen, Nicole L. Simone, Resa E. Lewiss, and Reshma Jagsi. 2020. "COVID-19 Medical Papers Have Fewer Women First Authors Than Expected." *eLife* 9. https://doi.org/10.7554/eLife.58807.

Armstrong, Elizabeth E., and Laura T. Hamilton. 2013. *Paying for the Party: How College Maintains Inequality.* Cambridge, MA: Harvard University Press.

Barley, Stephen R., and Pamela S. Tolbert. 1997. "Institutionalization and Structuration: Studying the Links between Action and Institution." *Organization Studies* 18 (1): 93–117.

Beasley, Maya. 2011. *Opting Out: Losing the Potential of America's Young Black Elite.* Chicago: University of Chicago Press.

Becker, Howard, Blanche Geer, Everett C. Hughes, and Anselm L. Strauss. 1961. *Boys in White: Student Culture in Medical School.* New Brunswick, NJ: Transactional.

Beisel, Nicola, and Tamara Kay. 2004. "Abortion, Race, and Gender in Nineteenth-Century America." *American Sociological Review* 69:498–518.

Bem, Sandra Lipsitz. 1983. "Gender Schema Theory and Its Implications for Child Development: Raising Gender-Aschematic Children in a Gender-Schematic Society." *Signs* 8:598–616.

Benard, Stephen, and Shelley J. Correll. 2010. "Normative Discrimination and the Motherhood Penalty." *Gender and Society* 24:616–46.

Berdahl, Jennifer L., Marianne Cooper, Peter Glick, Robert W. Livingston, and Joan C. Williams. 2018. "Work as a Masculinity Contest." *Journal of Social Issues* 74 (3): 422–48. https://doi.org/10.1111/josi.12289.

Berdahl, Jennifer, and J.-A. Min. 2012. "Prescriptive Stereotypes and Workplace Consequences for East Asians in North America." *Cultural Diversity and Ethnic Minority Psychology* 18:141–52.

Berdahl, Jennifer L., and Sue H. Moon. 2013. "Workplace Mistreatment of Middle Class Workers Based on Sex, Parenthood, and Caregiving." *Journal of Social Issues* 69 (2): 341–66.

Biernat, Monica. 2003. "Toward a Broader View of Social Stereotyping." *American Psychologist* 58 (12): 1019–27.

Biernat, Monica, and Kathleen Fuegen. 2001. "Shifting Standards and the Evaluation of Competence: Complexity in Gender-Based Judgment and Decision Making." *Journal of Social Issues* 57 (4): 707–24.

Biernat, Monica, and M. Manis. 1994. "Shifting Standards and Stereotype-Based Judgements." *Journal of Personality and Social Psychology* 66:5–20.

Bilimoria, Diana, and Abigail J. Stewart. 2009. "'Don't Ask, Don't Tell': The Academic Climate for Lesbian, Gay, Bisexual and Transgender Faculty in Science and Engineering." *NWSA Journal* 21 (2): 85–103.

Blair-Loy, Mary. 1999. "Career Patterns of Executive Women in Finance: An Optimal Matching Analysis." *American Journal of Sociology* 104 (5): 1346–97.

———. 2001. "It's Not Just What You Know, It's Who You Know: Technical Knowledge, Rainmaking, and Gender among Finance Executives." *Research in the Sociology of Work* 10:51–83.

———. 2003. *Competing Devotions: Career and Family among Women Executives*. Cambridge, MA: Harvard University Press.

———. 2010. "Moral Dimensions of the Work-Family Nexus." In *Handbook of the Sociology of Morality*, edited by Steven Hitlin and Stephen Vaisey. New York: Springer.

Blair-Loy, Mary, and Erin A. Cech. 2017. "Demands & Devotion: Cultural Meanings of (Over)work among Women in Science and Technology Industries." *Sociological Forum* 32 (1): 5–27.

Blair-Loy, Mary, Olga Mayorova, Pamela C. Cosman, and Stephanie Fraley. 2022. "Rubrics Are Susceptible to Gender Bias yet Their Use May Still Promote the Hiring of Women Faculty in Engineering." Unpublished manuscript. UC San Diego.

Blair-Loy, Mary, Laura Pecenco, and Erin Cech. 2013. *The Persistence of Male Power and Prestige in the Professions: Report on the Professions of Law, Medicine, and Science and Engineering.* San Diego: Center for Research on Gender in STEMM, UC San Diego.

Blair-Loy, Mary, Laura Rogers, Daniela Glaser, Anne Wong, Danielle Abraham, and Pamela C. Cosman. 2017. "Gender in Engineering Departments: Are There Gender Differences in Interruptions of Academic Job Talks?" *Social Sciences* 6 (1): 29.

Blair-Loy, Mary, and Amy S. Wharton. 2004. "Mothers in Finance: Surviving and Thriving." *Annals of the American Academy of Political and Social Science* 596:151–71.

Blair-Loy, Mary, and Stacy J. Williams. 2016. "Long Hours and the Work Devotion Schema: The Case of Executive Men in the United States." In *Work-Family Dynamics and the Competing Logics of Regulation, Economy and Morals*, edited by Berit Brandth, Sigtona Halrynjo and Elin Kvande. New York: Routledge.

———. 2017. "Devoted Workers, Breadwinning Fathers: The Case of Executive Men in the United States." In *Fathers in Work Organizations: Inequalities and Capabilities, Rationalities and Politics*, edited by M. Oechsle and B. Liebig. Berlin: Budrich.

Bloor, David. 1976. *Knowledge and Social Imagery.* New York: Routledge.

Bobo, Lawrence. 2000. "Reclaiming a DuBoisian Perspective on Racial Attitudes." *Annals of the American Academy of Political and Social Science* 568 (1): 186–202.

Bourdieu, Pierre. 1984. *Distinction: A Social Critique of the Judgment of Taste.* Translated by Richard Nice. Cambridge, MA: Harvard University Press.

Branch, E. H. 2016. *Pathways, Potholes, and the Persistence of Women in Science: Reconsidering the Pipeline.* Lanham, MD: Lexington.

Broverman, I. K., S. R. Vogel, D. M. Broverman, F. E. Clarkson, and P. S. Rosenkrantz. 1972. "Sex-Role Stereotypes: A Current Appraisal." *Journal of Social Issues* 28 (2): 59–78.

Budig, Michelle J., and Paula England. 2001. "The Wage Penalty for Motherhood." *American Sociological Review* 66 (2): 204–25.

Budig, Michelle J., and Melissa J. Hodges. 2010. "Difference in Disadvantage: Variation in the Motherhood Penalty across White Women's Earning Distribution." *American Sociological Review* 75:705–28.

Burrelli, Joan. 2008. *Thirty-Three Years of Women in S&E Faculty Positions.* Washington, DC: National Science Foundation, National Center for Science and Engineering Statistics.

Cajete, Gregory. 2000. *Native Science: Natural Laws of Interdependence.* Santa Fe, NM: ClearLight.

———. 2005. "American Indian Epistemologies." In *Serving Native American Students: New Directions for Student Service*, edited by Mary Jo Tippeconnic Fox, Shelly C. Lowe, and George S. McClellen. San Francisco: Jossey-Bass.

Canning, Elizabeth A., Katherine Muenks, Dorainne J. Green, and Mary C. Murphy. 2019. "STEM Faculty Who Believe Ability Is Fixed Have Larger Racial Achievement Gaps and Inspire Less Student Motivation in Their Classes." *Science Advances* 5 (2): eaau4734.

Castilla, Emilio. 2008. "Gender, Race, and Meritocracy in Organizational Careers." *American Journal of Sociology* 113 (6): 1479–526.

Castro, Athena R., and Christopher S. Collins. 2021. "Asian American Women in STEM in the Lab with 'White Men Named John.'" *Science Education* 105 (1): 33–61.

Cech, Erin A. 2007. "Dilbert in Stilettos: The Character of Deterrants Facing Women in Engineering." In *Gender and Engineering: Strategies and Possibilities*, edited by I. Welpe, J. Larkin and B. Reschka. Bern: Peter Lang.

———. 2013a. "Ideological Wage Gaps? The Technical/Social Dualism and the Gender Wage Gap in Engineering." *Social Forces* 91 (4): 1147–82.

———. 2013b. "The (Mis)Framing of Social Justice: Why Meritocracy and Depoliticization Hinder Engineers' Ability to Think about Social Injustices." In *Engineering Education for Social Justice: Critical Explorations and Opportunities*, edited by Juan C. Lucena, 64–87. New York: Springer.

———. 2014. "Culture of Disengagement in Engineering Education?" *Science, Technology, and Human Values* 39 (1): 42–72.

———. 2015. "Engineers and Engineeresses? Self-Conceptions and the Development of Gendered Professional Identities." *Sociological Perspectives* 58 (1): 56–77.

———. 2021. *The Trouble with Passion: How Searching for Fulfillment at Work Fosters Inequality*. Berkeley: University of California Press.

Cech, Erin A., and Mary Blair-Loy. 2010. "Perceiving Glass Ceilings? Meritocratic versus Structural Explanations of Gender Inequality among Women in Science and Technology." *Social Problems* 57 (3): 371–97.

———. 2014. "Consequences of Flexibility Stigma among Academic Scientists and Engineers." *Work and Occupations* 41 (1): 86–110.

———. 2019. "The Changing Career Trajectories of New Parents in STEM." *Proceedings of the National Academy of Sciences* 116 (10): 4182–87.

Cech, Erin A., Mary Blair-Loy, and Laura Rogers. 2017. "Recognizing Chilliness: How Cultural Schemas of Inequality Frame STEM Faculty's Views of Departmental Climates and Professional Cultures." *American Journal of Cultural Sociology* 6 (1): 125–60.

Cech, Erin A., Anneke Metz, and Jessi L. Smith. 2019. "Cultural Processes of Ethnoracial Disadvantage for Native American College Students." *Social Forces* 91 (1): 355–80.

Cech, Erin A., and Lindsey Trimble O'Connor. 2017. "'Like Second-Hand Smoke': The Toxic Effect of Workplace Flexibility Bias for Workers' Health." *Community, Work and Family* 20 (5): 543–72.

Cech, Erin A., Laura Pecenco, and Mary Blair-Loy. 2013. *Science and Technology Professions: The Status of Women and Men*. San Diego: Center for Research on Gender in STEMM, UC San Diego. https://crg-stemm.ucsd.edu/.

Cech, Erin A., and William R. Rothwell. 2018. "LGBTQ Inequality in Engineering Education." *Journal of Engineering Education* 107 (4): 583–610.

———. 2020. "LGBT Workplace Inequality in the Federal Workforce: Intersectional Processes, Organizational Contexts, and Turnover Considerations." *ILR Review* 73 (1): 25–60.

Cech, Erin A., Brian Rubineau, Susan Silbey, and Caroll Seron. 2011. "Professional Role Confidence and Gendered Persistence in Engineering." *American Sociological Review* 76:641–66.

Cech, Erin A., and Heidi M. Sherick. 2015. "Depoliticization and the Structure of Engineering Education." In *International Perspectives on Engineering Education*, edited by Steen Hyldgaard Christensen et al., 203–16. New York: Springer.

Cech, Erin A., and Tom Waidzunas. 2011. "Navigating the Heteronormativity of Engineering: The Experience of Lesbian, Gay, and Bisexual Students." *Engineering Studies* 3 (1): 1–24.

———. 2016. "LGBTQ@NASA: Workplace Climates, Employee Resource Groups, and Professional Credibility at the Space Agency." Working paper. Ann Arbor: University of Michigan.

———. 2021. "Systemic Inequalities for LGBTQ Professionals in STEM." *Science Advances* 7 (3): abe0933.

Charles, Maria. 2011. "What Gender Is Science." *Contexts* 10 (2): 22–28.

Chen, Anthony. 1999. "Lives at the Center of the Periphery, Lives at the Periphery of the Center: Chinese American Masculinities and Bargaining with Hegemony." *Gender and Society* 13:587–607.

Christopher, Karen. 2012. "Extensive Mothering: Employed Mothers' Constructions of the Good Mother." *Gender and Society* 26 (1): 73–96.

Cole, Elizabeth R. 2009. "Intersectionality and Research in Psychology." *American Psychologist* 64 (3): 170–80.

Cole, Jonathan R., and Steven Cole. 1973. *Social Stratification in Science*. Chicago: University of Chicago Press.

Collaborative on Academic Careers in Higher Education. 2008. *Selected Results from the COACHE Tenure-Track Faculty Job Satisfaction Survey*. Cambridge, MA: Harvard Graduate School of Education.

Collier, M., and M. Daniel. 2017. "The Production of Trans Illegality: Cisnormativity in the US Immigration System." *Sociological Compass* 13 (4): e12666.

Collins, Caitlyn. 2019. *Making Motherhood Work: How Women Manage Careers and Caregiving*. Princeton, NJ: Princeton University Press.

Collins, Patricia Hill. 2000. *Black Feminist Thought: Knowledge, Consciousness, and the Politics of Empowerment*. New York: Routledge.

Congressional Research Service. 2020. *US Research and Development Funding and Performance: Fact Sheet R443407*. https://crsreports.congress.gov/product/pdf/R/R44307.

Connell, R. W., and James W. Messerschmidt. 2005. "Hegemonic Masculinity: Rethinking the Concept." *Gender and Society* 19 (6): 829–59.

Cornell University. 2006. *Faculty Work Life Survey Results*. Cornell University.

Correll, Shelley J. 2001. "Gender and the Career Choice Process: The Role of Biased Self-Assessment." *American Journal of Sociology* 106 (6): 1691–730.

———. 2017. "SWS 2016 Feminist Lecture: Reducing Gender Biases in Modern Workplaces: A Small Wins Approach to Organizational Change." *Gender and Society* 31 (6): 725–50.

Correll, Shelley J., Stephen Benard, and In Paik. 2007. "Getting a Job: Is There a Motherhood Penalty." *American Journal of Sociology* 112 (5): 1297–339.

Corrice, A. 2009. "Unconscious Bias in Faculty and Leadership Recruitment." *Association of American Medical Colleges* 9 (2): 1–2.

Cott, Nancy. 1977. *The Bonds of Womanhood.* New Haven, CT: Yale University Press.

Cuddy, A. J. C., S. T. Fiske, and P. Glick. 2008. "Warmth and Competence as Universal Dimensions of Social Perception: The Stereotype Content Model and the BIAS Map." In *Advances in Experimental Social Psychology*, edited by M. P. Zanna, 61–149. New York: Academic.

Cuddy, Amy J. C., Susan T. Fiske, and Peter Glick. 2004. "When Professionals Become Mothers, Warmth Doesn't Cut the Ice." *Journal of Social Issues* 60:701–18.

Davies, Andrea Rees, and Brenda D. Frink. 2014. "The Origins of the Ideal Worker: The Separation of Work and Home in the United States From the Market Revolution to 1950." *Work and Occupations* 41 (1): 18–39.

de Melo-Martín, Inmaculada. 2013. "Patenting and the Gender Gap: Should Women Be Encouraged to Patent More?" *Science and Engineering Ethics* 19:491–504.

Des Jardins, Julie. 2010. *The Madame Curie Complex: The Hidden History of Women in Science.* New York: Feminist.

Diaz-Garcia, Cristina, Angela Gonzalez-Moreno, and Francisco Jose Saez-Martinez. 2013. "Gender Diversity within R&D Teams: Its Impact on Radicalness of Innovation." *Organization and Management* 15 (2): 149–60.

DiMaggio, Paul. 1997. "Culture and Cognition." *Annual Review of Sociology* 23: 263–287.

DiMaggio, Paul, and Walter W. Powell. 1983. "The Iron Cage Revisited: Institutional Isomorphism and Collective Rationality in Organizational Fields." *American Sociological Review* 48 (2): 147–60.

———. 1991. "Introduction." In *The New Institutionalism in Organizational Analysis*, edited by Walter W. Powell DiMaggio and J. Paul, 1–38. Chicago: University of Chicago Press.

DiTomaso, Nancy. 2012. *The American Non-Dilemma: Racial Inequality Without Racism.* New York: Russell Sage.

Dobbin, Frank. 2009. *Inventing Equal Opportunity.* Princeton, NJ: Princeton University Press.

Dobbin, Frank, and Alexandra Kalev. 2016. "Why Diversity Programs Fail." *Harvard Business Review* 94 (7). https://hbr.org/2016/07/why-diversity-programs-fail.

Domestic Policy Council. 2006. *American Competitiveness Initiative.* Office of Science and Technology Policy, Washington, DC.

Dow, Dawn Marie. 2019. *Mothering while Black: Boundaries and Burdens of Middle-Class Parenthood*. Berkeley: University of California Press.

Dryburgh, Heather. 1999. "Work Hard, Play Hard: Women and Professionalization in Engineering—Adapting to the Culture." *Gender and Society* 13 (5): 664–82.

Duhem, Pierre. 1996. "To Save the Phenomena: Essay on the Concept of Physical Theory from Plato to Galileo." In *Pierre Duhem: Essays in the History and Philosophy of Science*, edited by Ariew and Barker. Indianapolis: Hackett.

Eaton, Asia A., Jessica F. Saunders, Ryan K. Jacobson, and Keon West. 2019. "How Gender and Race Stereotypes Impact the Advancement of Scholars in STEM: Professors' Biased Evaluations of Physics and Biology Post-Doctoral Candidates." *Sex Roles* 82:127–41.

Ecklund, Elaine Howard, and Anne E. Lincoln. 2016. *Failing Families, Failing Science: Work-Family Conflict in Academic Science*. New York: New York University Press.

Ecklund, Elaine Howard, Anne E. Lincoln, and Cassandra Tansey. 2012. "Gender Segregation in Elite Academic Science." *Gender and Society* 26 (5): 693–717.

Edelman, Lauren B. 1990. "Legal Environments and Organizational Governance: The Expansion of Due Process in the American Workplace." *American Journal of Sociology* 95:1401–40.

Edelman, Lauren B., Christopher Uggen, and Howard S. Erlanger. 1999. "The Endogeneity of Legal Regulation: Grievance Procedures as Rational Myth." *American Journal of Sociology* 105:406–54.

Eglash, Ron. 2002. "Race, Sex, and Nerds: From Black Geeks to Asian American Hipsters." *Social Text* 20 (2): 49–64.

Eisenhart, Margaret A., Elizabeth Finkel, Linda Behm, Nancy Lawerence, and Karen Tonso. 1998. *Women's Science: Leading and Succeeding from the Margins*. Chicago: University of Chicago Press.

Ellemers, Naomi. 2001. "Individual Upward Mobility and the Perceived Legitimacy of Intergroup Relations." In *The Psychology of Legitimacy: Emerging Perspective on Ideology, Justice, and Intergroup Relations*, edited by J. T. Jost and B. Major. Cambridge, UK: Cambridge University Press.

———. 2018. "Gender Stereotypes." *Annual Review of Psychology* 69 (1): 275–98.

Ely, Robin J. 1994. "The Effects of Organizational Demographics and Social Identity on Relationships among Professional Women." *Administrative Science Quarterly* 39 (2): 203–38.

Enriquez, Laura E., and Abigail C. Saguy. 2016. "Coming out of the Shadows: Harnessing a Cultural Schema to Advance the Undocumented Immigrant Youth Movement." *American Journal of Cultural Sociology* 4 (1): 107–30.

Espiritu, Yen L. 1997. *Asian American Women and Men*. Thousand Oaks, CA: Sage.

Ezrahi, Yaron. 1971. "The Political Resources of American Science." *Social Studies of Science* 1:117–33.

Faulkner, Wendy. 2000. "Dualism, Hierarchies and Gender in Engineering." *Social Studies of Science* 30 (5): 759–92.

Fine, Eve, Jennifer Sheridan, Molly Carnes, Jo Handelsman, Christine Pribbenow, Julia Savoy, and Amy Wendt. 2014. "Minimizing the Influence of Gender Bias on the Faculty Search Process." *Advances in Gender Research* 19:267–89.

Flaherty, Colleen. 2020. "No Room of One's Own: Early Journal Submission Data Suggest COVID-19 Is Tanking Women's Research Productivity." *Inside Higher Ed*, April 21. https://www.insidehighered.com/news/2020/04/21/early -journal-submission-data-suggest-covid-19-tanking-womens-research-produc tivity.

———. 2021. "Multiple Black Professors Have Resigned in Recent Years over Racism." *Inside Higher Ed*, May 3. https://www.insidehighered.com/news/2021/05/03 /multiple-black-professors-have-resigned-recent-years-over-racism.

Fleck, Ludwick. 1979. *Genesis and Development of a Scientific Fact*. Translated by Fred Bradley. Edited by Robert K. Merton and Thaddeus J. Trenn. Chicago: University of Chicago Press.

Fligstein, Neil. 1990. *The Transformation of Corporate Control*. Cambridge, MA: Harvard University Press.

Foschi, Martha. 1989. "Status Characteristics, Standards, and Attributions." In *Sociological Theories in Progress: New Formulations*, edited by Joseph Berger, Morris Zelditch Jr., and Bo Anderson, 58–72. Newbury Park, CA: Sage.

———. 1996. "Double Standards in the Evaluation of Men and Women." *Social Psychology Quarterly* 59:237–54.

———. 2000. "Double Standards for Competence: Theory and Research." *Annual Review of Sociology* 26:21–42.

Foschi, Martha, Larissa Lai, and Kirsten Sigerson. 1994. "Gender and Double Standards in the Assessment of Job Applicants." *Social Psychology Quarterly* 57 (4): 326–39.

Fox, Mary Frank. 2001. "Women, Science, and Academia: Graduate Education and Careers." *Gender and Society* 15 (5): 654–66.

Fox, Mary Frank, Carolyn Fonseca, and Jinghui Bao. 2011. "Work and Family Conflict in Academic Science: Patterns and Predictors among Women and Men in Research Universities." *Social Studies of Science* 41:715–35.

Fox, Mary F., and Paula E. Stephan. 2001. "Careers of Young Scientists: Preferences, Prospects and Realities by Gender and Field." *Social Studies of Science* 31 (1): 109–22.

Freidson, Eliot. 1971. *The Professions and Their Prospects*. Beverly Hills, CA: Sage.

———. 2001. *Professionalism: The Third Logic*. Chicago: University of Chicago Press.

Friedland, Roger, and Robert R. Alford. 1991. "Bringing Society Back In: Symbols, Practices, and Institutional Contradictions." In *The New Institutionalism in Organizational Analysis*, edited by Walter W. DiMaggio and J. Paul, 232–63. Chicago: University of Chicago Press.

Fritz, Charlotte, and Sabine Sonnentag. 2006. "Recovery, Well-Being, and Performance-Related Outcomes: The Role of Workload and Vacation Experiences." *Journal of Applied Psychology* 91 (4): 936–45.

Gaddis, S. Michael. 2015. "Discrimination in the Credential Society: An Audit Study of Race and College Selectivity in the Labor Market." *Social Forces* 93 (4): 1451–79.

Galinsky, Adam D., Erika V. Hall, and Amy J. C. Cuddy. 2013. "Gendered Races: Implications for Interracial Marriage, Leadership Selection, and Athletic Participation." *Psychological Sciences* 24:498–506.

Gallimore, Alec D. 2019. "An Engineering School with Half of Its Leadership Female? How Did That Happen?" *Chronicle of Higher Education*, May 1. https://www.chronicle.com/article/an-engineering-school-with-half-of-its-leadership-female-how-did-that-happen/.

Garey, Anita I. 1995. "Constructing Motherhood on the Night Shift: 'Working Mothers' and 'Stay-at-Home Moms.'" *Qualitative Sociology* 18 (4): 415–37.

Gates, Gary, and Frank Newport. 2012. "Special Report: 3.4% of U.S. Adults Identify as LGBT." Gallup. http://www.gallup.com/poll/158066/special-report-adults-identifylgbt.aspx.

Gerson, Kathleen, and Sarah Damaske. 2020. *The Science and Art of Interviewing*. Oxford: Oxford University Press.

Gewin, Virginia. 2020. "The Time Tax Put on Scientists of Colour." *Nature* 583: 479–81.

Ginther, Donna K., Jodi Basner, Unni Jensen, Joshua Schnell, Raynard Kington, and Walter T. Schaffer. 2018. "Publications as Predictors of Racial and Ethnic Differences in NIH Research Awards." *PLOS ONE* 13 (11): e0205929.

Ginther, Donna K., and Shulamit Kahn. 2012. "Education and Academic Career Outcomes for Women of Color in Science and Engineering." Women in Science, Engineering, and Medicine, Washington, DC, October 8, 2012.

Ginther, Donna K., Walter T. Schaffer, Joshua Schnell, Beth Masimore, Faye Liu, Laurel L. Haak, and Raynard Kington. 2011. "Race, Ethnicity, and NIH Research Awards." *Science* 333 (6045): 1015–19.

Glavin, Paul, Scott Schieman, and Sarah Reid. 2011. "Boundary-Spanning Work Demands and their Consequences for Guilt and Psychological Distress." *Journal of Health and Social Behavior* 52 (1): 43–57.

Gorman, Elizabeth H. 2005. "Gender Stereotypes, Same-Gender Preferences, and Organizational Variation in the Hiring of Women: Evidence from Law Firms." *American Sociological Review* 70:702–28.

Gorman, Elizabeth H., and Julie A. Kmec. 2009. "Hierarchical Rank and Women's Organizational Mobility: Glass Ceilings in Corporate Law Firms." *American Journal of Sociology* 114 (5): 1428–74.

Gorman, Elizabeth H., and Rebecca L. Sandefur. 2011. "'Golden Age,' Quiescence, and Revival: How the Sociology of Professions Became the Study of Knowledge-Based Work." *Work and Occupations* 38 (3): 275–302.

Goulden, Marc, Karie Frasch, and Mary Ann Mason. 2009. *Staying Competitive: Patching America's Leaky Pipeline in the Sciences*. Berkeley: Center for American Progress, University of California.

Gramsci, Antonio. 1992. *Prison Notebooks*. Edited by Joseph A. Buttigieg. New York: Columbia University Press.

Grusky, David G., and Jesper B. Sorensen. 1998. "Can Class Analysis Be Salvaged?" *American Journal of Sociology* 103:1187–234.

Haas, Jack, and William Shaffir. 1991. *Becoming Doctors*. New York: Elsevier.

Halrynjo, Sigtona, and Selma Theresa Lyng. 2009. "Preferences, Constraints or Schemas of Devotion? Exploring Norwegian Mothers' Withdrawals of High-Commitment Careers." *British Journal of Sociology* 60 (2): 321–34.

Handley, Ian M., Elizabeth R. Brown, Corinne A. Moss-Racusin, and Jessi L. Smith. 2015. "Quality of Evidence Revealing Subtle Gender Biases in Science Is in the Eye of the Beholder." *Proceedings of the National Academy of Sciences* 112 (43): 13201.

Hanks, Andrew, and Kevin Kniffin. 2014. "Early Career PhD Salaries: The Industry Premium and Interdisciplinary Debate." *Applied Economics Letters* 21 (18): 1277–82.

Haraway, Donna. 1988. "Situated Knowledges: The Science Question in Feminism and the Privilege of Partial Perspective." *Feminist Studies* 14 (3): 575–99.

Harding, Sandra G. 1986. *The Science Question in Feminism*. Ithaca, NY: Cornell University Press.

———. 1991. *Whose Science? Whose Knowledge? Thinking from Women's Lives*. Ithaca, NY: Cornell University Press.

———. 1998. *Is Science Multicultural? Postcolonialisms, Feminisms, and Epistemologies*. Bloomington: Indiana University Press.

Hays, Sharon. 1996. *The Cultural Contradictions of Motherhood*. New Haven, CT: Yale University Press.

Herek, Gregory M. 1998. *Stigma and Sexual Orientation: Understanding Prejudice against Lesbians, Gay Men, and Bisexuals*. Thousand Oaks, CA: Sage.

Hermanowicz, Joseph. 1998. *The Stars Are Not Enough: Scientists—Their Passion and Profession*. Chicago: University of Chicago Press.

———. 2009. *Lives in Science: How Institutions Affect Academic Careers*. Chicago: University of Chicago Press.

Herzig, Rebecca. 2004. "The Matter of Race in Histories of American Technology." In *Technology and the African-American Experience*, edited by Bruce Sinclair. Boston: MIT Press.

Hirsch, J. E. 2005. "An Index to Quantify an Individual's Scientific Research Output." *Proceedings of the National Academy of Sciences* 102 (46): 16569–72.

———. 2007. "Does the H Index Have Predictive Power?" *Proceedings of the National Academy of Sciences* 104 (49): 19193–38.

Hochschild, Arlie Russell. 1983. *The Managed Heart: Commercialization of Human Feeling*. Berkeley: University of California Press.

———. 1997. *The Time Bind: When Work Becomes Home and Home Becomes Work*. New York: Metropolitan.

Hochschild, Jennifer. 1995. *Facing Up to the American Dream: Race, Class, and the Soul of the Nation*. Princeton, NJ: Princeton University Press.

Hoffman, Moshe, Uri Gneezy, and John A. List. 2011. "Nurture Affects Gender Differences in Spatial Abilities." *Proceedings of the National Academy of Sciences* 108 (36): 14786–88.

Hofstra, Bas, Vivek V. Kulkarni, Sebastian Munoz-Najar Galvez, Bryan He, Dan Jurafsky, and Daniel A. McFarland. 2020. "The Diversity-Innovation Paradox in Science." *Proceedings of the National Academy of Sciences* 117 (17): 9284–91.

Hughes, Thomas. 2004. *American Genesis: A Century of Invention and Technological Enthusiasm, 1870–1970.* Chicago: University of Chicago Press.

Hunter, Laura A., and Erin Leahey. 2010. "Parenting and Research Productivity: New Evidence and Methods." *Social Studies of Science* 40 (3): 433–51.

Hunzaker, M. B. Fallin, and Lauren Valentino. 2019. "Mapping Cultural Schemas: From Theory to Method." *American Sociological Review* 84 (5): 950–81.

Huutoniemi, Katri. 2012. "Communicating and Compromising on Disciplinary Expertise in the Peer Review of Research Proposals." *Social Studies of Science* 42 (6): 897–21.

Hyde, Janet S., and Janet E. Mertz. 2009. "Gender, Culture, and Mathematics Performance." *Proceedings of the National Academy of Sciences* 106 (22): 8801.

Jacobs, Jerry A. 2014. *In Defense of Disciplines: Interdisciplinarity and Specialization in the Research University.* Chicago: University of Chicago Press.

Jacobs, Jerry A., and Kathleen Gerson. 2004. *The Time Divide: Work, Family, and Gender Inequality.* Cambridge, MA: Harvard University Press.

Jacobs, Jerry A., and Sarah E. Winslow. 2004. "The Academic Life Course, Time Pressures and Gender Inequality." *Community, Work and Family* 7 (2): 143–61.

Johnson, Cathryn, Barry Markovsky, Michael Lovaglia, and Karen Heimer. 1995. "Sexual Orientation as a Diffuse Status Characteristic: Implications for Small Group Interaction." *Advances in Group Processes* 12:115–37.

Johnson, David R. 2017. *A Fractured Profession: Commercialization and Conflict in Academic Sciences.* Baltimore, MD: Johns Hopkins University.

Jordan, John M. 1994. *Machine-Age Ideology: Social Engineering and American Liberalism, 1911–1939.* Chapel Hill: University of North Carolina Press.

Judge, T. A., J. Kammeyer-Mueller, and R. D. Bretz. 2004. "A Longitudinal Model of Sponsorship and Career Success: A Study of Industrial-Organizational Psychologists." *Personnel Psychology* 57:217–303.

Kalev, Alexandra, Frank Dobbin, and Erin Kelly. 2006. "Best Practices or Best Guesses? Assessing the Efficacy of Corporate Affirmative Action and Diversity Policies." *American Sociological Review* 71 (4): 589–617.

Kang, Sonia K., Katherine A. DeCelles, Andras Tilcsik, and Sora Jun. 2016. "Whitened Resumes: Race and Self-Presentation in the Labor Market." *Administrative Science Quarterly* 61(3): 469–502.

Kelly, Erin, and Phyllis Moen. 2020. *Overload: How Good Jobs Went Bad and What We Can Do About It.* Princeton University Press.

Kelly, K., and L. Grant. 2012. "Penalties and Premiums: The Impact of Gender, Marriage, and Parenthood on Faculty Salaries in Science, Engineering, and Mathematics (SEM) and Non-SEM Fields." *Social Studies of Science* 42:869–96.

Kemelgor, Carol, and Henry Etzkowitz. 2001. "Overcoming Isolation: Women's Dilemmas in American Academic Science." *Minerva* 39 (2): 239–57.

King, Molly M., Shelley J. Correll, Jennifer Jacquet, Carl T. Bergstrom, and Jevin D. West. 2017. "Men Set Their Own Cites High: Gender and Self-Citation Across Field and Over Time." *Socius* 3 (January). https://doi.org/10.1177 /2378023117738903.

Kitchener, Caroline. 2020. "Women Academics Seem to Be Submitting Fewer Papers during Coronavirus. 'Never Seen Anything Like It,' Says One Editor." *The Lily*, April 24.

Kluegel, James R., and Eliot R. Smith. 1986. *Beliefs about Inequality: Americans' Views of What Is and What Ought to Be.* New York: DeGruyter.

Kmec, Julie A. 2013. "Why Academic STEM Mothers Feel They Have to Work Harder Than Others on the Job." *International Journal of Gender, Science and Technology* 5 (2): 79–101.

Kmec, Julie A., Matt L. Huffman, and Andrew M. Penner. 2014. "Being a Parent or Having a Parent? The Perceived Employability of Men and Women Who Take Employment Leave." *American Behavioral Scientist* 58 (3): 453–72.

Kmec, Julie A., Lindsey Trimble O'Connor, and Scott Schieman. 2014. "Not Ideal: The Association between Working Anything but Full Time and Perceived Unfair Treatment." *Work and Occupations* 41 (1): 63–85.

Knobloch-Westerwick, Silvia, Carroll J. Glynn, and Michael Huge. 2013. "The Matilda Effect in Science Communication: An Experiment on Gender Bias in Publication Quality Perceptions and Collaboration Interest." *Science Communication* 35 (5): 603–25.

Knorr-Cetina, Karin. 1999. *Epistemic Cultures: How the Sciences Make Knowledge.* Cambridge, MA: Harvard University Press.

Kolev, Julian, Yuly Fuentes-Medel, and Fiona Murray. 2019. "Is Blinded Review Enough? How Gendered Outcomes Arise Even Under Anonymous Evaluation." NBER Working Paper no. 25759.

Krapf, Matthais, Heinrich W. Ursprung, and Christian Zimmermann. 2017. "Parenthood and Productivity of Highly Skilled Labor: Evidence from the Groves of Academe." *Journal of Economic Behavior and Organization* 140:147–75.

Kreeger, Pamela K., Amy Brock, Holly C. Gibbs, Jane Grande-Allen, Alice H. Huang, Kristyn S. Masters, Padmini Rangamani, Michaela R. Reagan, and Shannon L. Servoss. 2020. "Ten Simple Rules for Women Principal Investigators during a Pandemic." *PLOS Computational Biology* 16 (10): e1008370.

Kuenzi, Jeffrey J. 2008. "Science, Technology, and Engineering, and Mathematics (STEM) Education: Background, Federal Policy, and Legislative Action." *Congressional Research Service Reports*, Paper 35.

Kuhn, Thomas S. 1962. *The Structure of Scientific Revolutions.* Chicago: University of Chicago Press.

Kunda, Gideon. 2006. *Engineering Culture: Control and Commitment in a High-Tech Corporation Revised Edition.* Philadelphia: Temple University Press.

Lam, Alice. 2010. "From 'Ivory Tower Traditionalists' to 'Entrepreneurial Scientists'? Academic Scientists in Fuzzy University—Industry Boundaries." *Social Studies of Science* 40 (2): 307–40.

Lamont, Michele. 1992. *Money, Manners and Morals*. Chicago: University of Chicago Press.

———. 2009. *How Professors Think: Inside the Curious World of Academic Judgment*. Cambridge, MA: President and Fellows of Harvard University.

Lamont, Michele, and Patricia White. 2005. *Workshop on Interdisciplinary Standards for Systematic Qualitative Research*. National Science Foundation Workshop, Washington, DC, May 20.

Larson, Magali S. 1977. *The Rise of Professionalism: A Sociological Analysis*. Berkeley: University of California Press.

Larson, Richard C., Navid Ghaffarzadegan, and Yi Xue. 2014. "Too Many PhD Graduates or Too Few Academic Job Openings: The Basic Reproductive Number R(0) in Academia." *Systems Research and Behavioral Science* 31 (6): 745–50.

Latour, Bruno. 1987. *Science in Action: How to Follow Scientists and Engineers Through Society*. Cambridge, MA: Harvard University Press.

Latour, Bruno, and Steve Woolgar. 1986. *Laboratory Life: The Construction of Scientific Facts*. Princeton, NJ: Princeton University Press.

Lauer, Mike. 2019. *NIH Annual Snapshot—FY 2018 by the Numbers*. Bethesda, MD: Office of Extramural Research (Extramural Nexus), National Institutes of Health.

Laursen, Sandra, and Ann E. Austin. 2020. *Building Gender Equity in the Academy: Institutional Strategies for Change*. Baltimore: Johns Hopkins University Press.

Leahey, Erin. 2006. "Gender in Productivity." *Gender and Society* 20 (6):754–80.

———. 2007. "Not by Productivity Alone: How Visibility and Specialization Contribute to Academic Earnings." *American Sociological Review* 72 (4): 533–61.

Lee, Robert. 1999. *Orientals: Asian Americans in Popular Culture*. Philadelphia: Temple University Press.

Lee, Sooho, and Barry Bozeman. 2005. "The Impact of Research Collaboration on Scientific Productivity." *Social Studies of Science* 35 (5): 673–702.

Leicht, Kevin T. 2016. "Market Fundamentalism, Cultural Fragmentation, Postmodern Skepticism, and the Future of Professional Work." *Journal of Professions and Organization* 3:103–17.

Leslie, Larry, Gregory T. McClure, and Ronald L. Oaxaca. 1998. "Women and Minorities in Science and Engineering: A Life-Sequence Analysis." *Journal of Higher Education* 69 (3): 239–76.

Leslie, Sarah-Jane, Andrei Cimpian, Meredith Meyer, and Edward Freeland. 2015. "Expectations of Brilliance Underlie Gender Distributions across Academic Disciplines." *Science* 347 (6219): 262–65.

Levine, Sheen S., Evan P. Apfelbaum, Mark Bernard, Valerie L. Bartelt, Edward J. Zajac, and David Stark. 2014. "Ethnic Diversity Deflates Price Bubbles." *Proceedings of the National Academy of Sciences* 111 (52): 18524–529.

Lincoln, Anne E., Stephanie Pincus, Janet Bandows Koster, and Phoebe S. Leboy. 2012. "The Matilda Effect in Science: Awards and Prizes in the US, 1990s and 2000s." *Social Studies of Science* 42 (2): 307–20.

Lisnic, Rodica, Anna Zajicek, and Brinck Kerr. 2019. "Work–Family Balance and Tenure Reasonableness: Gender Differences in Faculty Assessment." *Sociological Spectrum* 39 (5): 340–58.

Liu, Sida. 2020. "Professional Impurities." In *Professional Work: Knowledge, Power, and Social Inequalities*, edited by Elizabeth H. Gorman and Steven P. Vallas, 147–67. Bingley: Emerald.

Long, J. Scott, Paul D. Allison, and Robert McGinnis. 1993. "Rank Advancement in Academic Careers: Sex Differences and the Effect of Productivity." *American Sociological Review* 58 (5): 703–22.

Long, J. Scott, and Mary Frank Fox. 1995. "Scientific Careers: Universalism and Particularism." *Annual Review of Sociology* 21:45–71.

Lundquist, Jennifer H., Joya Misra, and KerryAnn O'Meara. 2012. "Parental Leave Usage by Fathers and Mothers at an American University." *Fathering: A Journal of Theory, Research, and Practice about Men as Fathers* 10 (3): 337–63.

Madera, Juan M., Michelle R. Hebl, Heather Dial, Randi Martin, and Virgina Valian. 2019. "Raising Doubt in Letters of Recommendation for Academia: Gender Differences and Their Impact." *Journal of Business and Psychology* 34 (3): 287–303.

Maliniak, Daniel, Ryan Powers, and Barbara F. Walter. 2013. "The Gender Citation Gap in International Relations." *International Organization*, August, 1–34.

Mars, Matthew M., Kate Bresonis, and Katalin Szelényi. 2014. "Science and Engineering Doctoral Student Socialization, Logics, and the National Economic Agenda: Alignment or Disconnect?" *Minerva* 52 (3): 351–79.

Marx, Karl, Friedrich Engels, and C. J. Arthur. 1974. *The German Ideology*. London: Lawrence and Wishart.

Mason, Mary Anne, Nicholas Wolfinger, and Marc Goulden. 2013. *Do Babies Matter? Gender and Family in the Ivory Tower*. New Brunswick, NJ: Rutgers University Press.

McBrier, D. B. 2003. "Gender and Career Dynamics within a Segmented Professional Labor Market: The Case of Law Academia." *Social Forces* 81 (4): 1201–66.

McCall, Leslie. 2005. "The Complexity of Intersectionality." *Signs* 30:1771–800.

———. 2013. *The Undeserving Rich: American Beliefs about Inequality, Opportunity, and Redistribution*. New York: Cambridge University Press.

McGlynn, Terrence P. 2017. "Identity Matters: Communicating About Equity and Opportunity for Students in Minority-Serving Institutions." *Annals of the Entomological Society of America* 110:480–83.

McIlwee, Judith S., and J. Gregg Robinson. 1992. *Women in Engineering: Gender, Power, and Workplace Culture*. Albany: State University of New York Press.

Merton, Robert K. 1973. *The Sociology of Science: Theoretical and Empirical Investigations*. Chicago: University of Chicago Press.

Mervis, Jeffrey. 2017. "Data Check: US Government Share of Basic Research Funding Falls Below 50%." *Science*, March 9. https://www.science.org/news/2017/03/data-check-us-government-share-basic-research-funding-falls-below-50.

Meyer, John W., and Brian Rowan. 1977. "Institutionalized Organizations: Formal Structure as Myth and Ceremony." *American Journal of Sociology* 83 (2): 340–63.

Milkman, Katherine L., Modupe Akinola, and Dolly Chugh. 2012. "Temporal Distance and Discrimination: An Audit Study in Academia." *Psychological Science* 23 (7): 710–17.

Milojević, Staša, Filippo Radicchi, and John Walsh. 2018. "Changing Demographics of Scientific Careers: The Rise of the Temporary Workforce." *Proceedings of the National Academy of Sciences* 115 (50): 12616–23.

Misra, Joya, Celeste Vaughan Curington, and Venus Mary Green. 2020. "Methods of Intersectional Research." *Sociological Spectrum* 41 (1): 1–20.

Misra, Joya, Jennifer Hickes Lundquist, and Abby Templer. 2012. "Gender, Work Time, and Care Responsibilities among Faculty." *Sociological Forum* 27 (2): 300–23.

Misra, Joya, Laurel Smith-Doerr, Nilanjana Dasgupta, Gabriela Weaver, and Jennifer Normanly. 2017. "Collaboration and Gender Equity among Academic Scientists." *Social Sciences* 6 (1): 25.

MIT. 1999. "A Study on the Status of Women Faculty in Science at MIT." *MIT Faculty Newsletter.*

Moen, Phyllis, Erin L. Kelly, and Rachelle Hill. 2011. "Does Enhancing Work-Time Control and Flexibility Reduce Turnover? A Naturally Occurring Experiment." *Social Problems* 58:69–98.

Morimoto, Shauna A., and Anna Zajicek. 2012. "Dismantling the 'Master's House': Feminist Reflections on Institutional Transformation." *Critical Sociology* 40 (1): 135–50.

Morrill, Calvin. 2008. "Culture and Organization Theory." *Annals of the American Academy of Political and Social Science* 619:5–40.

Moss Kanter, Rossabeth. 1977. *Men and Women of the Corporation.* New York: Basic.

Moss-Racusin, Corinne A., John F. Dovidio, Victoria L. Brescoll, Mark J. Graham, and Jo Handelsman. 2012. "Science Faculty's Subtle Gender Biases Favor Male Students." *Proceedings of the National Academy of Sciences* 109 (14): 16474–79.

Motro, D., J. B. Evans, A. P. J. Ellis, and L. Benson III. 2021. "Race and Reactions to Women's Expressions of Anger at Work: Examining the Effects of the 'Angry Black Woman' Stereotype." *Journal of Applied Psychology.* Advance online publication.

Motro, Daphna, Jonathan Evans, Aleksander P. J. Ellis, and Lehman Benson. 2019. "Race and Reactions to Negative Feedback: Examining the Effects of the 'Angry Black Woman' Stereotype." *Academy of Management Proceedings*, August 2019, 11230.

Nathan, Max, and Neil Lee. 2013. "Cultural Diversity, Innovation, and Entrepreneurship: Firm-level Evidence from London." *Economic Geography* 89 (4): 367–94.

National Academies of Sciences, Engineering, and Medicine. 2018. *Sexual Harassment of Women: Climate, Culture, and Consequences in Academic Sciences,*

Engineering, and Medicine. Washington, DC: National Academies Press. https://doi.org/10.17226/24994.

———. 2021. *The Impact of COVID-19 on the Careers of Women in Academic Sciences, Engineering, and Medicine.* Edited by Eve Higginbotham and Maria Lund Dahlberg. Washington, DC: National Academies Press.

National Academy of Engineering. 2004. *The Engineer of 2020: Visions of Engineering in the Century.* Washington, DC: National Academies.

National Academy of Sciences. 2000. *Who Will Do the Science in the Future? A Symposium on Careers of Women in Science.* Edited by National Academy of Sciences Committee on Women in Science and Engineering. Washington, DC: National Academies.

———. 2007. *Beyond Bias and Barriers: Fulfilling the Potential of Women in Academic Science and Engineering.* Edited by National Academy of Science Committee on Maximizing the Potential of Women in Academic Science and Engineering, National Academy of Engineering, and Institute of Medicine. Washington, DC: National Academies.

———. 2011. *Expanding Underrepresented Minority Participation: America's Science and Technology Talent at the Crossroads.* National Academy of Sciences, Washington, DC.

National Center for Science and Engineering Statistics. 2019a. *Doctorate Recipients from US Universities: 2019.* Washington, DC: National Science Foundation.

———. 2019b. *Women, Minorities, and Persons with Disabilities in Science and Engineering.* Washington, DC: National Science Foundation. ncses.nsf.gov/wmpd.

———. 2021. *Women, Minorities, and Persons with Disabilities in Science and Engineering.* Washington, DC: National Science Foundation. ncses.nsf.gov/wmpd.

National Research Council. 2015. *Enhancing the Effectiveness of Team Science.* Edited by Cooke and M. L. Hilton. Committee on the Science of Team Science, N.J. Board on Behavioral, Cognitive, and Sensory Sciences, Division of Behavioral and Social Sciences and Education. Washington, DC: National Academies Press.

National Science Foundation. 2008. *Women, Minorities and Persons with Disabilities in Science and Engineering.* Washington, DC: National Science Foundation, Division of Science Resources Statistics. http://www.nsf.gov/statistics/wmpd/pdf/tab9-37.pdf.

———. 2012a. *Science and Engineering Indicators 2012.* Washington, DC: National Science Foundation. http://www.nsf.gov/statistics/seind12/.

———. 2012b. *Women, Minorities and Persons with Disabilities in Science and Engineering.* Washington, DC: National Science Foundation, Division of Science Resources Statistics. http://www.nsf.gov/statistics/wmpd/sex.cfm#degrees.

———. 2013. *Women, Minorities and Persons with Disabilities in Science and Engineering.* Washington, DC: National Science Foundation, Division of Science Resources Statistics. https://www.nsf.gov/statistics/women/.

———. 2018. *Definitions of Research and Development: An Annotated Compilation of Official Sources.* Washington, DC: National Science Foundation. https://www.nsf.gov/statistics/randdef/.

―――. 2019. *Women, Minorities, and Persons with Disabilities in Science and Engineering: 2019. Special Report.* National Science Foundation Report 19-304. Washington, DC: National Science Foundation, National Center for Science and Engineering Statistics.

Newport, Cal. 2016. *Deep Work: Rules for Focused Success in a Distracted World.* New York: Grand Central.

Norton, Matthew. 2019. "Meaning on the Move: Synthesizing Cognitive and Systems Concepts of Culture." *American Journal of Cultural Sociology* 7:1–28.

Nye, David E. 1997. *Electrifying America: Social Meanings of a New Technology.* Boston: MIT Press.

O'Meara, KerryAnn, and Corbin M. Campbell. 2011. "Faculty Sense of Agency in Decisions about Work and Family." *Review of Higher Education* 34 (3): 447–76.

O'Meara, KerryAnn, Dawn Culpepper, and Lindsey L. Templeton. 2020. "Nudging toward Diversity: Applying Behavioral Design to Faculty Hiring." *Review of Educational Research* 90 (3): 311–48.

O'Neill, Olivia Amanda, and Nancy P. Rothbard. 2017. "Is Love All You Need? The Effects of Emotional Culture, Suppression, and Work-Family Conflict on Firefighter Risk Taking and Health." *Journal of Academy of Management Journal* 60 (1): 78–108.

Ong, Maria, Carol Wright, Lorelle Espinosa, and Gary Orfield. 2011. "Inside the Double Bind: A Synthesis of Empirical Research on Undergraduate and Graduate Women of Color in Science, Technology, Engineering, and Mathematics." *Harvard Educational Review* 81 (2): 172–209.

Owen-Smith, Jason, and Walter W. Powell. 2001. "To Patent or Not: Faculty Decisions and Institutional Success at Technology Transfer." *Journal of Technology Transfer* 26 (1): 99–114.

Page, Scott E. 2008. *The Difference: How the Power of Diversity Creates Better Groups, Firms, Schools, and Societies.* Princeton, NJ: Princeton University Press.

―――. 2017. *The Diversity Bonus How Great Teams Pay Off in the Knowledge Economy.* Princeton, NJ: Princeton University Press.

Pang, Alex Soojung-Kim. 2016. *Rest: Why You Get More Done When You Work Less.* New York: Basic.

Pascoe, C. J. 2005. "Dude, You're a Fag." *Sexualities* 8:329–46.

Perez, Caroline Criado. 2019. *Invisible Women: Data Bias in a World Designed for Men.* New York: Abrams.

Perlow, Leslie A. 2001. "Time to Coordinate: Toward an Understanding of Work-Time Standards and Norms in a Multicountry Study of Software Engineers." *Work and Occupations* 28 (1): 91–111.

Pfirman, Stephanie, and Melissa Begg. 2012. "Trouble by Interdisciplinarity?" *Science Careers*, April 6. https://doi.org/10.1126/science.caredit.a1200040.

Pierce, Jennifer L. 1996. *Gender Trials: Emotional Lives in Contemporary Law Firms.* Berkeley: University of California Press.

Posselt, Julie R. 2020. *Equity in Science: Representation, Culture, and the Dynamic of Change in Graduate Education.* Palo Alto, CA: Stanford University Press.

Price, J. 2010. "The Effect of Instructor Race and Gender on Student Persistence in STEM Fields." *Economics of Education Review* 29:901–10.

Puritty, Chandler, Lynette R. Strickland, Eanas Alia, Benjamin Blonder, Emily Klein, Michel T. Kohl, Earyn McGee, Maclovia Quintana, Robyn E. Ridley, Beth Tellman, and Leah R. Gerber. 2017. "Without Inclusion, Diversity Initiatives May Not Be Eenough." *Science* 357 (6356): 1101–2.

Pyke, Karen, and Denise Johnson. 2003. "Asian American Women and Racialized Femininities 'Doing' Gender across Cultural Worlds." *Gender and Society* 17:33–53.

Quillian, Lincoln. 2006. "New Approaches to Understanding Racial Prejudice and Discrimination." *Annual Review of Sociology* 32:299–328.

Ragin, Charles C. 1987. *The Comparative Method: Moving Beyond Qualitative and Quantitative Strategies*. Berkeley: University of California Press.

Reid, Erin. 2015. "Embracing, Passing, Revealing, and the Ideal Worker Image: How People Navigate Expected and Experienced Professional Identities." *Organization Science* 26 (4): 997–1017.

Reskin, Barbara. 2003. "Including Mechanisms in Our Models of Ascriptive Inequality." *American Sociological Review* 68 (1): 1–21.

Rhoten, Diana, and Stephanie Pfirman. 2007. "Women in Interdisciplinary Science: Exploring Preferences and Consequences." *Research Policy* 36 (1): 56–75.

Rhoton, Laura A. 2011. "Distancing as a Gendered Barrier: Understanding Women Scientists' Gender Practices." *Gender and Society* 25:696–718.

Ridgeway, Cecilia L. 2009. "Framed Before We Know It: How Gender Shapes Social Relations." *Gender and Society* 23 (2): 145–60.

———. 2011. *Framed by Gender: How Gender Inequality Persists in the Modern World.* Oxford: Oxford University Press.

Ridgeway, Cecilia L., and Shelley J. Correll. 2004. "Unpacking the Gender System: A Theoretical Perspective on Gender Beliefs and Social Relations." *Gender and Society* 18 (4): 510–31.

Rivera, Lauren A. 2017. "When Two Bodies Are (Not) a Problem: Gender and Relationship Status Discrimination in Academic Hiring." *American Sociological Review* 82:1111–38.

Roach, Michael, and Henry Sauermann. 2017. "The Declining Interest in an Academic Career." *PLOS ONE* 12 (9). https://doi.org/10.1371/journal.pone.0184130.

Roe, Anne. 1953. *The Making of a Scientist.* New York: Dodd Mead.

Rosette, Ashleigh Shelby, Christy Zhou Koval, Anyi Ma, and Robert Livingston. 2016. "Race Matters for Women Leaders: Intersectional Effects on Agentic Deficiencies and Penalties." *Leadership Quarterly* 27 (3): 429–45.

Rosette, Ashleigh Shelby, and Robert W. Livingston. 2012. "Failure Is Not an Option for Black Women: Effects of Organizational Performance on Leaders with Single versus Dual-Subordinate Identities." *Journal of Experimental Social Psychology* 48 (5): 1162–67.

Roth, Louise Marie. 2004. "The Social Psychology of Tokenism: Status and Homophily Processes on Wall Street." *Sociological Perspectives*. 47 (2): 189–214.

Rudman, L. A. 1998. "Self-Promotion as a Risk Factor for Women: The Costs and Benefits of Counterstereotypical Impression Management." *Journal of Personality and Social Psychology* 74 (3): 629–45.

Rudman, Laurie A., and Kris Mescher. 2013. "Penalizing Men Who Request a Family Leave: Is Flexibility Stigma a Femininity Stigma?" *Journal of Social Issues* 69 (2): 322–40.

Salazar, Martiza, and Theresa Lant. 2018. "Facilitating Innovation in Interdisciplinary Teams: The Role of Leaders and Integrative Communication." *Informing Science: The International Journal of an Emerging Transdiscipline* 21:157–78.

Sandefur, Rebecca. 2001. "Work and Honor in the Law: Prestige and the Division of Lawyers' Labor." *American Sociological Review* 66:382–403.

Sarsons, Heather. 2017. "Recognition for Group Work: Gender Differences in Academia." *American Economic Review Papers and Proceedings* 107 (5): 141–45.

Schiebinger, Londa. 1999. *Has Feminism Changed Science?* Cambridge, MA: Harvard University Press.

Schilt, Kristen, and Laurel Westbrook. 2009. "Doing Gender, Doing Heteronormativity: 'Gender Normals,' Transgender People, and the Social Maintenance of Heterosexuality." *Gender and Society* 23 (4): 440–64.

Schippers, Mimi. 2007. "Recovering the Feminine Other: Masculinity, Femininity, and Gender Hegemony." *Theory and Society* 36 (1): 85–102.

Schleef, D. J. 2006. *Managing Elites: Professional Socialization in Law and Business Schools*. Oxford: Rowan and Littlefield.

Seron, Carroll, Susan Silbey, Erin Cech, and Brian Rubineau. 2018. " 'I Am Not a Feminist, but . . .': Hegemony of a Meritocratic Ideology and the Limits of Critique among Women in Engineering." *Work and Occupations* 45 (2): 131–67.

Settles, I. H., L. R. Warner, N. T. Buchanan, and M. K. Jones. 2020. "Understanding Psychology's Resistance to Intersectionality Theory Using a Framework of Epistemic Exclusion and Invisibility." *Journal of Social Issues* 76:796–813.

Sewell, William H., Jr. 1992. "A Theory of Structure: Duality, Agency, and Transformation." *American Journal of Sociology* 98 (1): 1–29.

Seymour, Elaine, and Anne-Barrie Hunter. 2019. *Talking about Leaving Revisited*. Basel: Springer.

Shafran, Jon. 2017. "Bodies of Science: Gendered Impression Management Strategies among Private Sector Life Scientists and Technologists." PhD diss., University of California.

Shapin, Steven. 2008. *The Scientific Life: A Moral History of a Late Modern Vocation*. Chicago: University of Chicago Press.

———. 2010. *Never Pure: Historical Studies of Science as If It Was Produced by People with Bodies, Situated in Time, Space, Culture, and Society, and Struggling for Credibility and Authority*. 2nd ed. Baltimore: Johns Hopkins University Press.

Shapin, Steven, and Simon Schaffer. 1985. *Leviathan and the Air Pump*. Princeton, NJ: Princeton University Press.

Shauman, Kimberlee A. 2017. "Gender Differences in the Early Employment Outcomes of STEM Doctorates." *Social Sciences* 6 (1): 24.

Sheltzer, Jason M., and Joan C. Smith. 2014. "Elite Male Faculty in the Life Sciences Employ Fewer Women." *Proceedings of the National Academy of Sciences* 111 (28): 10107–12.

Siegel, D. J. 2015. *The Developing Mind: How Relationships and the Brain Interact to Shape Who We Are*. 2nd ed. New York: Guilford.

———. 2018. *Aware: The Science and Practice of Presence; The Groundbreaking Meditation Practice*. New York: TarcherPerigee.

Sinclair, Bruce. 2004. "Integrating the Histories of Race and Technology." In *Technology and the African-American Experience*, edited by Bruce Sinclair, 1–17. Boston: MIT Press.

Smith-Doerr, Laurel. 2004. *Women's Work: Gender Equality vs. Hierarchy in the Life Sciences*. Boulder, CO: Lynne Rienner.

Sommers, Samuel R. 2006. "On Racial Diversity and Group Decision Making: Identifying Multiple Effects of Racial Composition on Jury Deliberations." *Journal of Personality and Social Psychology* 90 (4): 597–612.

Sonnentag, Sabine. 2003. "Recovery, Work Engagement, and Proactive Behavior: A New Look at the Interface between Nonwork and Work." *Journal of Applied Psychology* 88 (3): 518–28.

Stainback, Kevin, Sibyl Kleiner, and Sheryl Skaggs. 2016. "Women in Power Undoing or Redoing the Gendered Organization?" *Gender and Society* 30 (1): 109–35.

Stainback, Kevin, Donald Tomaskovic-Devey, and Sheryl Skaggs. 2010. "Organizational Approaches to Inequality: Inertia, Relative Power, and Environments." *Annual Review of Sociology* 36:225–47.

Steinpreis, Rhea E., Katie A. Anders, and Dawn Ritzke. 1999. "The Impact of Gender on the Review of the Curricula Vitae of Job Applicants and Tenure Candidates: A National Empirical Study." *Sex Roles* 41 (7–8): 509–28.

Stephan, Paula. 2012. *How Economics Shapes Science*. Cambridge, MA: Harvard University Press.

Stewart, Abigail, and Danielle LaVaque-Manty. 2008. "Advancing Women Faculty in Science and Engineering." In *Gender and Occupational Outcomes: Longitudinal Assessments of Individual, Social, and Cultural Influences*, edited by H. M. G. Watt and J. S. Eccles, 299–322. Washington, DC: American Psychological Association.

Stewart, Abigail, and Virginia Valian. 2018. *An Inclusive Academy: Achieving Diversity and Excellence*. MIT Press.

Stolzenberg, E. B., M. K. Eagan, H. B. Zimmerman, J. Berdan Lozano, N. M. Cesar-Davis, M. C. Aragon, and C. Rios-Aguilar. 2019. *Undergraduate Teaching Faculty: The HERI Faculty Survey 2016–2017*. Los Angeles: Higher Education Research Institute.

Stone, Pamela, and Lisa Ackerly Hernandez. 2013. "The All-or-Nothing Workplace: Flexibility Stigma or 'Opting Out' among Professional-Managerial Women." *Journal of Social Issues* 69 (2): 235–56.

Sue, Derald Wing, and Lisa Beth Spanierman. 2020. *Microaggressions in Everyday Life*. 2nd ed. Hoboken, NJ: Wiley.

Sutton, John R., Frank Dobbin, John W. Meyer, and W. Richard Scott. 1994. "The Legalization of the Workplace." *American Journal of Sociology* 99:944–71.

Sy, T., L. M. Shore, J. Strauss, T. H. Shore, S. Tram, P. Whiteley, and K. Ikeda-Muromachi. 2010. "Leadership Perceptions as a Function of Race-Occupation Fit: The Case of Asian Americans." *Journal of Applied Psychology* 95 (5): 902–19.

Tajima-Peña, Renee. 1989. "Lotus Blossoms Don't Bleed: Images of Asian Women." In *Making Waves: An Anthology of Writing by and about Asian American Women*. Boston: Beacon.

Talbot, Margaret. 2021. "Is It Really Too Late to Learn New Skills?" *New Yorker*, January 11.

TallBear, Kim. 2014. "Indigenous Scientists Constitute Knowledge across Cultures of Expertise and Tradition: An Indigenous Standpoint Research Project." In *RE:MINDINGS: Co-Constituting Indigenous/Academic/Artistic Knowledges*, edited by Johan Gärdebo, May-Britt Öhman, and Hiroshi Maryuama, 173–91. Uppsala: Uppsala University.

Thébaud, Sarah, and Catherine J. Taylor. 2021. "The Specter of Motherhood: Culture and the Production of Gendered Career Aspirations in Science and Engineering." *Gender and Society* 35 (3): 395–421.

Tilcsik, A. 2011. "Pride and Prejudice: Employment Discrimination against Openly Gay Men." *American Journal of Sociology* 117 (2): 586–626.

Tilly, Charles. 1999. *Durable Inequality*. Berkeley: University of California Press.

Tomaskovic-Devey, Donald. 1993. "The Gender and Race Composition of Jobs and the Male/Female, White/Black Pay Gaps." *Social Forces* 92:45–76.

Traweek, Sharon. 1988. *Beamtimes and Lifetimes: The World of High Energy Physicists*. Cambridge, MA: Harvard University Press.

Trice, Harrison Miller. 1993. *Occupational Subcultures in the Workplace*. Ithaca, NY: ILR.

Trower, Cathy A. 2008. "Amending Higher Education's Constitution." *Academe*, September–October, 16–19.

Trower, Cathy A., and R. P. Chait. 2002. "Faculty Diversity: Too Little for Too Long." *Harvard Magazine*, March–April. https://www.harvardmagazine.com/2002/03/faculty-diversity.html.

Turco, Catherine J. 2010. "Cultural Foundations of Tokenism: Evidence from the Leveraged Buyout Industry." *American Sociological Review* 75 (6): 894–913.

US News and World Report. 2014. "National Universities Rankings." http://colleges.usnews.rankingsandreviews.com/best-colleges/rankings/national-universities?int=9ff208.

———. 2016a. "Best Global Universities Rankings." http://www.usnews.com/education/best-global-universities/rankings?page=2.

———. 2016b. "National Universities Rankings." http://colleges.usnews.rankingsandreviews.com/best-colleges/rankings/national-universities.

UCLA. 2003. *Final Report: UCLA Gender Equity Data Committee*. http://www.fac
ulty.diversity.ucla.edu/gendeq/comittees/docs/GenderEquityDataCommit
teeReport.pdf.

Valian, Virginia. 1998. *Why So Slow? The Advancement of Women*. Cambridge, MA:
MIT Press.

Vallas, Steven Peter, and Daniel Lee Kleinman. 2008. "Contradiction, Convergence
and the Knowledge Economy: The Confluence of Academic and Commercial
Biotechnology." *Socio-Economic Review* 6 (2): 283–311.

Vandello, Joseph A., Vanessa E. Hettinger, Jennifer K. Bosson, and Jasmine Siddiqi.
2013. "When Equal Isn't Really Equal: The Masculine Dilemma of Seeking
Work Flexibility." *Journal of Social Issues* 69 (2): 303–21.

Waidzunas, Tom. 2015. *The Straight Line: How the Fringe Science of Ex-Gay Therapy
Reoriented Sexuality*. Minneapolis: University of Minnesota Press.

Warikoo, Natasha K. 2016. *The Diversity Bargain and Other Dilemmas of Race, Ad-
missions, and Meritocracy at Elite Universities*. Chicago: University of Chicago
Press.

Weber, Max. 1946. "Science as a Vocation." In *From Max Weber: Essays in Sociology*, edited by H. H. Gerth and C. Wright Mills, 129–56. New York: Oxford
University Press.

———. 1958. "Science as a Vocation." *Daedalus* 87 (1): 111–34.

Weeden, Kim A. 2002. "Why Do Some Occupations Pay More than Others? Social
Closure and Earnings Inequality in the United States." *American Journal of
Sociology* 108:55–101.

Weeden, Kim A., and David B. Grusky. 2005. "The Case for a New Class Map."
American Journal of Sociology 111:141–212.

Wenneras, Christine, and Agnes Wold. 1997. "Nepotism and Sexism in Peer-
Review." *Nature* 387 (22): 341–43.

West, Jevin D., Jennifer Jacquet, Molly M. King, Shelley J. Correll, and Carl T.
Bergstrom. 2013. "The Role of Gender in Scholarly Authorship." *PLOS ONE*
8 (7): e66212.

Whalley, Peter. 1986. *The Social Production of Technical Work: The Case of British
Engineers*. London: Macmillan.

Wharton, Amy S., and Mary Blair-Loy. 2006. "Long Work Hours and Family Life:
A Cross-National Study of Employees' Concerns." *Journal of Family Issues*
27:415–36.

Wharton, Amy S., Sarah Chivers, and Mary Blair-Loy. 2008. "Use of Formal and
Informal Work-Family Policies on the Digital Assembly Line." *Work and Occupations* 35:327–50.

Wharton, Amy S., and Mychel Estevez. 2014. "Department Chairs' Perspectives on
Work, Family, and Gender: Pathways for Transformation." In *Gender Transfor-
mation in the Academy*, vol. 19, *Advances in Gender Research*, edited by Vasilikie
Demos, Catherine White Berheide, and Marcia Texler Segal, 131–50. Bingley:
Emerald Group.

Whittington, Kjersten Bunker, and Laurel Smith-Doerr. 2005. "Gender and Commercial Science: Women's Patenting in the Life Sciences." *Journal of Technology Transfer* 30:355–70.

———. 2008. Women Inventors in Context: Disparities in Patenting across Academia and Industry. *Gender and Society* 22:194–218.

Wilensky, Harold L., and Ladinsky Jack. 1967. "From Religious Community to Occupational Group: Structural Assimilation among Professors, Lawyers, and Engineers." *American Sociological Review* 32:541–61.

Williams, Christine L. 2014. "The Glass Escalator: Hidden Advantages for Men in the 'Female' Professions." *Social Problems* 39 (3): 253–67.

Williams, Joan. 2010. *Reshaping the Work-Family Debate: Why Men and Class Matter*. Cambridge, MA: Harvard University Press.

Williams, Joan C., Mary Blair-Loy, and Jennifer L. Berdahl. 2013. "Cultural Schemas, Social Class, and the Flexibility Stigma." *Journal of Social Issues* 69 (2): 209–34.

Williams, Joan, and Heather Boushey. 2010. *The Three Faces of Work-Family Conflict: The Poor, the Professionals, and the Missing Middle*. Center for American Progress. San Francisco: UC Hastings College of the Law.

Williams, Joan, and Rachel Dempsey. 2014. *What Works for Women at Work: Four Patterns Working Women Need to Know*. New York: New York University Press.

Williams, Joan C., Su Li, Roberta Rincon, and Peter Finn. 2016. *Climate Control: Gender and Racial Bias in Engineering?* San Francisco: Center for WorkLife Law and Society of Women Engineers.

Williams, Joan, Katherine W. Phillips, and Erika V. Hall. 2014. "Double Jeopardy? Gender Bias Against Women of Color in Science." *Tools for Change: Boosting the Retention of Women in the STEM Pipeline*. http://www.uchastings.edu/news /articles/2015/01/double-jeopardy-report.pdf.

Wingfield, Adia Harvey. 2020. "Systemic Racism Persists in the Sciences." *Science* 369 (6502): 351. https://doi.org/10.1126/science.abd8825.

Xie, Yu, and Kimberlee A. Shauman. 1998. "Sex Differences in Research Productivity: New Evidence about an Old Puzzle." *American Sociological Review* 63 (6): 847–70.

———. 2003. *Women in Science: Career Processes and Outcomes*. Cambridge, MA: Harvard University Press.

Xu, Yonghong Jade. 2008. "Gender Disparity in STEM Disciplines: A Study of Faculty Attrition and Turnover Intentions." *Research in Higher Education* 49 (7): 607–24.

Young, Michael. 1958. *The Rise of the Meritocracy*. Harmondsworth: Penguin.

Zambrana, Ruth Enid, Adia Harvey Wingfield, Lisa M. Lapeyrouse, Brianne A. Dávila, Tangere L. Hoagland, and Robert Burciaga Valdez. 2017. "Blatant, Subtle, and Insidious: URM Faculty Perceptions of Discriminatory Practices in Predominantly White Institutions." *Sociological Inquiry* 87 (2): 207–32.

Zerubavel, Eviatar. 1997. *Social Mindscapes: An Invitation to Cognitive Sociology*. Cambridge, MA: Harvard University Press.

Zippel, Kathrin. 2017. *Women in Global Science: Advancing Academic Careers through International Collaboration*. Palo Alto, CA: Stanford University Press.

Index

Abbott, Andrew, 177n17, 185n53, 186nn55–56, 186n58, 187n60, 187n62, 187n64, 187n68, 187nn70–71, 188n88, 190n133, 207n43, 209n10
academic excellence: and fairness, 159–60; vs. minority status, 12, 119–20; and transparency, 6, 159–60
academic freedom, 28, 35, 128–30, 149, 201n1
academic science: collaboration in, 130; commercialization of, 189n118; culture of, 2, 81; devaluation in, 6; equitable practices in, 6; excellence of, 12; and industry, collaborations, 130; marginalization in, 6; meanings and values of, 3; and meritocracy, 1; as sanctified, 127
aerospace science, 23
African American scientists: and cultural biases about intellectual inferiority of, 26; and grant funding, 8, 106–7, 134, 166–67, 179n134. *See also* Black faculty/ scientists
anti-Semitism, in US scientific culture, 204n3
Aristotle, 24–25, 126
Asian faculty, 103, 118; and grant funding, 120–21; and leadership roles, 178n23; and productivity, 81; and research respect, 198n21; self-conceptions

among, 174; and tenure, 98; as underrepresented minority (URM), 160
Asian men, 6, 37–38, 83, 86–87, 94, 117–18, 124, 127, 135–37, 139, 156, 160, 166, 190n126, 198n24
Asian women, 6, 12–13, 41, 88, 91, 94, 177n16, 178n23, 199n24, 199nn29–30, 200n36
assertiveness. *See under* scientific excellence schema
astronomical studies, and physics, 23
autonomy, 28, 33, 46, 66, 186n56

Becker, Howard, 186n59, 188n88
Berdahl, Jennifer, 199n29, 201n43
biases: cultural, 3, 26, 28, 38, 142; across different demographic groups, 81; and discrimination, 6; and excellence, 38, 94, 133–35, 142; false accusations of, 139; and identity politics, 133–35; and inequalities, 2, 31, 33–34, 125, 149; and innovation, 142; and innovation, restrictions, 142; about LGBTQ professionals, 31, 33–34; and mothers/motherhood, 21; in organizations, 28, 185n51; and prejudice, 6, 149; and productivity, 38, 181n58, 190n132; and professional culture(s), 27–28, 33–34, 95; and racial/ ethnic minorities, 2, 26, 31,

biases (*cont.*)
33–34, 114–15, 190n134; research on, 175n3; and scientific excellence, 133–35; and scientific merit, 149; sexual, 2, 204n21; social, 27–28; societal-level, 28; and stereotypes, 33–34, 123, 156; unconscious, 115, 123; about women, 2, 31, 33–34, 114–15, 190n134; and work devotion, 66

Biernat, Monica, 189n100, 200n31, 204n28

"big science," 25

biochemistry, 29

Black faculty/scientists: and creative brilliance, proof of, 87; and diversity, 12; and grant funding, 107, 134; and potential violations of purity of scientific excellence and devotion, 127; and stereotypes, 26; and tenure, 98; as underrepresented minority (URM), 6, 18, 21, 95, 100, 102–4, 114, 118, 134, 136, 166, 178n23, 190n126, 202n5. *See also* African American scientists

Black students, in STEM, 178n25

Branch, E. H., 177n18, 177n20, 202n4

brilliance, creative. *See under* scientific excellence schema

Budig, Michelle J., 179n39

calling, scientific. *See* scientific calling

caregiving. *See* family responsibilities

case university, 2–3, 6, 16, 60, 103, 131, 136–37, 151, 155, 160, 183n5, 198n19, 202n3, 202n7; falls short, 21–22; tenure at, 98, 201n2

Castilla, Emilio, 181n56, 209n23

Cech, Erin A., 154, 161, 176n15

CFA. *See* confirmatory factor analysis (CFA)

Charles, Maria, 183n9

childrearing. *See* family responsibilities; parents/parenthood

cisgender individuals, 28

cisnormative beliefs, 204n18

closure: and jurisdiction, 30; and merit, 205n9; and professional cultures, 29–30; and socialization, 186n53, 186n56

cluster sampling, 166, 211n58

collaboration: in academic science, 130; and collegiality, 118, 145; with departmental colleagues, 14; impeded, 18; and informal discussions, 136; and innovation, 6, 18, 90, 142–45; and

knowledge, 143; and mentorship, 12, 14, 119, 141, 146; and objectivity, 130; and peer review, 80; and productivity, 90; and professional relationships, 144; and professional/social integration, 90; and promotion, 118; vs. self-promotion, 6; and social connections, 151; and tenure, 188. *See also* professional relationships; team science

collegiality: and collaboration, 118, 145; and merit, 140, 150; and promotion, 118; and scientific excellence, 77, 80, 124; and tenure, 118; valued, 150. *See also* professional relationships

commercialization: of academic science, 189n118; of faculty research, 130, 205n19

commitment: and dedication, 65; to devotion, 127, 139; to discovery, 70; to diversity, 68–69, 75, 91–93, 117, 200n35; to education, 160; to excellence, 161; to objectivity, 3, 18, 161, 180n41; to science, 65, 141; to scientific excellence, 127, 139; to scientific knowledge, 35; singular, 65; to STEM, 3; to vocation, 65; of women to work, 188n82; and work devotion, 3, 15, 65; and worthiness, 128

competence: and assessments, 142; as culturally defined and assessed, 30; and expertise, 31; and skill, 32; and worthiness, 4, 7, 13, 31–33

computer science: and excellence, 70–71; women in, 5, 177n19, 184n35

confirmatory factor analysis (CFA), 211n61

conflicts of interests, 130–31, 175n5

Connell, R. W., 178n31, 184n32

Cornell Survey Research Institute, 163

Correll, Shelley J., 179n39, 183n11, 185n50, 189n99, 200n31, 207n60

COVID-19 pandemic, 52, 150, 191n2

creative brilliance. *See under* scientific excellence schema

crowdsourcing, 90, 118–19

cultural beliefs: and cultural schemas, 3–5, 155, 158–59; and inequalities, 2; and inequalities within professional occupations, 2; and merit, 158–59; and merit in professions, 158–59; and minority-meritocracy trap, 123–24; perpetuated, 157; and political power,

24; preexisting, 157; professional, 157; and scientific excellence, 3–5, 81; and work devotion, 3–4

cultural schemas, 12–17, 176n12, 182n68, 187n78, 187n79, 190n133, 209n17, 209n19, 210n44; consequences of, 15, 125–26, 139–49; and cultural beliefs, 3–5, 155, 158–59; as emotional and moral, 31, 158; as hegemonic, 7–9; and inequalities, 6, 13, 158–59; and merit, 7, 31–33, 125–26, 139–49, 151, 162; and reality, 31; in STEM, 19, 33–38; term, usage, 158

Curie, Marie, 190n123

Damaske, Sarah, 178n32, 210n43, 211n60

dedication: and commitment, 65; and gender, 161, 192n12; and hours worked, 191n2; and marginalization, 192n18; of mothers, 57; multidimensional scale, 41–42, 161, 167, 191n7, 192n12; and passion, 40; and racial/ethnic minorities, 161, 192n12; scale, 167, 191n10; to science as vocation, 65; to scientific discovery, 9; and scientific excellence, 161; to vocation, 34–35, 65; and work devotion, 42, 65, 129, 176n15, 189n119, 191n10

demographic measures, 63, 168–69, 192n14, 192n17

depoliticization, 26–27, 96, 109–11, 113, 127, 140, 146–47, 203n14; and objectivity, 75, 124. See also politics

devaluation: in academic science, 6; cultural, 11, 26, 66; and disrespect, 5–6, 21, 123, 125, 200n34; and diversity, 17, 26, 74–75, 81, 91–93, 109; and exclusion, 117, 139; of family responsibilities, 185n51; and hegemonic femininity, 38; of identities, particular, 208n2; and inequalities, 196n45, 208n2; and innovation, 13; and innovation, damages to, 13; of LGBTQ professionals, 6, 91; and marginalization, 5–6, 125–26, 146, 161; and material disadvantage, 66; of merit, 65; of mothers' work commitment, 125, 196n45, 208n2; as persistent, 139; professional, 5–6, 144, 161, 165; of racial/ethnic minorities, 161; and scientific excellence, 17–18; and underrepresented minorities (URMs), 12, 139, 178n24;

vulnerable to, 122; of women, 5, 28, 38, 88–89, 161

devotion: commitment to, 127, 139; to discovery, 1; and excellence, 1–18, 37, 125, 127–28, 139, 142, 151, 184n26; and scientific excellence, 18, 125, 127, 139, 151, 184n26; singular, 131–33; to vocation, 32, 41, 53, 131–33, 184n26; by women, to work, 188n86, 191n9. See also family devotion; work devotion schema

DiMaggio, Paul, 176n10, 181n61, 209n17, 209n19

discovery. See scientific discovery

discrimination: and biases, 6; gender, 21; and inequalities, 27; and LGBTQ professionals, 21; and prejudice, 6; and racial/ethnic minorities, 21; and women, 21

disparities: education, 101; and inequalities, 101

disrespect: and devaluation, 5–6, 21, 123, 125, 200n34; and exclusion, 85–86; and gender, 5–6, 200n34; of LGBTQ professionals, 22, 135; and marginalization, 22; of racial/ethnic minorities, 22; of women, 5–6, 22, 177n21. See also respect

diversity: commitment to, 68–69, 75, 91–93, 117, 200n35; and devaluation, 17, 26, 74–75, 81, 91–93, 109; discouraged, 18; in education, 138; and equity, 150–51; and gender, 75; and grant funding, 120–21; in hiring, 75, 119–23, 133–34, 138; and inclusion, 113, 164, 185n51, 207n62; and inequalities, 27, 37, 138; and innovation, 18, 151; and LGBTQ professionals, 27, 91–93; and mentorship, 140, 147, 150; and neutrality, 27; as political, 12; and productivity, 81, 83; and professional culture(s), 137; promoting, 74–75, 120, 150, 161–62, 170, 197n14; and public welfare, 26; and racial/ethnic minorities, 27, 75, 120; and recruitment, 139; and respect, 200n34; and scientific excellence, 17–18, 68–69, 74–75, 91–93, 95–96, 108–10, 119, 121–23, 137–39; and scientific work, 108–10; and social justice, 37, 180n41; and social welfare, 91; special programs promoting, 120; training, 150–51; valued, 150; and women, 27, 133–34

Dobbin, Frank, 185n51, 208n64
double standards, 161, 200n31, 208n4

Ecklund, Elaine Howard, 183n13, 184n26, 189n106, 189n110, 190n134, 191n3, 193n21, 193n23, 195nn35–36, 210n36
education: commitment to, 160; disparities, 101; diversity in, 138; and equality, 138
Einstein, Albert, 36
Einstein, Mileva Maric, 36
engineering: as craftwork done by men, 25; and formalization of training, 23; nano-, 29; as profession, 25; and professional licensure, 187n69; and traditional set of knowledge, 71; women in field, 177n19. *See also* science; STEM
England, Paula, 179n39
Enlightenment, 24, 35, 126–27
equality: and education, 138; and meritocracy, 5. *See also* inequalities
equity: cultural construction of, 185n51; and diversity, 150–51; and inclusion, 150–51. *See also* inequities
Estevez, Mychel, 179n36
ethnography, 186n59
evaluation: and fairness, 114, 139; and inequalities, 7–8; and merit, 33, 208n7; and objectivity, 139; and productivity, 183n5
excellence: academic, 6, 12, 119–20, 159–60; of academic science, 12; and biases, 38, 94, 133–35, 142; commitment to, 161; and computer science, 70–71; (mis)conceiving, 81–93; cultural conceptions/constructions/foundations of, 3, 22–27, 75, 114; definitions of, 3, 114; demands of, 140; and devotion, 1–18, 37, 125, 127–28, 139, 142, 151, 184n26; dogma of, 150; historical foundations of, 22–27; and identity politics, 133–35; manifesting, 75–80; and merit, 1–18, 31–33, 139, 157–59; and meritocracy, 159; and objectivity, 3, 18, 95, 98, 137, 161; and professional culture(s), 31–34, 37–38; research, 75, 86, 99–100, 106, 123, 128–29, 157, 175n1; in science, 33; social foundations of, 22–27; and tenure, 98, 129; and transparency, 6; Western traditions of, 37; and work devotion, 139. *See also* professional

excellence schema; scientific excellence schema
exclusion: and devaluation, 117, 139; and disrespect, 85–86; of LGBTQ professionals, 21, 135; and marginalization, 21; of racial/ethnic minorities, 21, 178n24; of women, 21. *See also* inclusion

factor analysis, 196n5, 211n61
fairness: and academic excellence, 159–60; and evaluation, 114, 139; of hiring, 20, 98, 123, 183n8; and meritocracy, 195n42; and objectivity, 22, 111; of promotion, 2–3, 20, 98, 114, 123, 183n8; and salaries, 195n42; of tenure process, 96–98, 114; and transparency, 2–3, 20, 96–98, 114, 159–60, 202n3
family devotion: cultural expectations of, 55; mothers'/womens' responsibility for, 58, 131–33; schema, 36, 53, 194n34; and work devotion, 61, 66
family responsibilities, 2, 18, 21, 79, 125, 132, 195n34, 207n62; devaluation of, 185n51; and work devotion, 45–46, 48, 54, 56, 59–60, 64, 67. *See also* parents/parenthood
fathers/fatherhood, 40–41, 45–47, 49–52, 54–59, 61–62, 66, 131–32, 179n39, 191n3, 193n23, 193n27, 193n29, 194n31, 206n27, 208n62. *See also* mothers/motherhood; parents/parenthood
Faulkner, Wendy, 204n7, 207n47
femininity, hegemonic, 38
firefighting, as mission-driven occupation, 205n13
flexibility stigma, 36, 45–48, 63–65, 67, 167–68, 196n45, 211n62
Fox, Mary F., 180n45, 180n53, 189n110, 204n22, 207n40, 207n49

gender, 2; cis-, 28; and dedication, 161, 192n12; deeply-rooted beliefs about, 24–26; and demographic measures, 168; and depoliticization, 109; and discrimination, of women, 21; and disrespect, 5–6, 200n34; diversity, 75; and diversity, 75; diversity in hiring and promotion, 75; and favoritism, 208n4; and grant evaluations, 107–8, 134; harassment, 5–6, 177n21, 200n34; identity, 114, 177n16, 187n78, 204n18; and inequalities, 17,

19, 21, 196n45; as invisible, 108–10, 134; nonconforming men, 5, 177n21; and parenthood, 42, 51, 63, 79, 193n23, 195n42, 207n62; and promotion, 208n4; and recruitment, 109–10; and scientific worth, 110; signifiers in names, 108–9; stereotypes, 38, 184n35, 199n27. *See also* sexual identity

Gerson, Kathleen, 178n32, 195n36, 210n43, 211n60

Ginther, Donna, 107, 178n33

Gorman, Elizabeth H., 180n41, 183n11, 186n56, 190n133, 208n4, 209n10

harassment. *See* gender: harassment; sexual harassment

Harding, Sandra G., 184nn19–21, 184n25, 184n36, 188nn92–93, 208nn7–8, 208n68

Hays, Sharon, 193n28, 194n34, 205n25

hegemonic, term usage, 7

hegemonic femininity, 38

hegemonic masculinity, 24–26, 184n32, 190n133

heteronormativity, 34, 91–92, 94, 125, 139, 142, 156, 204n18

heterosexism, 12–13, 18, 19, 21–22, 24–28, 37–38, 57, 83, 87, 91–94, 111–12, 124, 127, 133–34, 139, 156, 160, 162, 180n41, 185n48

Hidden Figures (film), 184n35

hiring: beliefs about, 98–100; diversity in, 75, 119–23, 133–34, 138; fairness of, 20, 98, 123, 183n8; gender-based favoritism of, 208n4; and meritocracy, 121; as meritocratic, 19, 22, 115–16, 125; and publishing, 125; and research excellence, 99–100, 106; and underrepresented minorities (URMs), 134. *See also* recruitment

Hochschild, Arlie Russell, 200n32

homophily, 208n4

homophobia, 92

ideal engineer, 24–26, 93

ideal scientist, 24–26, 28, 34, 72, 93, 184n26, 189n106; as inspired genius, 24

ideal worker norms, 34, 45, 185n51, 193n22

identity: devaluation of, 208n2; gender, 114, 177n16, 187n78, 204n18; and

LGBTQ professionals, 110–13, 127, 135–37, 206n34; nerd, 185n43; and objectivity, 127; political, 96; subcultural, 185n43. *See also* identity politics; sexual identity

identity politics: and bias, 133–35; and merit, 125, 139, 146; and scientific excellence, 18, 133–35. *See also* political identity

inclusion: and diversity, 113, 164, 185n51, 207n62; and equity, 150–51; and innovation, 126; and minority women, 94; and respect, 44, 83, 94, 200n34; of underrepresented minorities (URMs), 135; and work devotion, 44. *See also* exclusion

individualism, 5, 7, 11, 13, 15, 24, 33, 140, 144, 148, 151, 205n14

inequalities: and biases, 2, 31, 33–34, 125, 149; and cultural beliefs, 2; and cultural schemas, 6, 13, 158–59; and devaluation, 196n45, 208n2; and discrimination, 27; and diversity, 27, 37, 138; and educational disparities, 101; and evaluation, 7–8; existing patterns of, 124; and gender, 17, 19, 21, 196n45; intercategorical intersectional analysis of, 208n2; and LGBTQ professionals, 17, 19, 21, 27, 33–34, 37; and merit/meritocracy, 5–6, 125, 189n103, 191n134; and neutrality, 27; as persistent, 2, 31; and professional culture(s), 17, 22, 28, 31, 33–34, 156, 158–59, 187n76; and professional excellence, 37; and racial/ethnic minorities, 2, 7–8, 17, 19, 21, 27, 33–34, 37, 182n69; racialized economic, 101; reproduction of, 189n103; and scientific excellence, 13, 18, 37–38, 95–124; social, 22, 138, 180n56; as status quo, 5; in STEM, 5–6, 22, 33–34, 149, 155; and underrepresented minorities (URMs), 21, 96; and women, 27, 33–34, 37; and work devotion, 13, 36. *See also* equality

inequities: and departmental politics, 21; in salaries, 209n27; in STEM, 2; and underrepresented minorities (URMs), 109. *See also* equity

innovation: and biases, 142; and collaboration, 6, 18, 90, 142–45; and communal work, 142–45; and devaluation, 13; and diversity, 18, 151; impeded, 6, 18;

innovation (*cont.*)
  and inclusion, 126; and individualism,
    33; and knowledge advancement, 126;
    and problem solving, 15; scientific, 13,
    15, 146–47, 151, 160; undermined by
    overwork, 147–49. *See also* scientific
    discovery
interdisciplinarity, 5, 14, 29, 143, 147, 172,
    187nn65–66, 207n43
intersectionality, 17, 35, 41, 65, 74–75, 88,
    93–94, 155–56, 168, 171, 173, 182n68,
    192n15, 197n9, 197n13, 199n24,
    201n41, 208n2
intolerance, 190n134
isolation: and LGBTQ professionals, 21,
    136; and marginalization, 90; and preju-
    dice, 6; and racial/ethnic minorities, 6,
    190n134; and women, 190n134
isomorphism: and cultural continuity,
    181n61; institutional, 185n53; and
    organizational/professional cultures,
    185n53; professional, 160

Jacobs, Jerry A., 186n57, 187n65, 193n29,
    195n36, 195n43, 207n43

Kelly, Erin L., 180n51, 181n56, 189n107,
    207n53, 209n23
King, Molly M., 180n42, 181n58, 183n13,
    211n56
Kington, Raynard, 107, 178n33
Kmec, Julie A., 179n38, 180n41, 190n133,
    191n4, 193n22

Lamont, Michele, 175n1, 176n8, 180n56,
    183n7, 203n12, 204n1, 209n22,
    210n42, 211nn57–58
Latinx faculty: and creative brilliance, proof
    of, 87; cultural biases about intellectual
    inferiority of, 26; and diversity, 12;
    and potential violations of purity of
    scientific excellence and devotion, 127;
    and stereotypes, 26; and tenure, 98; as
    underrepresented minority (URM), 6,
    18, 21, 95, 100, 102–4, 114, 118, 134,
    136, 166, 178n23, 190n126, 202n5
LGBTQ professionals: biases against, 31,
    33–34; and concealment/invisibility,
    110–13, 135–37, 146; and covering/
    deemphasizing, 92, 113, 135–36; and
    demographic measures, 168; devalua-
tion of, 6, 91; and discrimination, 21;
    disrespect of, 22, 135; and diversity, 27,
    91–93; exclusion of, 21, 135; experi-
    ences of, 91–93, 110–13, 135–36; as
    fitting in and working harder, 200n39,
    206n33; and identities known/un-
    known, 110–13, 127, 135–37, 206n34;
    and inequalities, 17, 19, 21, 27, 33–34,
    37; and isolation, 21, 136; marginal-
    ization of, 6, 21–22, 90, 146; negative
    treatment of, 6; as parents, 208n62;
    political identity of, 96; prejudice
    against, 91; professional relationships
    of, 93, 113; and status beliefs, 185n48;
    stereotypes of, 21, 31, 33–34, 94; as
    threat to cultural norms, 127; as threat
    to STEM work, 25–26; as underrepre-
    sented minority (URM), 3, 5, 11, 17, 90,
    95, 125, 136, 183n14, 185n48, 208n2
Lincoln, Anne E., 183n13, 184n26, 189n94,
    189n106, 189n110, 190n134, 191n3,
    193n21, 193n23, 195nn35–36, 208n7,
    210n36

marginalization: in academic science, 6; and
    devaluation, 5–6, 125–26, 146, 161;
    and disrespect, 22; and exclusion, 21;
    and isolation, 90; of LGBTQ profession-
    als, 6, 21–22, 90, 146; of mothers, 146;
    and organizational dedication, 192n18;
    of racial/ethnic minorities, 21–22, 90,
    146, 161; and underrepresented minori-
    ties (URMs), 5, 124; of women, 5, 21–22,
    90, 146; and work devotion, 44
masculinity, hegemonic, 24–25, 184n32,
    190n133
mathematics, women in, 5, 177n19,
    184n35. *See also* STEM
McCall, Leslie, 208n2
mentorship: and collaboration, 12, 14, 119,
    141, 146; and diversity, 140, 147, 150;
    to majority-race men, 147; and promo-
    tion, 146; and racially minoritized
    students, 207n40; and role models,
    207n37; and scientific excellence,
    11, 14; valued, 150; and women, 12,
    207n40; and work devotion, 43
merit: and consequences, 125–51; cultural
    conceptions/constructions of, 3, 6, 17,
    19–38, 22, 31, 34, 189n103; cultural
    definitions of, 7, 16, 19, 22, 27–28, 31,

38, 93, 149, 158, 161, 189n103, 208n7; definitions of, 16–17, 22, 31–33, 151; misconceived/misperceived/mismeasured, 1–18, 68–94, 139–49, 151, 156; moralization of, 18, 125–51; paradox of, 22, 125; scientific, 2, 18, 27, 46, 66, 93, 96, 107, 110, 123, 141–51, 155, 158, 189n103; and scientific excellence, 17, 33, 68–94, 142; understandings of, 125; and work devotion, 31–32, 39, 65–66, 142. *See also* meritocracy; rewards

meritocracy: and academic science, 1; and academic STEM, 1, 18, 21, 95, 99–100, 123–24, 135; doubts about, 114–15, 150; faith in, as moral conviction, 135; and personnel actions and salaries, 195n42; and salaries, 195n42; and science, 1, 9, 20, 65, 107, 134, 183n8; and scientific excellence, 96–100; and tenure, 96–97; and transparency, 52; venerated, 159; widely endorsed, 18; widely held beliefs justifying, 96–100. *See also* merit; minority-meritocracy trap

minorities. *See* minority-meritocracy trap; minority women; racial/ethnic minorities

minority-meritocracy trap, 12, 18, 96, 119–21, 123–24, 134–35

minority women, 6, 12, 21, 41, 88, 91, 94, 150, 156, 166, 178n26, 190n134, 195n34, 200n35, 208n2. *See also* Asian women

Misra, Joya, 190n131, 193n26, 193n29, 199n26, 207nn42–43, 207n57, 208n1

Moen, Phyllis, 180n51, 181n56, 189n107, 207n53, 209n23

moralization, of merit, 18, 125–51

mothers/motherhood: avoiding or delaying, 53–54; and biases, 21; and commitment to families, 57, 66; covering or deemphasizing, 10; cultural construction of, 10–11, 205n24; dedication of, 57; and devaluation of work commitment, 125, 196n45, 208n2; and faculty positions, less likely to obtain, 193n23; and family devotion, 58, 131–33; and gender inequality, 196n45; as legitimate scholars, 179n38; marginalization of, 146; moral tension, and academic science careers, 52–53, 57, 66, 131; as neglectful, 190n123; and pregnancy, 61–65;

productivity of, 10, 50, 66; and promotion, 61; salaries of, 61–62, 179n39, 195n41, 209n27; scientific excellence of, 150; stigmatized, 11; and tenure, 61; as underrepresented minority (URM), 125, 136; and work devotion, 10, 17, 40–41, 50, 53–58, 61–67, 191n4. *See also* fathers/fatherhood; parents/parenthood

nanoengineering, 29

National Institutes of Health (NIH), 8, 106–8, 134, 166–67, 178–79nn33–34, 202n10

National Science Foundation (NSF), 170, 175n2, 181n67, 182n70, 196n45, 202n5, 202n8, 210n39, 228–29

National Survey of the Changing Workforce (NSCW), 163

Native American faculty: cultural biases about intellectual inferiority of, 26; and potential violations of purity of scientific excellence and devotion, 127; and stereotypes, 26; as underrepresented minority (URM), 6, 21, 100, 102–4, 166, 178n23, 190n126, 202n5

Native American students, in STEM, 178n25

"nerd identity," 185n43

neuroscience, 29, 130, 143, 148

neurosurgery, 188n88

neutrality: and diversity, 27; and inequalities, 27; and merit, 142; and objectivity, 19–20, 27, 31, 127, 180n41; of STEM, 27

Newport, Cal, 207n54

Newton, Isaac, 24, 126

NIH. *See* National Institutes of Health (NIH)

novitiate (training period), 30, 128–29

objectivity: and collaboration, 130; commitment to, 3, 18, 161, 180n41; cultural norms of, 127; and depoliticization, 75, 124; and evaluation, 139; and excellence, 3, 18, 95, 98, 137, 161; and fairness, 22, 111; foundations of, 127; and identity, 127; and merit, 2, 123, 142; and neutrality, 19–20, 27, 31, 127, 180n41; and productivity, 165; professional norms of, 130; and rewards, 10; and science, 133; scientific, 124, 137; and scientific excellence, 95, 98; and scientific method, 109; threats to cultural norms of, 127; and transparency, 10

O'Meara, KerryAnn, 175n3, 193n21, 193n26, 207n57, 208n65
O'Neill, Olivia Amanda, 205n13
operationalization, scale, 41, 167–70
organizational culture(s): and isomorphism, 185n53; and professional culture(s), 28, 185n53, 185n51

paradox: cultural foundations of, 19; of merit, 22, 125; and moralized professional culture, 139; and STEM, 2; and underrepresented minorities (URMs), 139
parents/parenthood: and covering/deemphasizing, 59, 132; demands of, 54, 127; and demographic measures, 168–69; and family leave accommodations, 207n62; and gender, 42, 51, 63, 79, 193n23, 195n42, 207n62; and hours worked, 40; and ideal scientist concept, 184n26; and incursions of work at home, 205n22; and LGBTQ professionals, 208n62; scales, 169; stigmatized, 13–14, 45–52, 59–60, 67, 150; struggles of, 179n36, 191n3; and work devotion, 41, 49, 51, 54–58, 62–63, 192n14. *See also* family responsibilities; fathers/fatherhood; mothers/motherhood
passion: and addiction, 129; and career, 192n16; and dedication, 40; principle, 176n15, 205n14; scientific discovery as, 129; and work devotion, 4
"pedigree issues," 100–103
peer review, and collaboration, 80
people of color. *See* racial/ethnic minorities
physics, and astronomical studies, 23
Picture a Scientist (PBS documentary), 184n35
pipeline issues/narrative, 18, 95, 100–103, 106, 119, 133, 182n70, 202n4
Plato, 24–25, 126
political identity, 96. *See also* identity politics
political power, and cultural beliefs, 24
politics: and cultural beliefs, 24; and culture, 20, 127, 156; and diversity, 12; and markets/profit, 2, 159; and power, 24; and science, 22; and STEM, 22–24, 27; vagaries of, 20. *See also* depoliticization
Posselt, Julie R., 178n27, 178n32, 187nn65–66, 202n4, 206n35, 207n38, 207n58, 209n11, 210n37

prejudice: and biases, 6, 149; and discrimination, 6; and isolation, 6; against LGBTQ professionals, 91; and racial/ethnic minorities, 6
problem solving: and idea development, 151; and innovation, 15; and knowledge creation, 151; and work devotion, 43
productivity: and biases, 38, 181n58, 190n132; and collaboration, 90; demands of, 147; and diversity, 81, 83; and evaluation, 183n5; and grant success, 40, 135, 164, 169, 194n30; indices as warped indicators of, 145–47; and leaves taken, 193n26; of mothers, 10, 50, 66; and objectivity, 165; and publishing, 50–51, 194n30; and recruitment, 163; scales, 169; scholarly, 10–11, 16, 33, 38, 40, 50, 52, 61, 81–83, 87, 123, 132, 155, 164–67, 181n57, 198n19, 206n26, 208n7; and self-conceptions, 81; and social integration, 90; and visibility, 162–64
professional culture(s): and autonomy/self-regulation, 28, 186n56; and beliefs, 2; and biases, 27–28, 33–34, 95; and closure, 29–30; and core tasks, 29; and diversity, 137; and excellence, 31–34, 37–38; and inequalities, 17, 22, 28, 31, 33, 156, 158–59, 187n76; as institutionalized, 25; as insulated and perpetuated, 186n53; and isomorphism, 185n53; and jurisdiction, 29–30; of medicine, 186n59; and merit, 22, 27–31, 183n5; moralized, 18, 139; and organizational culture(s), 28, 185n53, 185n51; and paradox, 139; as social collectives, 28; of STEM, 2, 16, 22, 33–34, 95, 109, 123, 142, 156–57, 210n44; and success, 172; and work devotion, 41
professional excellence schema: cultural judgments of, 38; and merit, 31–33; nonconformity as threat to, 31; and professional culture(s), 31–34, 37–38; in STEM, 33–34; and work devotion schema, 31–38. *See also* scientific excellence schema
professional purity, 18, 29, 96, 108–10, 124, 125–27, 136
professional relationships: and collaboration, 144; devaluation of, 144; of LGBTQ professionals, 93, 113. *See also*

collaboration; collegiality; socialization, professional; team science

promotion: academic reviews for, 96, 116, 146; beliefs about, 96–98; and collegiality/collaboration, 118; fairness of, 2–3, 20, 98, 114, 123, 183n8; gender-based favoritism of, 208n4; and interdisciplinary work, 29; and mentorship, 146; as meritocratic, 96–97, 115–16; and motherhood, 61; and publishing, 145; and research output, 128; and respect, 63, 79; and underrepresented minorities (URMs), 134. *See also* salaries; tenure

public welfare, and diversity, 26. *See also* social welfare

purity. *See* professional purity; science: and purity

race. *See* racial/ethnic minorities; racialization; racism

racial/ethnic minorities: and acting white, 185n43; and biases, 2, 26, 31, 33–34, 114–15, 190n134; and citizenship status, 177n23; and dedication, 161, 168, 192n12; and demographic measures, 168; and depoliticization, 109; devaluation of, 161; and discrimination, 21; and disrespect, 22; and diversity, 27, 75, 120; diversity in hiring and promotion, 75; exclusion of, 21, 178n24; exploitation of, 26; and grant funding, 107–8, 120, 134; and inequalities, 2, 7–8, 17, 19, 21, 27, 33–34, 37, 182n69; as invisible, 108–10, 134; and isolation, 6, 190n134; and lower-income backgrounds, 101; marginalization of, 21–22, 90, 146, 161; national origin of, 182n69; political identity of, 96; and prejudice, 6; and recruitment, 109–10; and research credit, 11; and scientific worth, 110; signifiers in names, 108–9; and status beliefs, 185n48; stereotypes about, 26, 31, 33–34, 38, 94, 123, 184n35; and subcultural identities, 185n43; and tenure, 98; term, usage, 177n23; as threat to cultural norms, 127; as underrepresented minority (URM), 2–3, 5, 6, 11, 17, 18, 21, 90, 95, 100–108, 117–19, 122–24, 125, 160, 175n3, 180n43, 181n67, 183n14, 185n48, 202n8. *See also* Asian faculty;

Asian men; Asian women; Black faculty/scientists; Latinx faculty; minority women; Native American faculty

racialization, 26, 28, 101, 139, 178n23, 184n35, 199n29

racism, 21, 115, 139, 142

rationality, 126, 185n51

recruitment: and cluster sampling, 211n58; and diversity, 139; and gender, 109–10; and productivity, 163; and racial/ethnic minorities, 109–10. *See also* hiring

regression models, 42, 46, 62–64, 82, 84, 171, 173, 179n39, 180n43, 192n18, 192n14, 192n17, 193n27, 197n7, 197n9, 197n12, 198n24

relational qualities/skills. *See under* scientific excellence schema

research teams, 89, 128. *See also* team science

respect: and advancement/promotions, 63, 79; and diversity, 200n34; and inclusion, 44, 83, 94, 200n34; and integration, professional, 83, 90, 117; and rewards, 84. *See also* disrespect

rewards: and merit/meritocracy, 1, 19–20, 22, 30, 96, 107, 123, 125, 150; and objectivity, 10; and recognition, 19–20, 68, 87, 116, 133; and respect, 84; and scientific excellence, 85, 93–94, 99, 123, 133; and transparency, 10

Ride, Sally, 26

Rivera, Lauren A., 203n15

role-incumbent schemas, and ideal fit, 190n133

salaries, 168, 176n9, 209n26; academic reviews for, 146; and assertive self-conceptions, 11, 69; as fair and meritocratic, 195n42; inequities in, 209n27; of women and mothers, 179n39, 195nn41–42, 209n27. *See also* promotion

scale operationalization, 41, 167–70

Scholarly Production Indices (SPI) database, 16, 40, 50, 81, 132, 134–35, 155, 164–67, 194n30, 206n26

science: aerospace, 23; big, 25; commitment to, 65, 141; as creative, 71; dedication to, 65; dissent in, 24, 204n6; dominant Western approaches to, 23–24, 27–28, 34, 37, 151, 183n18; excellence in,

science (*cont.*)
33; as institutionalized profession,
25; and meritocracy, 1, 9, 20, 65, 107,
134, 183n8; and objectivity, 133; and
politics, 22; and purity, 96, 108–10;
as systematic, 71; and technology, 22;
term, usage, 175n2; truth in, 24, 71,
126–27, 144, 184n30; as vocation, 65,
131–33, 191n8; women in, 177n19,
188n86, 190n123. *See also* academic science; engineering; neuroscience; STEM
Science (journal), 7–8, 106–7, 166–67
science, technology, engineering, and math
(STEM). *See* STEM
science and technology studies (STS), 22,
155–57, 208n7
scientific calling, 18, 34, 40, 125, 128–31
scientific discovery: as aspiration, 141;
as buffered, 2; commitment to, 70;
complex and interdisciplinary world of,
14; and creative brilliance/creativity, 70,
148; dedication to, 9; devotion to, 1;
impeded, 15; as passion, 129; and pride,
140; and self-promotion, 73. *See also*
innovation; scientific method
scientific excellence schema, 1–5, 172–73;
alternative approaches to, 151; and
assertiveness, 1, 5, 17, 69, 72–73, 77–78,
87–88, 93, 145, 169, 180n41, 196n4,
196n5, 198n19, 199n28; as bad for professionals and innovation, 15; characteristics of, 7, 172, 190n129; consequences
of, 11–15, 17, 81–85; and creative
brilliance, 1, 5, 17, 24, 37–38, 68, 70–71,
74, 77, 83, 85–87, 126, 141, 147–48,
180n41, 196nn3–4; cultural roots of, 18,
19, 24, 106; culture of, 2; defense of, 18,
95–124; defined, by faculty, 1, 70–75;
definition/description, 4, 7; demands
of, 79; faculty critiques of, 113–17; as
hegemonic, 7–9, 93–94; manifesting,
75–80; and merit, 17, 33, 68–94, 142;
misconceiving/mismeasuring, 81–93,
114; purity of, 18, 96, 108–10, 124, 125–
27, 136; and relational qualities/skills,
17, 73–74, 88–90, 169–70; in STEM,
36–38, 184n26; and underrepresented
minorities (URMs), 12, 119–21. *See also*
professional excellence schema
scientific method, 109, 127. *See also*
scientific discovery

SCOPUS (online bibliographic database),
164–65, 169, 181n57, 210n50, 210n52
self-conceptions, 12, 69, 81–85, 88, 94,
169–71, 173–74, 196n1, 197nn8–9,
197n12, 198n19, 199n28, 199n30,
200n33, 200n36
Sewell, William H., Jr., 187n79
sexism, 20–21, 115, 139, 142, 204n21
sexual harassment, 177n21, 200n34,
204n21. *See also* gender: harassment
sexual identity, 2, 11, 16, 25–26, 41, 92–93,
98, 110, 112–14, 133, 156. *See also*
gender
sexual minorities, 2, 13, 110–11
sexual orientation, 111–12
Shapin, Steven, 182n3, 183n17, 184n28,
184n31, 188n90, 189n95, 189n115,
189n117, 190n125, 204nn3–6, 208n7
Sheltzer, Jason M., 180n45, 180n53,
204n22, 207n40, 207n49
Smith-Doerr, Laurel, 183n11, 210n37
social integration, 90
socialization, professional, 29–32, 43–44,
158, 183n5, 186n53, 186n56, 187n73,
205n10; and networks, 21, 32, 38,
80, 93, 198n18. *See also* professional
relationships
social justice, and diversity, 37, 180n41
social sciences disciplines/professions,
175n2, 176n14
social welfare, and diversity, 91. *See also*
public welfare
sociology, 157, 162, 209n19
Socrates, 24, 126
SPI database. *See* Scholarly Production Indices (SPI) database
STEM: core beliefs of, 2–3; and corporate profitability, 189n107; cultural
conceptions/structures of, 22–27, 151;
excellence, 22–27; hegemonic ideas as
taken for granted, 7–8; and meritocracy,
1, 18, 21, 95, 99–100, 123–24, 135; and
paradox, 2; as political, 22–24, 27; and
positive change, 149–51; and professions as product of cultural and political
processes, 22–24; scientific excellence schema in, 36–38, 184n26; and
scientific life, 33; social construction
of, 26–27, 33; and success, 172; term,
usage, 175n2; and values systems of as
Western cultural constructs, 24; work

devotion schema in, 34–36, 184n26. *See also* engineering; mathematics, women in; science; technology

STEM Inclusion Study, 75, 161–62, 181n63, 183n5, 191n7, 192n12, 198n17, 210n39

Stephan, Paula, 175n5, 180nn45–46, 180n53, 182n4, 182n69, 183n6, 183n10, 184n27, 186n57, 187n65, 189n110, 195n38, 204n22, 205n14, 205nn16–17, 207n40, 207n42, 207n46, 207n49, 209n25

stereotypes, 161, 178n23, 188n88, 190n126, 190n133; of Asian men, 198n24; of Asian women, 88, 94, 199n29; and biases, 33–34, 123, 156; cultural, 26; gender, 38, 184n35, 199n27; of LGBTQ professionals, 21, 31, 33–34, 94; negative, 119; racial/ethnic, 26, 31, 33–34, 38, 94, 123, 184n35; of women, 31, 33–34, 94; of women of color, 94

Stewart, Abigail, 175n3, 183n12, 185n48, 189n99, 206n32, 206n36, 207n58, 208n65, 210n37

stigma, flexibility. *See* flexibility stigma

Stone, Pamela, 193–94n29

STS. *See* science and technology studies (STS)

team science, 5, 29, 144, 187n66. *See also* collaboration; professional relationships; research teams

technology: and aerospace science, 23; and science, 22; women in, 177n19, 188n86, 190n123. *See also* science and technology studies (STS); STEM

tenure: and academic freedom, 149, 201n1; and collegiality/collaboration, 118; and excellence, 98, 129; and fairness, 96–98, 114; and interdisciplinary work, 29; and job security, 128, 149, 157; as meritocratic, 96–97; and motherhood, 61; and racial/ethnic minorities, 98; and research excellence/output, 128–29, 157; reviews, 96–98, 116, 201nn1–3. *See also* promotion

transparency: and academic excellence, 6, 159–60; and accountability, 150; and excellence, 6; and fairness, 2–3, 20, 96–98, 114, 159–60, 202n3; and meritocracy, 52; and objectivity, 10; and rewards, 10

Turco, Catherine J., 188n82

Turing, Alan, 25–26

underrepresented minorities (URMs), 136, 139, 180n43, 181n67, 202n8. *See also specific minority/minorities*

Valian, Virginia, 175n3, 183n11, 185n48, 189n99, 206n32, 206n36, 207n58, 208n65, 210n37

Vandello, Joseph A., 180n41

vocation: commitment to, 65; dedication to, 34–35, 65; devotion to, 32, 41, 53, 131–33, 184n26; long hours of, 4; science as, 65, 131–33, 191n8; scientific, 32, 34–36, 41, 65, 126, 131–33, 176n14, 184n26; service to, 35; single-mindedness of, 4

Weber, Max: on anti-Semitic strain in US scientific culture, 204n3; on men as academic scientists, 36, 176n14; on scientific vocation, 35, 176n14

Weeden, Kim A., 186n55, 187n71, 187n76

Wharton, Amy S., 179n36, 181n56, 185n51, 189n104, 191n5, 193n22, 195n34, 209n23

white faculty, 177n23, 177n16; self-conceptions among, 174

white men, 6, 11–12, 15–17, 21, 27, 114, 127, 133, 161, 165–66, 181n58, 185n48, 190n134, 190n126, 190n132, 198n24, 208n4

white women, 6, 11–12, 14, 21, 26, 88, 91, 94, 127, 133–34, 150, 166, 178n23, 190n126, 190n134, 199n24, 199n28, 199n30, 200n33, 200nn35–36, 205n25

Williams, Joan, 176n12, 183n11, 188n79, 188n81, 188n83, 188n85, 190n124, 191nn5–6, 193n24, 195nn36–37, 195n41

women: biases about, 2, 31, 33–34, 114–15, 190n134; commitment of, to work, 188n82; in computer science, 5, 177n19, 184n35; and demographic measures, 168; devaluation of, 5, 28, 38, 88–89, 161; and devalued hegemonic femininity, 38; and discrimination, 21; disrespect of, 5–6, 22, 177n21; and diversity, 27; as diversity hires, 133–34; and domesticity, 36; in engineering, 177n19; exclusion of, 21; and extra

women (*cont.*)
emotional work to fit in professional networks, 198n18; and family devotion, 58, 131–33; and genius, relationship to, 36; and inequalities, 27, 33–34, 37; and isolation, 190n134; as less valued and less rewarded, 28; marginalization of, 5, 21–22, 90, 146; and mathematics, exceptional abilities of, 184n35; in mathematics, 5, 177n19; and mentoring/teaching, 12, 207n40; political identity of, 96; and potential violations of purity of scientific excellence and devotion, 127; presumed compassion and emotionality of, 25; and research credit, 11; salaries of, 179n39, 195nn41–42, 209n27; in science and technology, 177n19, 188n86, 190n123; and status beliefs, 185n48; stereotypes of, 31, 33–34, 94; as threat to cultural norms, 127; as underrepresented minority (URM), 3, 5–6, 11, 17, 18, 21, 90, 95, 100–108, 114, 117–19, 123–24, 125, 134, 136, 166, 175n3, 178n23, 183n14, 184n32, 185n48, 190n126, 190n134, 202n7, 208n2; and work devotion, 188n86, 191n9. *See also* minority women; mothers/motherhood; white women

women of color. *See* minority women

work dedication. *See* dedication

work devotion schema, 205n14; and academic science, 3; adherence to, 17; as bad for professionals and innovation, 15; characteristics of, 7; coercive side of, 17; consequences of, 9–11, 15, 17, 39–67; cultural roots of, 18, 19; definition/description, 3, 7; demands of, 10, 191n9; elements of, 189n119; as hegemonic, 7–9, 41; institutionalization of, 67; and merit, 31–32, 39, 65–66, 142; as powerful cultural frame, 41; and professional excellence schema, 31–38; purity of, 18, 125–27, 136; in STEM, 34–36, 184n26; and underrepresented minorities (URMs), 12

work-family. *See* family responsibilities

worthiness: and commitments, 128; and competence, 4, 7, 13, 31–33; scientific, 79, 110

Zippel, Kathrin, 177n18, 177n20, 185n46, 187n66, 207n42

Lightning Source UK Ltd.
Milton Keynes UK
UKHW020620180522
403143UK00008B/22